The BEST TRAVEL WRITING
Volume 11

TRUE STORIES
FROM AROUND THE WORLD

TRAVELERS' TALES

THE **BEST**
TRAVEL WRITING
Volume 11

TRUE STORIES
FROM AROUND THE WORLD

Edited by
JAMES O'REILLY, LARRY HABEGGER,
AND SEAN O'REILLY

INTRODUCTION BY ROLF POTTS

Travelers' Tales
An imprint of Solas House, Inc.
Palo Alto

Art Direction: Kimberley Nelson Coombs
Cover Photograph: © Xuanhuongho, Shutterstock. Rowboat on water lily pond on the Mekong Delta, Vietnam
Interior Design and Page Layout: Scribe, Inc.
Production Director: Susan Brady

ISBN: 978-1-60952-117-2
ISSN: 1548-0224
E-ISBN: 978-1-60952-118-9

First Edition
Printed in the United States
10 9 8 7 6 5 4 3 2 1

Table of Contents

Introduction

Picturesque World

ROLF POTTS

Earlier this year, while road tripping through the American South, I wandered into a New Orleans bookstore and wound up dropping $250 on a nineteenth-century travel tome entitled *Picturesque World*. I typically wouldn't have spent that much on an unwieldy old book, but something about it sent me into an imaginative reverie that felt a little bit like time travel.

Most any journey can, at moments, have a way of making a traveler feel like he's navigating a blurred line between present and past. Walk through the urban slums at the outskirts of modern Mumbai, and you can get a sense of what New York's Lower East Side might have felt like in 1900; lose your smartphone in Copenhagen and you may well find yourself trapped in 1999 (that distant age when travelers still used paper maps and the kindness of strangers to find their way around). In New Orleans, I often saw the present-day city through the lens of the previous decade, when I'd spent the first few months of 2005 living out of a rented apartment at the edge of the French Quarter, blissfully unaware that hurricane-triggered floods would soon transform everything around me. Discovering the two-volume heft of *Picturesque World* in Beckham's Bookshop on Decatur Street sent me back even further in time. Paging through the book's exquisitely detailed engravings of landscapes and monuments and village vistas from distant lands, I felt like I'd discovered some long-forgotten steampunk incarnation of Instagram.

At first glance the Instagram comparison might seem spurious, since *Picturesque World* clearly was designed for an elite readership. Published by Boston's Estes & Lauriat in 1878, the two 576-page volumes are bound in blind-tooled Moroccan goat leather and accented with gilt-stamp detailing and gold-painted endpapers. Its full title reads: *The Picturesque World; Or, Scenes in Many Lands: With One Thousand Illustrations on Wood and Steel of Picturesque Views from All Parts of the World. Comprising Mountain, Lake and River Scenery, Parks, Palaces, Cathedrals, Churches, Castles, Abbeys, and Other Views Selected from the Most Noted and Interesting Parts of the World; With Original and Authentic Descriptions by the Best Authors.*

Picturesque World was assembled at a time when the very definition of travel writing was shifting. For millennia, going back to Herodotus and beyond, the bulk of travel writing was at heart an empirical endeavor, dutifully describing faraway peoples and places for the imaginations of the home audience. By the late nineteenth century, however, the rise of new engraving and photographic technology meant that the reading public could see the world in pictures rather than envisioning it from text descriptions. *National Geographic* debuted one decade after the release of *Picturesque World*, and before long the monthly geographical magazine came to be known more for its full-page photographs than for its scientific data. Around the same time, the Exposition Universelle in Paris sparked a fad for picture postcards, which by the turn of the century were being sold in the billions in Europe and North America.

As images of the world continued to proliferate in mass media, cultural critics on both continents began to wonder if something was being lost in the process. Much like Plato once worried that writing would stunt people's ability to memorize, early twentieth-century academics and newspaper editors worried that images would impoverish the imagination, inhibit cultural literacy, and oversimplify our understanding of the world. In 1906, American writer John Walker Harrington satirically suggested that the world was succumbing to a disease known as "postal carditis," asserting that "unless such manifestations are checked, millions of persons of now normal lives and irreproachable habits will become victims of faddy degeneration of the brain."

More than a century later, it's easy to draw parallels between that *fin de siècle* image boom and the current-day ubiquity of digital photographs on picture-sharing apps like Instagram. Century-old anxieties that postcards might trivialize one's understanding of the world reverberate in current-day critiques of social media—with the added concern that "selfie culture" lends a veneer of narcissism to the equation. Whereas the postcards of previous generations were inscribed with "wish you were *here!*" sentiments, artfully filtered Instagram photos imply something along the lines of "don't you wish you were *me?*" In this way, critics worry, as more and more travelers reflexively post scenery-fringed selfies to social media, journeys have become less about an inquiry into other places than a roving performance of the Self.

While I can appreciate this concern, I would contend that a degree of superficiality has always been a part of travel, particularly as it has become more and more accessible for middle-class tourists over the past two centuries. The engravings in *Picturesque World* triggered my fascination not because they were somehow purer than the travel photos one sees on Instagram, but because they are *essentially the same* as their social media equivalents. Search Instagram for photos of Angkor Wat or the Taj Mahal, the Pantheon or the Parthenon, and you'll find tens of thousands of digital snapshots that share the exact same angles, lighting, and framing as the images in *Picturesque World*. Regardless of whether these pictures feature a selfie, the most viral social-media travel photos have a way of depicting places in terms of iconic beauty (i.e. the "picturesque") rather than experiential nuance.

Around the time *Picturesque World* first appeared in libraries and bookstores, conventional wisdom held that ongoing advances in photographic technology and scientific empiricism would soon render travel writing obsolete. What this assumption overlooked, of course, was that the best travel writing had always shrugged off the conceit of objectivity and embraced a personal point of view. The ancient Egyptian traveler Wenamun is memorable less for his description of the Mediterranean than for his weeping jag of homesickness in Lebanon; the fourth-century Galician pilgrim Egeria is at her most profound when she expresses gratitude for the kindness of strangers who showed her hospitality in the Sinai; the fourteenth-century Moroccan wanderer Ibn Battuta is most relatable when he longs for the lifestyle of a simple weaver on an idyllic island in the Maldives. And, around the time *Picturesque World* was published, the most telling travel book was not some exhaustive colonial monograph, but Mark Twain's *The Innocents Abroad*, which exuded self-deprecating chagrin at the prescribed rituals of tourism.

In a way, the flood of travel images stretching from Instagram back to *Picturesque World* has freed travel writing from the pretense of objective description and underscored its importance as a subtle, open-ended, ragged-edged undertaking. Beholden neither to the panic-driven tropes of news journalism or the forced cheerfulness of tourism publicity, the best travel writing blends reportage with reflection, seeking out the complex humanity of places through a subjective, self-questioning personal lens. Simple attention counts for more than overarching analysis, and wrestling with questions is more important than outlining answers.

The travel stories collected in this book illustrate how, on the road, the most vivid lens into a place and its people is often revealed in the smallest moments and the simplest encounters. For Laura Resau, this means consenting to wear a traditional Quichuan dress while going out on the town with her indigenous host in Ecuador; for Darrin Duford, this means exploring the idiosyncrasies of Panamanian culture through a quixotic quest to find a new Panama hat; for Amber Paulen, this means gaining perspective on her own life by baking bread with a self-described "spinster" in Italy. Mario Kaiser's experience of Iran is transformed by the fact that, against all conventional wisdom, he and his wife have chosen to travel there in the throes of their honeymoon; in Malaysia, Christina Ammon learns that what at first feels like an exasperating inconvenience—her truck breaking down in an obscure provincial town—can, in time, be a window into the joys of friendship with the people who live in an unfamiliar place.

Many of the stories in this book show how, as first-world travelers, the most affecting lessons we learn in distant lands often involve people who don't enjoy the same privileges that we do. Olga Pavlinova Olenich discovers this while sharing a train compartment with a Moldovan migrant whose travels are motivated not by leisure, but the promise of "illegal" work in Portugal; Michael Sano gains perspective when, far from his out-of-the-closet life in San Francisco, he falls into an ambiguous flirtation with a young gay man in the conservative confines of small-town Nicaragua. Time and movement also have a way helping us understand our relationship to distant places: for James Michael Dorsey this means experiencing Baja California by bus; for Glenda Reed, approaching the Marquesas Islands by sailboat; for Peter Wortsman, digging deeper into the idiosyncrasies of France as his language skills improve over the course of many years. The passage of time also takes on a poignant resonance when—in an inversion of the dynamic insinuated by *Picturesque World* or Instagram—Marcia DeSanctis reflects on how, as often as not, the most powerful narrative contained in a travel photograph is not found in the subject it depicts, but in the person who chose to leave herself out of the frame.

In the end, the best travel writing risks a kind of vulnerability that is intrinsic to experiencing the world in a meaningful way. In the essay that concludes this book, Don George's emotional epiphany during a moment of rain-sodden exhaustion in Cambodia reveals how, in travel, getting "closer to the wild heart of life" is often inseparable from embracing uncertainty and keeping your eyes open in unfamiliar places. "I follow the compass of my heart," he writes, "venturing off the map, making connections, asking questions, going deeper, trying to penetrate the essence of a place, so that I can understand it better and bring back precious pieces to share."

So long as this attitude underpins the journey, travel writing will always remain relevant.

⚬ ⚬ ⚬

Rolf Potts has reported from more than sixty countries for the likes of National Geographic Traveler, Slate, Outside, The New Yorker, The Believer, Sports Illustrated, *and the Travel Channel. He is perhaps best known for promoting the ethic of independent travel, and his book on the subject,* Vagabonding: An Uncommon Guide to the Art of Long-Term World Travel, *has been through twenty-four printings and translated into several foreign languages. His newest book,* Marco Polo Didn't Go There: Stories and Revelations From One Decade as a Postmodern Travel Writer, *won a Lowell Thomas Award from the Society of American Travel Writers, and became the first American-authored book to win Italy's prestigious Chatwin Prize for travel writing. Each July he can be found in France, where he is the program director at the Paris American Academy's creative writing workshop.*

꙳ ꙳ ꙳

Flight Behavior

The annual sandhill crane migration
helps explain why and how we leave.

*E*cstatic is not a word I would use to immediately describe Hal, though on a predawn morning in central Nebraska, standing together in an unheated viewing blind along the Platte River, it is precisely this word he provokes. He stands rapt before his camera, his fingers flitting over buttons he'll soon use to focus and zoom and shoot, in clear possession of an enthusiasm I have seen only in the very young, and in this way, he defies expectation. Hal is seventy-six, for one, with hair the consistency of a child's—peach fuzz, fading out—and a hunched demeanor that suggests, regardless of whatever might've come before, a life now lived stuck in stagnation. He is slow to speak, he tells me, and slower still to move. The skin on his hands is translucent, nearly blue, and covered in the minutiae of burst blood vessels and liver spots that conjure a certain sense of pointillism, as if he is a man made of many things—colors and experiences alike—though up close, as he is now, he looks remarkably ordinary.

Ordinary in a sense, although today, Hal and I are one with the Earth. This is what was advertised to us on posters—in the lobby, at the front desk, adhered with blue putty to bathroom stalls—and what our tour guide, Bill, reminded us as he led us first through prairie grass and then winding through mulch into these woods where we now stand. It was cold then, unfathomably dark, and carried with it the silence of 4:15 A.M., and so it was with some apprehension that we moved, sluggishly, via a small red laser attached by carabineer to Bill's denimed hip, its beam so subtle in shape and shade that I worried aloud that I might trip.

Hold steady, Hal told me, simply, as if intent alone could do the trick.

We stand now in a place unassuming but miraculous: a small, thatched viewing blind not more than thirty feet from the winding bank of a particularly shallow stretch of the Platte. This is south-central Nebraska, the middle of America, the middle of absolutely nothing, a place that appears, in many ways, apathetic to either coast, thousands of acres of empty farmland giving rise to a Burger King and a Taco Bell, a few blinking traffic lights, and "Grandpa's Steakhouse." But every spring without exception, this town of Gibbon, Nebraska—or, more specifically, the famed Rowe Sanctuary, owned and operated by the National Audubon Society—manages to draw in several thousand people, all of them out-of-towners from the Florida Keys or Cincinnati, Dubuque, Iowa or the Carolinas. They come from Canada or they come from Texas, Washington state or Washington, D.C., flocking by minivan—almost always blue—to see what has been hailed as "one of the world's greatest natural wonders" by *National Geographic* and "one of fifteen of nature's most spectacular shows" by CNN. Gibbon, Nebraska is right up there with the aurora borealis, with South Korea's Cherry Blossom Festival, with the Great Migration crossing, in which half a million wildebeests traverse the Masai Mara River, which separates Kenya from Tanzania. Just last week, in fact, the *CBS Evening News* aired a special segment on this very place, with anchorman Scott Pelley offering that it is, frankly, "awe-inspiring." Despite the world's often terrible or grizzly news, here, he said, was a blip of footage "of nature [going] along as planned," complete with its own "rhythm, sound and beauty," dazzling unique and indifferent to humans.

That beauty that Pelley speaks of—the thing that everyone has come to see—appears at first as a swatch of gray, uniform and blurred. There is a prehistoric cooing, a rising noise as the sky fills with light. And then, in one smooth gesture, an estimated six hundred thousand sandhill cranes lift their wings and then their legs to rise in unison above the river, the prairie, and bulbous trees. It is like this every year: for reasons we cannot know, Bill tells us, they select this particular stretch of river, this exact same swatch of trees and yellowed land, as their only prolonged stop in what will prove a several thousand-mile migration, a custom so engrained it is as if a part of bone, or beak, or feather.

I am not from this part of the country, though perhaps this goes without saying. I am from New England, a town thirty miles from a grocery store, a place whose economy thrives from felling timber, a little farming, some welding, some forestry. The woods there are dense and dark; there is no vastness like Nebraska's vastness. There is no kindness like you find here.

Like the birds and nearly everyone, really, my time here in Nebraska is temporary. Unlike the birds, however, I have no final destination—no place I feel my body drawn to. I am young and often feel younger, explorative in the way I think the young cannot help but be. Upon arriving in this state two weeks ago, in fact, I had never even heard of the sandhill cranes, but since then, they are all I hear: they purr in every cornfield, every pasture, every plain. They purr, yes, absolutely; there is no other verb to describe their constant noise. The first time I heard it, it was like a choir—echoing, without barrier, across the infinite and vast nothingness. I rolled my window down, stopped my car along the shoulder.

Nebraska, is what I thought, simply.

And yet while my knowledge of their existence remains relatively new, I take great comfort in their migration. It is one of the largest in the world, Bill tells us, certainly the largest bird migration in North America, and in Nebraska at this time of year, it is all anyone can talk about.

Have I been out to the Rowe?

Have I made my appointment to see the birds?

An appointment, as it were, consists of twenty-three dollars paid in advance for a man like Bill, his carabineer, and expertise.

"Do not talk," he advised us earlier. "Do not cough. Try not to sneeze."

Any movement, however subtle, threatens startling the birds and, beyond disrupting their natural schedule, risks a premature departure before the sun is up for us all to see it.

"How disappointing," Bill reminds us, "how sad to have all of this be in vain."

Our viewing blind, then—and our careful concealment within its hay-stuck walls—is of particular significance: we must take on the appearance of the land, because it is precisely the land the birds know and trust.

"Keep in mind," Bill told us earlier, "these birds are far smarter than we even know. We can't even begin to mine that depth."

That depth, he advised us all, is what has brought the sandhill cranes to Gibbon, Nebraska every year for at least the last several thousand. Likely more, he says, even if we can't prove it. According to a poster hanging in the sanctuary's gift shop, the oldest known sandhill crane fossil is an estimated two and a half million years old, or double the oldest remains of the majority of birds still alive today.

"Let's put it this way," he said, "these birds predate us all."

Their antiquity, then, makes them valuable, their permanence a symbol of significance. The land here has been built up, the highway now an ashy stroke connecting eight hotels to another eight. And yet the birds continue coming, and with them, many thousands of tourists who pay great money and drive great distances to stand in a frigid viewing blind and watch them, to bear witness in this way, to take photographs and shape memories and buy postcards they'll soon mail home.

And in this time, the birds gain back over 20 percent of their body weight, just enough to sustain them for the coming months as they travel farther north. It is here, in Nebraska, for these four weeks that span mid-March to early April, that the birds feast and rest, feast and rest. They eat bugs, Bill tells us, rodents, frogs, snakes. They eat seeds and corn and berries and, on occasion, the smallest of mammals. They spend their nights roosting in the river, so recognizant are they that they know that to remain alive is to hear predators coming: coyotes, foxes, bobcats, even the occasional raccoon. When they once again take flight, it is with the sustenance of Nebraska, the sustenance of America, this place that proves the only thing connecting the places they have been—namely, California and Mexico—and the places they will go: northern Michigan and Canada, Alaska, even Siberia.

"Siberia?" I'd asked earlier, standing in the lobby, as we waited for the last of us to pee. That traced geography—to my mind—required a level of concentration I felt unaccustomed to at 4 A.M.

"Yes," Bill said. "Yes. Many will go on to travel as far as Siberia."

Siberia, indeed.

So I have paid fifty-six dollars to see them twice—once at dawn and once at dusk—and I've driven many hours and bought a guidebook and booked a hotel room beside a pool, because I trust, the way humans are wont to, that this payment will translate into experience: into the birds, unfathomably significant, and my place—there, beside them—as they rise.

As a tourist, I learned quickly, it is not possible to lodge within nineteen miles of the roosting birds or even Gibbon—proximity to this portion of the Platte is reserved for Nebraskans who've long owned homes along the river: families, mostly, it seems to me. Tourists are required to stay in the neighboring Kearney, pronounced *carnie,* in their Holiday Inn or Howard Johnson, Wingate, Best Western, or Ramada. There are, in fact, twenty-one hotels in Kearney, all of them seemingly apropos of nothing at most any other time of the year. But in spring, for these four weeks, they create a cluster of illumination—a modern-day Northern Star, instructing tourists where to go.

Kearney makes me think of a man with missing teeth, his denim overalls, his aluminum doublewide. I think broken lawn chairs in the front yard, a Chihuahua that barks until someone yells.

A woman in pink hair rollers, predictable stereotypes, predictable people.

But last night, pulling into town as late as I did at the suggestion of a bird enthusiast I'd met at a rest stop, I found first a Thai restaurant and then a Mexican grocery, an Italian buffet and half a dozen big-box stores: Target and Best Buy and Wal-Mart, plus a CVS, Rite-Aid, and Home Depot. Here, it seems, is what this part of Nebraska can offer visitors when it cannot offer the sandhill cranes: a good meal and a choice of rooms and your friendly neighborhood pharmacy, all conveniently located just off the highway.

And, when in season, of course, the sandhill cranes.

But it was precisely Kearney's distance that made us nervous—what if we overslept? What if there was highway construction? Which is why, upon arriving a full hour early, I found myself in good company in the sanctuary's lobby. And while one might argue that it is not terrifically easy to make a friend at this hour of the morning, I found I befriended Hal nearly immediately. We were the only two there alone, and we took notice of this immediately.

"Isn't it a little early for someone like you?" Hal joked, implying my young age. Around us, older couples shared single Styrofoam cups of free coffee and embraced for warmth, and Bill began to take roll.

Indeed, our group of twenty or so bird enthusiasts had a median age, I'd guess, of sixty—mostly women in mauve windbreakers and men wearing navy sweatpants with bed-fussed hair. The women's coifs were permed, or going gray, or nearly absent, trimmed so short along their scalp that they reminded me of my brother's buzz cuts—how, when he was small, he'd sit at the backyard picnic table as our father ran an electric razor over his sun-soaked skin, blond hair falling in patches to the hot cement.

These women thought of children, too—they spoke at length about "grandbabies." Their recitals, their vocabularies. Their voices peaked when they found a parallel: Susan's granddaughter in Missouri was enrolled in a jazz and hip-hop class, just like Mildred's granddaughter in southern New Jersey. And *how about that,* they clucked with joy.

These couples were lifelong bird lovers, watchers, amateurs, some, maybe, experts. I was, of course, no bird enthusiast, and in fact, remained rather indifferent about most things. I was the only one of us under forty, having turned twenty-seven the previous month. Hal guessed twenty-five and I felt a swell of pride that when I corrected him, as if those years could really matter. I spent them mostly fumbling, spending money I barely had.

How invigorating, then, to spend the past two weeks seeing what felt like everything: wind turbines churning in silent violence, wind turbines that rest, stagnant, against the sky. I've seen lobster crates roped down to eighteen-wheelers and lighthouses, erect and red against green earth. I am in search of ecstasy, though of course I do not call it that. And yet it is precisely that very term that implies what I am after: a concrete sense of experience, to feel outside myself. The town where I come from expects that all will choose to stay. It is a quiet but crushing confine, meant, I think, to provide comfort, though its comfort does not speak to me. In fact, the idea of lifelong stagnation is so great a fear, I fear it could crush me.

So there is solace in these birds; in their constant, annual movement.

And it is precisely this sense of movement that I have begun to actively seek. These two weeks, I have traveled 1,572 miles, some twenty-four highway hours, and spent the evenings in dimly lit bars at quiet exits just off the highway, and while not ecstaticism, necessarily, I've found the pleasure inherent to these experiences unparalleled to all else I've known. There is a quiet beauty in being lost, in being but one body flitting between two transitory spaces, and Hal champions me for this—how, despite my age and the early hour, I have shown up here regardless.

He says, "Birds aren't normally of interest to someone your age."

A real trooper is what he calls me.

But I am not the only one. At his last count, Bill informs us, the Rowe Sanctuary estimated a hundred and seventy thousand cranes sleeping beside us in the darkness. Two weeks ago, it was half a million, and by this time next week, only a few thousand will remain. It is a predictable occurrence—their departure from these Plains—and it is hard not to envy them for that freedom, how it is *expected* that they will go

Standing shivering against the viewing's plywood, the window covers open, the sound near tangible, Hal tells me he was an army brat—a truth he shares with nearly everyone, he tells me, because it implies a certain sense of impermanence.

"We always lived all over. Every land you could think to live: China and Vietnam, very briefly in Korea."

Texas, too, he says. And he spent a little time in western Florida.

"I didn't much enjoy the heat," he says, "which is why I live now in Kansas."

I think about Kansas and imagine it an arid place, prairie-like and hot. Not tumbleweeds, exactly, but lizards flat like pancakes on the roads, foxes and prickly wildflowers, certainly. Hal tells me that in Kansas, there are no lizards, and that the heat is only cumbersome in summer—the winters, he says, are cold.

"And anyway, it's the change I like," he says. "So I take the few months of heat like I take everything."

This is not Hal's first time viewing the cranes, though it is the first time he has come alone. Next month, he says, will mark the one-year anniversary of her death—his wife of forty-seven years. This springtime viewing of the birds in flight was something they did with regularity; last year, his wife was here to stand beside him, just like all the many years before, and they watched the birds take off together—their wings extended in perfect angles, their bodies gleaning, alit with light.

It was still so smooth in the quiet dawn, he said, that the water mirrored their departure.

"Birds everywhere," he said. "On the ground, horizon, sky."

He explained that during their most recent visit, Hal and his wife learned that the sandhill cranes are believed to pair for life, though their guide conceded it was nearly impossible to trace each partnership from year to year. Still, Hal tells me, enthusiasts take comfort in the birds' likeness: their elegance so much like our own, we flatter, their shared inclination for monogamy. Very few roam alone, and there's a lesson, Hal tells me, in that. His eyes narrow when he looks at me. He stacks his sneakers one on top of the other for warmth.

They are a creature, he reflects, open to love, to company lifelong and migratory, and I, too, prefer this idea of pairing, how the birds can be nomadic and, yet, not alone.

"I met my wife," he says, "and everything about the world I knew changed."

He meant, among other things, his world of impermanence. Unlike Hal, who saw in travel a certain freedom, his wife feared the dangers of mobility—she would not fly, would not board a boat, and once famously called the ranger's station outside of Yosemite to inquire about the road's stability.

Are they steep or winding? she wanted to know.

Hal tells me this and laughs; it is a part of her, he says, he learned to love. And it was worth it, all those years, to give up the open road, the atlas stained with grease and coffee, the paper-wrapped hamburger with its softened pickles and grated onions. It was enough to be beside her. But in the eleven months since her death, he has seized his own vitality—visiting first their daughter in San Diego, then their youngest son in Baltimore, and most recently, he took part in an eight-hour, elaborate bird-watching tour along the California coast, a package that promised viewings of more than a hundred and fifty birds. Hal counted a hundred and forty-four, but he says he wasn't about to complain. When I ask him which was his favorite, he pauses.

"Hard to say," he says. Then, "The pelicans."

In June he'll fly to Anchorage to spend four weeks in remote Alaska, camping outside of Denali with his two sons and both their wives. He did the same trip as a young man, he tells me, long before the government thought to expand Denali. It was smaller then; you could sleep beside the mountains.

By fall, he'll be in Maine—more specifically, Kennebunkport—where he'll watch the leaves catch fire, the most impressive display of foliage the nation has to offer. They are colors I know well, and when I offer this to him, he says, *Soon I'll know them, too.*

"The things I never saw," he said. "All these things I never did."

However far from her I am now, I am reminded of a woman I met many months ago on a plane. We sat, stalled, on the tarmac of Charlotte Douglas International; she was but bone beneath her blanket. When finally I inquired where she was headed, her face lit, jubilant.

"Maine," she said. She was ninety-eight, visiting—for one last time—each of her five adult children in their respective homes across the country. Her itinerary freighted her down the West Coast and to southern Texas, to Minnesota and Lynchburg, Virginia. It spanned well over a month, and at its culmination: a nursing home.

But when I expressed condolences, she said there was no need.

"This is just the way it goes," she said, "if you are lucky."

If you are lucky. If you get to live before the living stops.

It seems to me a matter of perspective: the way we choose to think about a life, about a landscape or loved one or circumstance. After all, even from the farthest edge of our viewing blind, Hal and I see only darkness: there are no birds or beaks or wings. We know and trust that they are there—we have a rising sense of their frenetic noise—but without the glint of sun cannot see their multitude, those birds, all several hundred thousand, converging and veering across the Platte.

As we approach our third hour within the warming viewing blind, Bill tells us to, at last, "hush up." Prepare our cameras, he ushers softly. Their prehistoric noise, he notes, has built.

Hal pushes his elbow into my stomach, ecstatic.

"Get ready," he says—as if I am his child, as if I stand on tiptoes at his feet. As if the very years that have brought him here with regularity have altogether faded away, have rendered him open, once again, to an altogether new experience. Hal is not old or without love; he is, above all, held captive by its renewal, by these birds preparing to rise from murky darkness, however traveled, however weary.

I raise my binoculars to my face and unexpectedly lower my camera. It is not, I know, what matters. I have come to see the birds, and when at last they finally rise, they do so in unison, their wings extended at an enormous length, their density above the river like a churning turbine, roiling quickly, rising up.

A single blade of gray, interrupting this empty landscape.

"Amazing," Hal says to me, and *amazing,* I repeat. There's no way for me to know it now, but three months from this quiet morning, I'll find myself in a parking lot in Fairbanks, Alaska—a place I've chosen to see because of Hal. Nothing about it will seem out of the ordinary: it is simple yellow grass that gives way to birch. But it's here, in Creamer Field, I'll read that the sandhill cranes land, having at last reached Alaska.

And have I heard of them, a stranger will ask? Have I ever heard of sandhill cranes?

"Yes," I'll say, and will think of Hal: there in Denali, many miles south, beside his daughters, beside his sons. Beside the comfort that he seeks—that he knowingly extracts—from the art of movement. I remember the origin of *ecstatic:* that it means, quite literally, "to be or stand outside"—of oneself, one's environment, one's consciousness, I suppose, or in a viewing blind along the Platte, many hundred miles from one's origin.

That day in Nebraska, Hal said to me, *The world requires no audience*. And while I could admit that that seemed true, that it would indeed go on without our presence, it seems nothing if not miraculous when our lives align so that we might bear witness.

When we begin to notice, for the first time, that we are not altogether different, or alone.

～ ～ ～

Amy Butcher is an essayist and author of Visiting Hours, *a 2015 memoir that earned starred reviews and praise from* The New York Times Sunday Review of Books, *NPR,* The Star Tribune, Kirkus Reviews, Glamour, Cosmopolitan, *and others. Most recently, her work was awarded grand prize in the 2016 Solas Awards' "Best of Travel Writing" series, earned a notable distinction in* Best American Essays 2015, *and was awarded grand prize in the 2014 Iowa Review Award in nonfiction as judged by David Shields. Her 2016 op-ed, "Emoji Feminism," published in* The New York Times Sunday Review, *inspired Google to create thirteen new female-empowered emojis, due out later this year. Additional work has appeared in* The New York Times, The Iowa Review, Guernica, Gulf Coast, Fourth Genre, The Rumpus, *The Paris Review online, Tin House online, and Brevity, among others, and has been anthologized in* Tell It True: The Art and Craft of Creative Nonfiction *and* The Best Of Vela. *She is a recent recipient of Colgate University's Olive B. O'Connor Creative Writing fellowship as well as grants and awards from the Kimmel Harding Nelson Center for the Arts, the Academy of American Poets, Word Riot Inc., and the Stanley Foundation for International Research. She currently teaches a range of courses on the essay and literary journalism at Ohio Wesleyan University and annually at the Sitka Fine Arts Camp in Sitka, Alaska.*

❧ ❧ ❧

The Good Captain

When the sea is calm, every ship has a good captain.
—Sailing proverb

I watched the sleeping ocean from a corner of the cockpit. In the deep darkness, blind waves broke and collapsed in rhythmic, drawn-out hisses, luring me to sleep as they misted me with spray. Even in sleep, the ocean swell rolled forward, constant, like a shark that never stops swimming. I had felt that I could go on forever too, sailing west without stopping across the great expanse of the Pacific.

Then a few hours before sunset, a faint smudge had floated into view amidst the clouds on the horizon. A Marquesan island, hazy through the atmosphere, marked our entry into Polynesian waters. Sighting land awakened in me dormant memories: limitless freshwater, a bed that didn't move, the quiet pleasure of a walk. Having sailed day and night for three weeks, I'd already spent the time I'd wanted with the open ocean. Seeing land made me starved for landfall. But the distant island was not a port of entry, and we could not lawfully stop there. We had to carry on; we still had one more night till our destination. We were headed for Nuku Hiva, a dead volcano thousands of miles from any continent.

I had three hours and twenty-seven minutes before Chet would relieve me from my watch. After dawn, we'd trade places and I'd flop into one of the bunks he and I and Cyrille—the other hitchhiking crew member—all shared, the cushions still warm from his body. In the meantime I stared down the sky.

On night watch, the very real (albeit unlikely) possibility of annihilation is balanced against total boredom. I watched for signs of changing weather or a ship's light on the horizon. A 900-foot container ship cruises at around thirty nautical miles an hour with minimal crew to keep costs down. On autopilot, the captain literally asleep at the wheel, a container ship could run us down without ever knowing it had hit us.

In the groping dark, inky cumulus clouds were assembling behind us along the eastern horizon. The clouds could have been nothing, an annoying obstacle between me and the sunrise, or they could have been a squall, a localized storm. Without a moon, I couldn't tell. I could barely see the clouds—gobs of black in an even blacker sky.

A squall could bring strong winds that might tear sails, break rigging. We couldn't afford breakages so far from help. I turned away from the horizon and closed my eyes to relieve the painful pressure behind them, exhaustion from straining into the night. I just wanted an easy final watch. I didn't want the hassle of deciding whether the clouds were going to coalesce into a squall. If, in fact, a localized storm was forming behind us on the eastern horizon, the trade winds would blow the squall onto us. Then, I'd need to determine if we could ride it out, or if I would need to wake the captain. And waking the captain was the last thing I wanted to do.

Chet didn't like to be called "captain." He'd told Cyrille and me, "I don't want to create a weird dynamic. We're all just part of the crew." Once, after he made some unusually pointed request, I said as a joke, "Alright, Cap." Cyrille winked at me, but Chet cringed and went below without saying anything.

Still, on night watch by myself, when I needed to decide whether or not to wake the one person who charted our course, who rebuilt and rewired every inch of this boat, *his* boat, the one person ultimately in charge, I thought of him as captain.

For the most part, Chet was right: we were all just part of the crew, though as the newest member, I felt I had to prove myself. I knew Chet trusted me, but he trusted Cyrille more. Cyrille had joined the boat three months and 300 miles before me. His time on the boat showed; while I milled about gearing up the gumption to ask Chet what needed doing, there was Cyrille coming down the dock with a chipper smile and a cart full of potable water jugs anticipating our need to top up the fresh water tanks before Chet had asked. Cyrille was Johnny-on-the-goddamn-spot, a valuable member of the three-person team we had fast become. Still, I wanted to be first among equals.

I had connected with Chet—and by extension Cyrille— through *Latitude 38*'s online crew list. Other boats had dismissed me, saying they wanted young, strapping (they didn't explicitly say *male*) crew to help with heavy lifting. Those boats that did welcome me aboard wanted a cook and a maid, often asking if I would be open to a relationship. One captain old enough to be my grandfather declared himself a balding sex machine. Chet, thankfully, just wanted me to sail the boat. He was impressed that a twenty-six-year-old had a decade of sailing experience. I had a lot more if you counted the years I captained my childhood home, a fifty-foot sailboat, from the safety of my father's lap. I liked that Chet and Cyrille were only ten years older than I and European; I was hoping to sidestep American "bro culture." Chet was a certified skipper, and *Sudden Stops Necessary* (*Stops*, for short) was a seaworthy boat—big enough for three people, with a galley, a navigation station, two cabins that were already taken, and a salon for me to sleep in when we weren't underway. Chet and I emailed, Skyped, and checked references, until there was nothing left for me to do but fly down to Mexico for a get-to-know-you sail. Since that first night passage along the coast of Jalisco, the guys had trusted me to stand watch while they rested below.

First light glowed indigo on a distant edge of the horizon, while the clouds bled into a continuous line. Every fifteen minutes it was time to look again. If I saw a ship on the horizon ten miles away, closing half a sea mile a minute, I would have twenty minutes to determine if we were on a convergent course, devise a plan of action, and alter our heading to avoid a possible collision.

I stood to scan the horizon, and the cloud line behind us, now a fully fortified rampart, startled me with its height and solidity. I leaned closer and looked without blinking, trying to let in as much light as possible. Beneath the cloud line loomed the darkest corner of the sky. Pushed by a following wind and fast approaching, the clouds would soon be on top of us.

I circled my ankles, flexed my calves and checked the self-steering wind vane keeping us on course. *Stops* was steering itself. All was in order. I took one last look and went below. At the nav station, I turned on the radar as the deck lurched out from under my feet, and I stumbled backward, disoriented. A large swell rolled under *Stops's* hull. I grabbed at the edge of the chart table to keep from falling across the cabin, then leaned back hard in the opposite direction, as the counter-roll tried to throw me into the radar. *That was a big one. Pay attention.* If I let myself forget where I was, I could break a rib being flung across the cabin.

Embarrassed, despite the lack of observers, I shook off the large swell, assuming it to be the tallest wave in the set, and pulled myself toward the radar. I didn't consider, perhaps chose to ignore, a fact I knew: big waves are often pushed by big winds.

On the radar screen, large green blotches marred with red announced squall clouds with a lot of rain. Since a few degrees north of the equator, we had been skirting around and through the doldrums. The doldrums, or the intertropical convergence zone, are not a place marked on any chart. Between the reliable trade winds, they are a shifting region of low pressure known for days or weeks of windless calm punctuated by squalls. At first we had motor-sailed around the squalls, altering course a few degrees to dodge each pregnant, low-slung cloud. Then one afternoon we had come across a squall too big to avoid. Chet had taken the helm and driven straight through the gusty downpour. Since leaving the doldrums we'd been pounding through one squall after another.

North of the equator, I had known to expect a predictable burst of wind and rain. Squalls in the South Pacific, however, had taken on different personalities. Would this squall be calm, almost windless, absentmindedly dripping a wet, persistent drizzle? Or would it have no rain but a lot of wind, or both? A squall could push strong winds and a torrential deluge, a wall of enormous drops that rip into the water like gunfire, obscuring the horizon and shrinking the visible world around the boat. My favorite squalls started thick and close, then eased out, pulling back the curtain of rain to reveal undulating silver hills embossed with braille.

In the last few weeks, I'd sailed through more squalls than years I'd been alive, and still I didn't know what to make of this one. Sizable lakes of green and red pooled twenty miles wide on the radar screen, but size, as they say, doesn't tell you everything. We had double-reefed at dusk, significantly reducing our sail area to safely ride out the inevitable squalls. The only reason I would need to wake the captain was if the winds were going to be so strong that we needed to shorten sail even further. The radar, whose radio waves echoed off rain, but not wind, couldn't tell me either.

The captain lay a few feet from me in the salon and I let my eyes wander over his sleeping body. Chet was curled on his side in gray, checkered boxers, limp on top of his white sheet, unable to tell me what he wanted. The thought occurred to me, *Maybe he isn't really sleeping.* If he wasn't sleeping, I reasoned, I wouldn't technically be waking him. The steady rise and fall of his white t-shirt, however, confirmed he was asleep.

I sat there at the nav station in the captain's chair, watching him. A week before, we had sailed across the equator. Crossing the equator, a maritime rite of passage, transformed me forever from a *pollywog*, a rookie, into a *shellback*, an experienced sailor. I believed in tests of skill and willpower, and the possibility of arriving on the other side stronger, wiser, truer. Somebody different, somebody new. A person could cross a line that meant she had gained enough experience to know the answers in difficult situations. I believed that I'd already arrived at that other side, and I loathed myself for not knowing what to do now. The squall felt like a test whose sole purpose was to humiliate me. *If I were a better sailor*, I thought, *I would be able to reef single-handed, to handle this on my own.*

The waves were gathering force, and to keep from falling, I crawled on all fours back up the companionway ladder. The deck pitched at steep angles. All around me in the dim morning, more night than day, the gray surface of the ocean throbbed rhythmically, the pulse of waves visible only as movement. I couldn't see their height, but I could feel them growing. *Big winds*, I allowed myself to remember. If only the squall could wait till Chet's watch.

As the only girl on board *Stops*, I didn't want to sound the alarm unless I had a good reason. I had to divine the true nature of the squall as well as the moment when the captain wanted me to wake him, if it got bad. Too early and I was afraid he'd be angry, lose respect for me; too late and we'd be in trouble.

I could feel the squall's power even before it reached us. The steady wind speed hit thirty knots and gusts struck with surprising force. The sea around *Stops* heaped up as the wind tore the foaming tops off waves in white streaks. On land, this wind would throw whole trees into motion.

Adrenaline flaming through my veins screamed bigger winds were coming. I had to wake Chet. How could I have waited this long?

In the muffled quiet below deck, I crept toward Chet, trying not to disturb Cyrille, even as the stiff crinkle of my foul weather gear rustled to a roar. My shipmates' sleeping bodies appeared dead to the impending squall.

I shook Chet's shoulder. He pushed up his sleeping mask, "Have we reached Nuku Hiva?" Chet's instant lucidity made me wonder if he'd been sleeping at all. Maybe *Stops*'s increasingly agitated motion had woken him, or maybe he'd been awake anticipating landfall.

"I need your help." Chet leapt from his bunk

Back on deck the instrument panel showed wind speeds exceeding forty knots. The wind clawed down the backs of waves with a force that would tear limbs from trees. Though thick clouds blotted out the dawn, the squall was now clearly visible. Massive gray clouds stretched in a formidable front as far as I could see in either direction. Beneath this advancing army, winds beat the sea into a fury a few hundred yards behind us.

Chet's large eyes widened as he took in the mega-squall. The acid taste of imagined insults were on my tongue. *What's wrong with you? Why didn't you wake me sooner?* Chet's eyebrows pursed together, then fell back. He wasted no time squabbling. "Let's reef. You've got the wind vane?" For the captain, only our safety mattered.

With a hand on the wind vane's thin control lines, I steered *Stops* into the wind to take the burden off the sails. I braced my feet as the boat slammed headlong into oncoming waves. The mainsail swung close above my head, whipping itself in the wind, each crack of canvas cutting through me like a gunshot. No longer caught in the hand of the wind, the boat's machinery was a loose-flung thing, predictable only up to a point.

Chet threw himself about the winch, grinding down the mainsail even further, then folded and secured the sail. On his mark, I turned us back downwind. The mainsail, now smaller, filled and steadied us in the following seas. We rolled in more of the headsail and *Stops'* jerking motion lost its frantic edge. Practice had made us good at this.

Without saying a word Chet took the helm from me, unhitching the wind vane to steer by hand. Then a long, high-pitched cry let loose from the sky, and the squall hit. Strong winds blew seawater skyward and forced rain sideways, slant-ways, anyways but down. A gust tried to push the boat over, but 6,000 pounds of ballast in *Stops's* keel kept us upright. If we hadn't shortened sail, the gust could have knocked us down, slamming the boat on its side, the cockpit pitched vertical, the sails pushed all the way down against the waves.

Chet squinted into the wind and rain. He resembled a wet cat; his rain-drenched hair clumped into random hunks. But most of all it was his long, matted eyelashes, blinking away the water streaming into his partly closed eyes, that made me thankful not to be Captain. Instead, I was safe and relatively dry beneath the spray hood.

Though rousted from sleep minutes ago, Chet stood at the wheel without complaint. It was as if he'd been waiting for this opportunity to prove himself. *Chet Against the Squall.* There was an assuredness about him that spoke to his years of ocean racing. Here was the sailor who, when Royal Yachtmaster test officials turned off the GPS-enabled, electronic charts in the middle of the night, was able to find his location and pass his exam using only a depth sounder and paper charts to feel his way over the bottom.

I relaxed back into my corner of the cockpit, even as a coiled sense of unease pressed against my chest. Despite my best efforts, I'd woken him too late, though he didn't seem upset.

"Nice and wet," Cyrille said, spitting saltwater out of his mouth. Standing half out of the main hatch, he had caught the full brunt of a wave. The hollow clinking of winches would have amplified through the hull. That and *Stops'*s catapulting motion must have woken him.

Cyrille stepped into the cockpit wearing what he'd been sleeping in: swim trunks and nothing else. "You should really have a tether," Chet said. I'd made that mistake before, coming on deck in weather without the tedious safety gear—life jacket, tether, foul-weather pants and jacket—that the conditions required. I was glad it wasn't me this time.

Cyrille opened his mouth as if to say something, but just nodded his chin into his chest and went below. I knew that feeling; it was hard to be told what to do first thing in the morning when you just wanted to see what the commotion that woke you looked like, and harder still that Chet was always right.

A few minutes later Cyrille reemerged in full regalia. He sat in the small, dry-ish space beneath the spray hood opposite me and flashed a good-humored smile, wrinkling the corners of his eyes—the only hint of age. Cyrille seemed to greet each day with ease. He'd shrugged off the recession that had reclaimed his house. And then slipped out of half-ownership in a restaurant to be an extra hand on a racing yacht. That was two boats and six months ago. Though he was from Brittany, France's sailing capital, he hadn't sailed there and was learning as he went. I never caught him looking back, not once. How was that possible? I wished I could live as effortlessly.

The wind fell away and the sky opened, releasing large drops that relinquished themselves to gravity. The rain clattered against the silver surface of the ocean, hollowing out 10 million tiny craters. Waves sloshed against *Stops*'s hull with idle energy left over from the wind. "This is like sailing in England," Chet said in mock complaint. "You don't need to go to the South Pacific, it's rainy, dark, cloudy. Jesus, it's like the English Channel. Right?" He was playing around; he knew that of the three of us, only he had sailed there. He continued, "Look at this thing. Is it getting bigger, or . . ." Waggling his head, he said in a ludicrous falsetto, "We're gonna die."

If Chet was joking around, maybe he really wasn't angry? We shortened sail in time. The boat was intact. No one was hurt. Then why was I queasy with the thought of what could have happened? Instead of feeling elation for having survived the squall, fear hollowed out a hole behind my solar plexus. I'd made the cut, but barely. Maybe all those other captains who'd dismissed me had been right.

It didn't occur to me that I'd used my knowledge and skill to make a call that was well-timed *enough*, considering my exhaustion, my newness to South Pacific weather patterns, the vagaries of the ocean.

From far above, the sun murmured through clouds, raising the ceiling and brightening our morning. Then the rain subsided and the world expanded all the way to the horizon. There, like a forgotten promise, the hazy shadow of our destination floated between sea and sky. "Nuku Hiva," I pointed straight ahead excitedly. This time there was no question; I identified our barely discernable island with certainty.

"You haven't seen it yet?" Chet said, that same surety slapping a grin across his face. Apparently, while looking forward steering the boat, he had seen the island ages ago. For him, Nuku Hiva had always been there, poised near the ninth parallel for 3 million years. With my attention directed back towards the squall behind us, the island had snuck up on me.

The sea has amnesia. An hour after the sky had opened up, the trade winds returned and the waves relaxed back into a manageable size. Our bodies and the boat were dry. The only reminders of the squall were a gray ceiling of clouds and a cool, misty morning veiling Nuku Hiva.

Nuku Hiva's mass and density solidified as we approached. A dark mist on the horizon grew into the sleeping body of a blue-gray whale lumbering on the sea. I had been expecting the startling mountains that Tania Aebi, the first American woman to sail around the world, described in her 1989 book, *Maiden Voyage*. To me, however, Nuku Hiva at a distance was flat as a tabletop, the island's gently sloping volcanic rock slouching into the sea.

As we got closer, the island multiplied into a quintuplet of headlands separated by deep bays. One of those headlands marked the entrance to Taiohae (pronounced Tie-ee-oh-hay) Bay, where we would finally anchor.

With Chet at the wheel, I tried to make sense of our satellite position on the digital chart below deck in relation to the actual rock, dirt, and leaves off our starboard side. I was anxious to be the one to find our headland. I wanted to prove—to him and to myself—that I could do something right.

Eventually, Chet lost patience and gave Cyrille the helm. I was crestfallen. After consulting the chartplotter, Chet turned us in the direction he thought Taiohae Bay. Sure enough, the trail on the plotter corresponded exactly with our new heading. We were now aiming for our destination.

Large ocean waves couldn't penetrate the deep bay. The incessant motion that had rattled my body for more than three weeks began to ease. Standing in the cockpit became easy. I could walk around deck without holding a handrail. It was like breathing deeply when I hadn't realized I'd been holding my breath.

"Wanna take the helm?" Chet asked me.

"Really?" I didn't move, unable to believe that Chet wanted me to steer us into our first South Pacific port, the port that marked the end of our long and successful journey, a port that neither of us had ever seen before.

"It's an easy entrance," he said. Chet knew the island was steep-to, sloping downward toward the seafloor 13,000 feet below.

"There aren't any reefs or rocks to worry about?"

"You'll be fine." Chet's eyes were kind, vacant, expectant. He really did want to give me this honor. Besides, he needed to consult the sailing guide to decide where we'd drop anchor.

In one synchronized movement, Chet stepped away from the wheel and I slid in. I assumed the captain's stance, back tall, legs wide, hands firm. Though the ocean had emptied me of more energy than I thought I had, my senses sparked to alertness as my hands grasped the wheel. At the helm, my fears receded. I was driving and being driven, captain and passenger.

My hands hold the memory of every boat I have ever steered, though none are held so tightly as the first. From my father's lap, I clasped the knobby handles of the ship's wheel on my family's boat. The open wood grain, weathered in the sun, was smooth and rough in my small hands. I was always oversteering, turning the wheel too far and worrying us off course, then over correcting in the opposite direction. My father told me again and again to look straight ahead, to keep the mast in line with our destination. The fifty-foot sailboat swaggered back and forth as I found and lost and found our heading.

The morning we sailed into Taiohae Bay, I navigated a straight course. Cyrille prepped the anchor, and Chet surveyed the bay for a good place to drop the hook. In a few hours, I would walk the crescent footpath around the bay, waves smashing against the beach, then draining back through large, smooth stones in a silvery clatter reminiscent of rain.

≈ ≈ ≈

Glenda Reed is a writer, artist and adventurer. Her writing has received funding from the Jerome Foundation, the McKnight Foundation, and the Barbara Deming Memorial Fund among others. She was awarded a fellowship to the Loft Literary Center's 2-15-2016 Mentor Series. Reed is also a winner of The Moth StorySlam, and is currently working on a memoir about hitchhiking around the world on sailboats. This story was originally published in the Winter 2016 issue of Creative Nonfiction.

⊰≈ ⊰≈ ⊰≈

Love and Lies in Iran

Most people dream of spending their honeymoon on
exotic beaches. The author and his American bride
opted for a road trip through the land of the ayatollahs.

We raced through the darkness and didn't see it
coming. Mehdi sat erect behind the wheel, honking slower cars out of his way. But one car stayed in its lane;
it challenged his hierarchy. Mehdi honked, flashed, tailgated,
and when the other car slowly made way, he barreled into
the opening. Then something crashed, glass shattered, and the
other car's side-view mirror went flying through the air, leaving a trail of silvery dust glittering in its wake.

Mehdi laughed and kept going.

We sat in silence, and it unsettled Mehdi that my wife,
Gypsy, and I weren't laughing. He kept looking at us, anxious, it seemed, for approval, some kind of validation. And
then, suddenly, a car appeared next to us, honking, flashing,
pushing us to the edge of the road. Mehdi looked for a way
out, braking, accelerating, swerving, but the other car followed us like a shadow. He struggled for a while, then gave
up and slowed down. The other car cut him off, forcing us
to stop.

It was after midnight and we were cornered on a dark road somewhere in Iran. This is where our honeymoon ended and the epilogue began. Without turning around, I whispered to Gypsy not to move or say a word. Then I pushed the bag with the money deeper into the legroom, until it was no longer visible.

The other car's doors opened and two women got out. The woman on the passenger side screamed into her phone and started walking in circles, glowering at us in the glare of our car's headlights. The woman on the driver's side went to the trunk of her car, opened it and leaned in. She was heavy-set and wore her headscarf in a rigid style, showing no hair. Mehdi jumped out of the car and raised his arms in disbelief. The woman pulled a baseball bat out of the trunk, straightened herself and slowly walked toward him.

I knew that a honeymoon in Iran with an American bride would not be without complications, and that my being a German journalist wouldn't help. When two governments are as mistrustful of each other as those of the U.S. and Iran, their citizens are made to feel the suspicion whenever they enter the other country. The fact that we were living in Berlin might have made us look a little less suspicious, but I was prepared. In my pocket, I carried a piece of paper with the phone number of the Swiss Embassy in Tehran, which, in the absence of a U.S. Embassy, takes care of Americans and their consular needs. Missing from my emergency plan was the wrath of the Iranian women.

We had been sitting in this car like exhibition pieces in a museum of the Iranian Revolution—in the front, Mehdi and I, two bearded men in the back, Gypsy, a veiled woman. And suddenly the dominant male figure around which everything seemed to revolve in this country was gone. The man who minutes ago had his hands on the wheel was now standing in the street beseeching a woman who wanted to crack his skull.

When Gypsy and I made plans for our honeymoon, we weren't dreaming of lagoons and lonely beaches. We weren't drawn to riding elephants in India, or flying in a propeller plane across the Okavango Delta. We wanted to penetrate a hermetic country and find beauty behind its forbidding façade. We liked the idea of lovers subverting a state ruled by imperious men, and quickly fell for Iran.

The first conflict of our honeymoon erupted even before we departed, in the women's section of a department store in Berlin. We argued about a pair of shoes. To me, they looked like the shoes of a splay-footed ballerina—black and shiny, with ribbons glued to the tips. Their brand name was "Yessica," and I didn't like them. They made my wife appear small. I called them "mullah shoes." Gypsy bought them for seven euros.

We were standing in the middle of Berlin's hip Prenzlauer Berg neighborhood, and I felt as though the power of the Iranian mullahs extended all the way to the German capital. They had reprogrammed my wife.

I didn't know this side of Gypsy, this kind of submissiveness. She was born in the Dominican Republic and grew up in the Bronx, and she has the fearlessness of the underprivileged and Simone de Beauvoir's lust for arguing. She is also the daughter of a woman who used to carry a ladies' revolver in her purse, and who once shot into the ceiling of a bar where she had tracked down her husband, a woman sitting on his lap. And now Gypsy bought a pair of ugly shoes to please the mullahs, letting them decide when she was a woman and when a subject. I didn't understand. "You lack pragmatic intelligence," Gypsy said.

We knew that the dress code of the Islamic Republic of Iran was also enforced in Frankfurt, from the moment passengers entered an Iran Air plane. At the gate, we didn't notice it. We sat among Iranian women who only stood out because they were dressed more elegantly than the German women around them. But at some point they began to change. As boarding time approached, they slipped into overcoats and covered their hair with headscarves. They slowly disappeared.

A few Iranian women remained uncovered. They showed their hair, their necks, the shape of their bodies, and they weren't wearing mullah shoes. They walked around in high heels and didn't mind being followed by the looks of others. They seemed determined to hold on to their freedom for as long as they could.

Gypsy didn't dare to do that. She knew that, as an American, she would be watched with particular scrutiny, and she worried about offending anyone. She covered her head with a black scarf and pushed it back to reveal some hair, just as she had seen it in pictures of street life in Tehran. She knew the Iranian dress code in detail—she had been studying it for weeks. Sometimes during her dress rehearsals, she would stand in front of me, covered in a headscarf and an overcoat, and ask if I was still attracted to her. I didn't care for the coat, but I became enchanted by the way the scarf framed her face, the mystery it bestowed on her.

Gypsy knew that liberal Iranian women are smarter at interpreting the dress code than the mullahs are at writing it. She admired their mastery at stretching the rules, how they played with the fact that the boundaries of the permissible are fluid on a woman's body. But she also knew that plainclothes officers walk the streets, harshly enforcing the dress code. In their canon, women are only allowed to show their face and hands; their feet, if they dare to wear open shoes, have to be covered by opaque stockings.

We entered the plane, and my Dominican wife, who was raised in America, lived in Germany and bears the name of a vagabond, obeyed the Iranian dress code by covering herself in an overcoat sewed by Chinese hands and a scarf bought from a Kashmiri in India.

Gypsy understood the uncovered Iranian women and their longing for freedom, but the German women irritated her. She looked around the plane and none of them was wearing a headscarf. She found it disrespectful. The men on Iran's Guardian Council would have liked Gypsy, how she stood there in her headscarf, her opaque stockings and her mullah shoes, seething at the women of the West.

I kept quiet. In a strange way, I was indebted to Ayatollah Khomeini and the revolution he instigated. My life would have been different without him, shallower. I never would have met the first love of my life. He pushed her toward me, and if he were still alive, I would have to kiss his hand for it.

Her name was Mandana—the Everlasting. Her parents took her and fled to Germany after Khomeini seized power. We went to high school together, and she enraptured me in a hotel room in Warsaw. I was eighteen and knew nothing; she was nineteen and knew more. Our love lasted six years. I could have liberated her father from the brothers who kept calling from Iran, claiming they had found the perfect husband for his daughter. But I kept her waiting, and she left for Jerusalem with the one who promised to make her wait no more.

Observing Mandana's father, I studied the inner conflicts of an Iranian man. He used to work as a bartender, and had married Mandana's mother even though she was a divorced woman from the West. He loved his black Jaguar and a good whiskey. He worked tirelessly to give his beloved four daughters the best education possible. And he lied for me when he told his brothers that Mandana was already engaged.

His name was Faramarz, and he could be as tender as his name suggested: the one who forgives his enemies. He seemed like a prototype of the modern Iranian man, but his modernity had its limits. He wasn't supposed to know that Mandana took the pill. He wasn't supposed to know that she was lying in my bed when she purported to be staying at a girlfriend's place. He wasn't supposed to know any of the secret deals his wife struck with his daughters.

He knew it. He knew everything. But he had to pretend he knew nothing. At the time, I thought he was living in a lie. Years later, I understood that the lie was his armor in defending us against the liars, the cover behind which he gave us freedom. I never thanked him for it, and it haunted me.

Gypsy knew this part of my past. She understood that Mandana had played a crucial role in shaping me into the man she took as her husband, and she was grateful for it. She knew that it was Mandana who had kept my life from falling apart when I despaired over my parents' separation, and that it was Mandana who had pushed me to mend my relationship with my mother. This journey was a passage into our future that acknowledged the past.

We landed in Tehran and entered a quiet country. Freedom of speech was quietly suppressed. Dissidents were quietly arrested. A nuclear program was quietly developed. We detested the regime, but we believed in the beauty of the country. We believed that the Iranian people were different from the men who pretended to represent them.

It was the spring of 2009 and we had no idea of the turmoil that was coming. We couldn't know that, only months later, people would take to the streets to protest the manipulated results of a presidential election, only to see their uprising brutally crushed. Many would be arrested, many raped, bludgeoned, shot dead. We didn't know the face of Neda Agha-Soltan yet, the student who would lie dying in a street in Tehran, blood streaming across her cheeks, a sniper's bullet in her chest.

The apparatus of the Islamic Republic of Iran received the American bride with theatrical coldness. The photograph in her visa showed Gypsy smiling, and the immigration officer might have liked it. But he didn't open her passport. It was enough for him to see the golden eagle and the gilded words "United States of America." He grabbed the passport, gestured harshly in one direction and said, "Come!"

He led us to a desk where two men in elaborately embroidered uniforms were sitting, frozen in straight posture. They carried themselves with an abrasiveness that suggested they were in charge of handling sensitive cases. I presented my German passport, but they waved me off. I pulled out our marriage certificate, but it didn't help that it carried the seal of the City of New York. One of the officers took Gypsy's passport and disappeared, the other pointed to a bench by the wall and said, "Wait!"

We sat on this bench like defendants. It didn't surprise us that the American received special scrutiny, just like Iranians are singled out whenever they try to enter the U.S. But we were convinced that they had vetted Gypsy before issuing her visa, and the same was probably true for me. We didn't have anything to hide and knew that our governments would be there for us if we needed help. But after twenty minutes in abeyance, we became nervous. We began to strategize how to react if they separated us.

That is the frame of mind where dictatorial regimes like to have their visitors. They give you time to think, and watch as you slide into irrationality. Gypsy was now a woman without a passport, stateless in an arbitrary state. The officer kept staring at us from behind his desk; that seemed to be his task. Gypsy leaned over my shoulder and whispered, "My heart is going to jump out of my chest."

After a while, the other officer returned with Gypsy's passport. He placed it on the desk and took an inkpad and a sheet of paper out of a drawer. Then he asked for Gypsy's hand. Printed on the paper were two large and ten small squares.

He took Gypsy's hand and pressed the tip of her fingers on the ink pad, then on the paper—the individual fingerprints in the small squares, the whole hand in the large squares. When he was done, he pushed the passport across the desk and smirked. He seemed to enjoy the fact that the American now had to run around his country with ink on her fingertips, like a criminal.

I waited for him to ask for my hand, but he wasn't interested. When I asked why he took Gypsy's fingerprints but not mine, he looked amused and said, "Because America does it." Our eyes locked and we both laughed at the absurdity of the games governments play.

Gypsy and I got on a bus that took us into the city, and the first thing we saw were the illuminated minarets of the Khomeini Mausoleum, piercing like lances into the night sky. Khomeini followed us wherever we went, always watching. Our hotel in Tehran was named after Ferdowsi, a revered Persian poet, but we only ever saw Khomeini. He gazed at us from the wall behind the reception desk, and on the way to the elevator we passed a Khomeini painting and a Khomeini bust, then listened to an instrumental version of "Careless Whisper" as we ascended to our floor. Even the elevator music was from the time of Khomeini.

We entered our room and saw two single beds, a picture of Khomeini hanging in the middle. We thought it was a misunderstanding. Perhaps they had given us separate beds because Gypsy had not shed her family's name. We went back to the reception and explained to the concierge that we were on our honeymoon and would like to sleep in the same bed. He gave us a mystified look and said that Iranian couples sleep in separate beds.

We dismissed this Iranian tradition and pushed our beds together under Khomeini's beard. Then Gypsy undressed in front of him. The ayatollah had to look at a number of things during our honeymoon. Maybe that is why he always stared at us with such a grim face.

The next morning, as we walked around Tehran to get a feel for life in the city, Gypsy caught a glimpse of her reflection in a store window. She stopped, spun around and said, "I look elegant." It was a tender moment that demonstrated how porous the mullah's banishment of sensuality from public life was. They didn't seem to understand that the shrouds into which they forced women are like frames that emphasize their beauty. Or maybe they did.

In the afternoon, Gypsy and I argued about something, and she went for a walk by herself. I shouldn't have let her go, but it seemed like a good way to release some of the tension the all-pervading restrictions had caused between us. After an hour she came back to our room, stirred up. She dropped her purse and said, "They're hissing at me!" She was talking about the men. Gypsy was used to this in the streets of Santo Domingo, but there was something playful about the hissing of Dominican men. They would explain themselves. The hissing of Iranian men was desperate, and they didn't say a word. Their speechlessness frightened Gypsy.

The men's desperation made me think about the unintended effects of the dress code. Coming from Berlin, where I had tired a bit of women with candy-colored hair walking around barefoot and holding bottles of cheap beer, I appreciated the proper way Iranian women dressed. But I wondered if the strictness of the code created a suppressed erotic tension in the streets. There was a sense of the men feeling strangled, of wanting to break out, and I could see myself as one of them.

Gypsy studied the women and learned how they pushed the dress code's boundaries. The closer she looked, the more skin she saw. She noticed women who pushed their headscarves so far back that they almost fell off their heads. She saw sleeves that ended at the elbow. She glimpsed skinny jeans under overcoats cut so tight that they revealed more than they covered.

Gypsy remained covered; she didn't want to be seen as the loose American. Every morning, she disappeared under her overcoat and closed it all the way up to her neck. She spent more and more time in front of the mirror, and despaired over how far she could go. One particularly hot morning, she stood in front of me and asked, "Do you think I have to wear the coat?" I thought so and pulled up her coat's zipper. Gypsy looked down on herself and, sounding crestfallen, said, "I'm oppressed."

I, in contrast, felt almost liberated. I was aware that there is also a dress code for men. (When you Google "male dress code," the suggested search automatically includes "Iran.") But I was in no danger of being targeted by the chastity squads. The very style that had often earned me teasing from my friends—crisply ironed shirts rather than T-shirts, no bright colors, and never, ever shorts—was in perfect sync with the mullahs' definition of decency. I also lacked the dramatically spiked haircut popular among young men, for which some of them have been arrested. I was behind the Iranian curve, though, with my rejection of Texan-size belt buckles, and bell-bottoms that seemed to come straight out of *Saturday Night Fever*.

In the streets, the visible women stood in stark relief next to the invisible ones. The women that I once heard two young Iranian men call B.M.O.s—black moving objects—fluttered around completely covered up, showing only their eyes. "They could become pregnant and nobody would notice," Gypsy said. We soon learned that there are many things the invisible ones can do under their shrouds.

When one black moving object walked past us, we caught a glimpse of her uncovered feet in her open shoes. Her nail polish was a seductive scarlet. The discovery changed the way I looked at women. I began to understand the burning of Iranian men for a woman's ankles. They are the erotic zone in a disembodied country.

We began to see the abyss behind the veil, the revolts in the details. And then we saw two women prancing around the lobby of our hotel, dangerously uncovered. One of them had Cindy Crawford's hair and mole; she wore boots with heels capable of impalement. The other one had Amy Winehouse's winged eyeliner and aura of emaciation; she purred without pause into her phone. We saw this as our chance to join one of those infamous illegal parties raging behind Iran's closed doors, with dancing, alcohol, and other sins. But as we got closer, we stopped in our tracks. They were either transvestites or transgender women, pushing the boundaries in the safety of a hotel frequented by Westerners.

Deceit has always been the cloak of lovers in Iran, long before Khomeini seized power. The door of an old teahouse in the city of Yazd, an architectural jewel in the heart of the country, reminded us of that. In the old Persia, houses had separate door knockers for men and women. Men used a massive rectangular piece of iron to knock, while women touched a slender ring, announcing their arrival with a softer, gentler sound. But what was meant to keep men and women apart, opened the door for men who wanted to be with their beloved behind the façades of chastity. They knocked as women.

Khomeini didn't like the blurring of the line between man and woman, and he sought clarity. In 1984 he issued a fatwa allowing transsexuals to change their sex. To him, transsexuals were prisoners caught in the wrong body. He set out to liberate them and bestowed penises on male women, and vaginas on female men. It is a lesser-known part of the Ayatollah's legacy that the Islamic Republic of Iran has a budget for sex changes, allocating the equivalent of $122,000 for each person diagnosed with "gender identity disorder," the regime's term for transsexuality.

Khomeini became the god of plastic surgeons, and not just for transgendered people. The shroud under which he forced Iranian women reduced them to faces. He focused the male gaze on the one part of the female body that men could study in detail, and they were beguiled by the darkest eyes, immaculate brows, and beautiful noses. I liked the Iranian nose; there was something regal about it, mystical. But I made the same mistake as Khomeini. Many Iranian women don't want a nose that stands out from the frame of their scarf, a nose that exceeds the conventions of the West. They dream of a generic nose, a line in the face. This is how the Ayatollah created a promised land for plastic surgeons. For a few thousand U.S. dollars, they plane every bump in the Iranian face.

The operated women weren't hiding. We saw them everywhere: in the streets, in teahouses, at the mosque. They couldn't wait to exhibit their bandaged faces and show others that they were able to afford a small nose. The operated nose is the Iranian woman's Gucci purse.

And the nose was only the beginning. Step by step, plastic surgeons were conquering the body of the Iranian woman. After diminishing the nose, they moved on to pumping up lips and breasts to desperate-housewife levels. The veil turned out to be one of their best marketing tools, emphasizing the visible results of their work and covering the ones not to be seen.

The men, in a rare reversal, were beginning to follow the women's lead. Many of them are less educated than most women. They skip college in order to chase fast money, hoping it will enable them to purchase a captivating bride. But when it came to nose jobs, they were slowly catching up, showing off their freshly operated noses just as proudly as the women.

Gypsy shared my affection for the Iranian nose; she didn't like the operated men. Once, I saw her holding a rial bill dominated by a portrait of Khomeini. She moved her thumb across his face, as though she was caressing him. "He was a good-looking man," she said, gazing at Khomeini. She found his nose beautiful.

We traveled south and followed the road of addiction. The highway between Tehran and Kerman is the main artery of the drug trade in Iran, where an estimated 5 million people are addicted to opium and heroin. We didn't see any of that. All we saw was a dry, rocky landscape dotted by an endless gallery of portraits of supposed martyrs, sent to their death in the war with Iraq. Their faces lined the road like advertisements for an unnamed product.

At one rest stop, we saw a different kind of gallery. A truck driver opened the door of his cab, revealing that he was surrounded by pictures of half-naked women. When he got up, the body of another half-naked woman materialized, life-size and printed on the red cover of his seat. He had been sitting on her lap.

The mullahs have divided love into the allowed and the forbidden. Allowed love is a corset that suffocates lovers. That is why many seek refuge in forbidden love. Couples are not allowed to have sex before marriage, but if they do, there are solutions. Nobody ever asks the groom if he is still a virgin, and the bride can have her hymen stitched back together for a few hundred dollars.

Money is an important substance in Iranian love, a currency with the power to surpass the value of passion. The parents of a bride can demand a large sum for their daughter. The groom's family in return purchases the bride with a money-back guarantee, in case the marriage fails. A woman's value is meticulously assessed in the arithmetic of the law. In

life, as a bride, she is most precious. But if she dies and somebody is culpable in her death and forced to pay blood money,
she is worth only half as much as a man.

I gazed at Iranian love like a world behind glass. I was
traveling around the country with a woman who had chosen
me at a time when I had neither money nor the promise of
it. I didn't have to pay for her, and I was allowed to find out
if I liked sleeping with her before I married her. My love life
began to feel like a province of privilege.

Sleeping with a man who is not her own can be deadly for
an Iranian woman. An extra-marital affair can also lead a man
into death, but he can rely on the masculinity of the Iranian
state of law. In court, a woman's word, like her life, is only
worth half as much as that of a man.

That was the other Iran. We didn't see it, but we heard of it.
While we were savoring our honeymoon, seven women and two
men were waiting to be stoned to death for adultery and sexual
indecency. Their stonings were suspended, but when the time
comes, the accused have to descend into a pit—the women down
to their chest, the men down to their hips. The stonings have a
strict choreography, and the stones must not be too big. Justice is
supposed to descend slowly upon the indecent.

I have done things in my life that could have gotten me
stoned in this country. My indecency had not gone unpun-
ished, but I had gotten off comparatively cheap. I remembered the force with which a betrayed girlfriend once hit me
in the face. I remembered the gentle stoning I received from
Mandana. She threw the other woman's letters at me.

Later that night, Gypsy and I walked around Kerman and
saw a house with two blinking hearts on its façade, melting
into one. We suspected something wicked going on behind
these walls, and sneaked inside. But the club of hearts was not
a hotbed of vice; one couldn't buy love there, at least not the

fast way. It was a wedding ballroom, but one with a twist. The Iranian hierarchy was turned upside down in this house—the women were celebrating upstairs, the men downstairs.

The bride was beautiful. She had eyes black as coal, and the classic Iranian nose. She was dancing in a strapless gown. I never saw her; I wasn't allowed to go near her. Gypsy told me about her, after a group of giggling women had taken her upstairs. I was sitting downstairs with the other men, staring at our juice glasses.

I felt dirty in this aura of purity. The separation of men and women and the banning of alcohol and lust were the opposite of everything that was welcome at our own wedding. We had placed the voluptuous Turkish woman next to the divorced German man, hoping for attraction. My bride danced with other men. We drank Dominican rum in large amounts, and at five in the morning, a gay male friend was passionately kissing a woman.

All that was taboo in the lonely hearts club. The women offered Gypsy sweets; the men were brooding in their juice quarantine and ignored me. I felt like inciting them to storm the women's floor, but I learned that there were other ways for them to find solace. For Shiites, Iran's overwhelming majority, marriage can be a wide-open field, at least for men. There is room for up to four wives in their marriages, and if that is not enough, the husband can expand his portfolio with "temporary marriages." This kind of marriage may last up to ninety-nine years, but the more popular version lasts only a few hours. That is why Iranians also call it a "pleasure marriage."

The pleasure is the man's alone. He is not obliged to tell his wife about a temporary marriage, and all he has to discuss with his pleasure wife is the price. No written contract is required, which is also a pleasure for a man in a country where his word counts twice as much in court as that of a woman. If the man wants to, he can strike a temporary marriage agreement that includes how often he wants sex. The woman, however, is not entitled to any sexual demands, and she must not be married. She only has to be at least as old as Aisha when she became the third wife of the Prophet Muhammad. Aisha was nine.

The temporary marriage affords men a diverse sex life, where no adultery and no children out of wedlock exist. The wives in temporary marriages are usually divorced women, who are damaged goods in the permanent-marriage market. They need the money, and hope that the man stays with them for more than an hour, perhaps even leaves his first wife. They discreetly signal that they are available for a temporary marriage by wearing their chador inside out.

Wherever we went, we realized that this is not the norm but, rather, a possibility. It felt like a wand invented by a male-dominated regime trying to show a way out to the very men it is stifling, and we were reminded of that at the lonely hearts club, where the pleasure was the women's alone.

It was almost midnight, but there was still light inside the shop. An elderly woman wearing a black chador stood in front of a white wall, perfectly placed between portraits of Khomeini and Khamenei. When I stopped to take a photograph of her with the ayatollahs looking over her shoulder, she gestured for us to wait and called to someone in the back of the shop. Out came her smiling daughter, and a perilous conversation ensued. She told us about her forbidden love.

I cannot write where we met her; there would be terrible consequences if the guardians of Iran's order found her. She had a lyrical name and spoke good English; she liked the language and literature of her country's supposed enemy. She was in her early twenties and hungry for unrestricted love. But she was afraid they might come for her. There was always the fear of being arrested for the crime of having a boyfriend.

She told us about the night everything changed. She remembered it clearly, the time, the place, the sweet taste of ice cream on her lips. They had waited until night fell, thinking they would be safer under the cover of darkness. They drove to a quiet street, with her at the wheel, pretending to be sister and brother. They had just stopped when another car slowly passed by, with two men inside staring at them. After a while, the car came back and stopped behind them. The two men got out, approached their car and dangled handcuffs in front of the ice cream-eating couple.

The men weren't wearing uniforms and didn't identify themselves. They didn't have to. The couple knew that if they said a wrong word, they would be dragged to a building that everyone in the city knew—the prison of forbidden love. After their arrest, the parents would have had to pick up their indecent children. They would have had to pay a fine and sign a pledge that this will never happen again. "We don't have the right to eat ice cream," the young woman said, tears welling up in her eyes.

The mother looked at her daughter and took her hand. She didn't understand a word, but she seemed to know exactly what the daughter was telling us. Then she threw her thumb over her shoulder, pointing at Khomeini and Khamenei on the wall behind her, and shook her head. We went back to our hotel room and turned Khomeini's portrait around, making him face the wall.

It was the saddest night of our honeymoon, but something changed as we lay on another tradition-defying bed. A delicate confidence was seeping into the way we looked at the country, especially the women. There was a subcutaneous seething, a quiet determination to turn their rage into change—with a baseball bat if necessary. It reminded us of something a man had told us at a teahouse. We were cautious not to discuss anything with the slightest political undertone, but we eagerly listened to whatever people wanted to share. What the man told us sounded incredible at the time, but his words kept coming back to us as the mothers and daughters of Iran came into sharper focus. He said, "The women will bring the mullahs down."

The man with the golden microphone stood in front of a wall and sang. A small crowd of people gathered around him, looking enchanted as they listened to him. This made the man dangerous. He sang only love songs, but a policeman pushed through the crowd, bent over the loudspeaker and lowered the volume. The man smiled and kept singing. A few minutes later, two other policemen came and unplugged his microphone.

We were standing in a street in Shiraz, and the Iranian police state reminded us of its fearful nature. Shiraz is the city of poets, the heart of romantic old Persia, but we came only for Hafez. Iran's most beloved poet had written with breathless passion about love and lies in the time of despotism, and it moved us. He called himself a "serf of love," drank heavily, and dreamed of soaking prayer rugs with wine. Hafez lived in the fourteenth century, when mosque and state were one and the mullahs ruled with an arbitrary fist similar to the Iran of the twenty-first century. We read his poems and felt as though he was still alive.

> *Preachers who preen in prayer-niche and pulpit,*
> *when in private, quite another matter do they practice*
> *than they preach!*

The Hafez mausoleum is a place of pilgrimage for lovers. Newlyweds come from all over the country to be close to Hafez, and we followed them. We placed our hands next to theirs on the cold marble of his tomb and listened to them recite the Qu'ran's first *surah*. While they vowed to worship Him alone, we whispered a worldly wish, desiring a child.

There was something about Hafez that made people feel safe. At no other place did we see so many couples touch each other—holding hands, embracing each other, exchanging chaste kisses. And in the park surrounding the mausoleum we saw men that, former president Ahmadinejad once claimed, don't exist in Iran. Following the trend of the time, they had carefully modeled their hair to look like ransacked birds' nests. But something was different about them. Their eyebrows were a little too perfect, their t-shirts a little too tight, their nails a little too filed, and one of them sat on another's lap. We sat with them for a while, and one of them confided to Gypsy that they were "admirers of men." Then we saw some of them look at two policemen walking by as if they were their secret fantasy.

Young men and fire. A lot of them seemed to be playing with it, especially in matters of love. But the gay men reveling in Hafez's shadow, despite being persecuted by a homophobic regime, seemed almost privileged when we came across another generation of young men. On the road from Shiraz to Isfahan we stopped at a white building adorned with Iranian flags; it seemed to be decorated in celebration of something. Inside were the tombs of three soldiers who had fallen in the war with Iraq. It was a shrine to their deaths, silent on their lives. On the pristine white walls surrounding the tombs were photographs that documented their transformation from soldiers to martyrs. The first images showed nervous, smiling young men up to their chests in murky water, each holding a rifle over their head like a monstrance. The last images showed bodies that were missing something. An arm. A leg. A head.

In Isfahan we wanted to let go of all this. The sadness of having ice cream. The danger of golden microphones. The decency guards wielding feather dusters at the mosque, tapping women they deemed insufficiently covered. The air was clear and the night warm, and we felt like tourists again. But the men had a way of drifting toward us. We walked across the Bridge of 33 Arches and watched a man having his portrait drawn by a street artist. When the man noticed us, he pointed at the drawing and asked, "Beautiful?" He was unhappy with the size of his nose, even though the artist had drawn it smaller than it actually was. We sat down for our own portrait, and the artist, giving us the Iranian treatment, drew our noses smaller than they actually were. When we said goodbye, he reached out and shook Gypsy's hand. He was the first man in Iran who touched her.

Under the bridge was a teahouse with a beautiful view of the river, the glow of the city reflecting on its surface. Teahouses are the Iranian substitute for bars, a placebo for those who want to talk and mingle in a country where drinking alcohol is forbidden. The place was bustling with large groups of friends and families, and watching them engage in passionate discussions, it became obvious why the regime had shut down teahouses around the country. It was there that we met Mehdi and his brother Muhammad. They brought us saffron ice cream and told us about each of their difficulties finding a bride.

Mehdi and Muhammad were in their early thirties and their father was getting nervous that his sons still weren't married. He was putting pressure on them. The problem was money—they had too much of it. Coming from a wealthy family, the brothers felt that what attracted most women to them was their buying power. It's the luxury problem of privileged men in a society where brides come with a price tag. "Maybe I should marry a foreigner," Mehdi said.

As a man with a foreign bride, I was not in a position to argue against marrying one. But I didn't want Mehdi to give up on an Iranian bride, and I told him about the women in New York I had pursued in vain. Claiming that Gypsy was an exception to the rule, I said that, over there, I often felt that a man's value partly depended on his net worth. Gypsy put her hand on Mehdi's and nodded. He looked at her in disbelief. We talked late into the night and wanted to take a photograph to remember it by. Gypsy placed herself between the brothers, but they didn't fit into the frame. They kept their distance from the woman in the middle and stood next to her like soldiers at roll call, arms pressed against their flanks. I motioned for them to get closer to Gypsy. The brothers looked over their shoulders, as if planning a crime, and then, beaming, moved in and put their arms around Gypsy.

The man I came to call Little Shah didn't want to be in the picture. He had heard us speak English and hovered around our table, but now he kept his distance. Mehdi knew him; he was a regular at the teahouse. His English had a tinge of an American accent, which he seemed to cultivate, and he watched us like somebody who knew us. He was dressed in a black pinstriped suit with a shiny veneer of neglect, as though he had not taken it off in a long time. He wore it like his past.

His name was the same as that of the last Shah of Iran, Mohammed Reza. When we went for a walk along the Zayandeh River, which irrigates the fields and dreams of the people along its banks, he followed us and told us his story. He said he used to work as a journalist and, as punishment for writing the truth, was thrown into jail for several years. Now he worked at a police station. He cleaned it.

I viewed the Little Shah in the conditional. He had a black briefcase that he hugged like a pillow and said things that make a person cautious in a surveillance state. He told us that he had seen us in the morning near our hotel and overheard us speak German and Spanish, and he tried to impress us by speaking a little bit of both. He knew what had recently been on the cover of *Der Spiegel*, a magazine

I have written for. He wanted to know if I had brought a laptop and foreign newspapers.

Maybe he was an unrefined spy; maybe he was just a ragged man cleaning the dirt of those who had broken him. I didn't know what to make of him. We said goodbye, pretending to be exhausted from our honeymoon, but the Little Shah wasn't done with us. He asked us to give him just a few more minutes. He sat down on a small brick wall, pulled a school notebook and a fountain pen from his briefcase, and wrote a poem for us.

> *People tell me that windows*
> *have no feelings and no heart.*
> *But when a window fogs up*
> *and I write the words*
> *"I love you"*
> *on the glass,*
> *the window begins to cry.*

The following night, we went back to the teahouse. Mehdi had asked us to meet him there. He wanted to drive us to a popular spot in the mountains that he said has the most beautiful view of Isfahan. As I sat down on the passenger seat, he put a plastic bag full of money between my feet. I looked at the bag in amazement, and he laughed and said inside were the day's earnings from his uncle's business.

As we drove out of the city and saw it turn into a sea of lights behind us, Mehdi tried to impress us with his racing, pushing other cars out of the way. We ignored it, until everything came to a stop and we saw the woman with the baseball bat walking toward Mehdi. She was taller than him.

The road lay in front of us like a stage in a play about the future of Iran. In the spotlight stood a man at the moment when everything crashed and his hubris caught up with him. Mehdi raised his arms higher and pleaded with the woman, but she didn't say a word. She held the bat in front of her chest like a scepter and stared at him.

Mehdi slowly retreated, came back to the car and reached into the bag with the money. He grabbed as many bills as he could, walked back to the woman and waved the bills in front of her, begging her to take them. The woman lowered her bat, turned around and got into her car. She sped off and left Mehdi standing in the street with a handful of money, a small, humiliated man.

᷾᷾᷾   ᷾᷾᷾   ᷾᷾᷾

Mario Kaiser is a writer of narrative nonfiction. A former reporter and editor for Die Zeit *and* Der Spiegel, *his work has also appeared in* The International New York Times, Guernica, *and* Narratively. *He is a recipient of the Henri Nannen Prize, the Kurt Schork Award in International Journalism, and the Kurt Tucholsky Prize for Literary Journalism. "Love and Lies in Iran" originally appeared in* Narratively. *You can follow Mario at @MarioKaiserNYC.*

LAURA RESAU

~ ~ ~

Playing Dress-Up in the Andes

An embarrassing fashion disaster heals
old wounds and creates new bonds.

"Suck in your belly," María commands.

I obey. Arms extended, I'm standing before her in my underwear, legs bare, torso covered in a loose white blouse, trimmed with ample lace and embroidered flowers. María wraps several yards of fabric around my lower half, followed by a long strip of woven fabric around my waist—a *faja*. She tugs tightly, securing the top of the skirt fabric, as though winching a tourniquet.

We're in the bedroom of her yellow cement house nestled in the Andes mountains of Otavalo, Ecuador, preparing for a night on the town. Most tourists zip in and out of this cozy *pueblo*, spending only a whirlwind Saturday at the craft market—one of the biggest and oldest in South America—snapping photos of woven rugs and fuzzy ponchos and dazzling Otavaleña Indian women.

But I'm here for a whole week, staying with one of these women, and quickly learning that there's more to the frills and glitter than meets the eye. I've spoken with tourists who assume these outfits are just part of a shiny exotic-Andean-market façade, unaware that all the lace and cotton and wool hold layer upon layer of meaning.

María tugs tighter, and I let out a squeak as my compromised lungs struggle for breath. The musty smell of alpaca sweaters envelops us—merchandise piled on the bed that she sells on trips to Colorado, where I first met her. We're the same age—early thirties—but beyond that, our lives have been drastically different. She was a child slave, denied education, while I spent my coddled American girlhood devouring books. Before meeting María, I'd only read about slavery; back then, it seemed like something distant, centuries and continents away.

Now it feels much closer. Over the past three years, María has bravely revealed her deepest self to me, every scar and spark, inside and out, and entrusted me to shape this material into a book.

But standing here in my half-dressed, corseted state, I am the one exposed. She is clearly enjoying my discomfort, in an impish way.

With a ruthless giggle, she orders, "Suck in your belly some more, Laurita!"

"But Mari, I can't breathe!"

"Ay, Laurita," she sighs. "It has to be tight or else the skirt falls off." She motions to her own *anacos,* a black layer on top, a cream one beneath, both firmly held up by a purple *faja.*

"But how can I fit any food in my stomach?"

"It's just for a few hours," she laughs, tossing waist-long hair over her shoulder. She pulls the *faja* tighter still, until my ribs are on the verge of cracking.

Secretly, I consider tearing off the fabric, releasing my gut, and changing into a pair of comfy sweatpants. It occurs to me, though, that dressing up in her clothes could be useful to our book-in-progress. Our project has already given me the unique experience of slipping out of my own life and into María's—entering her mind, heart, and even body, from the beauty mark near her lip to the whip scars on her calves. The only thing missing, I realize as I stand half-mummified in yards of fabric, has been wearing María's clothes. Frankly, it hadn't occurred to me before. I had a vague notion that indigenous people would frown at me, a gringa posing as an Otavaleña. But this dress-up session was María's idea—girls playing makeover, then going out for a night on the town. And she's obviously taking pleasure in it. Her playfulness is infectious, transforming us into giddy teens. I have only one sibling, a brother, but I imagine this is how it would feel to have a giggly, slightly tormenting sister.

María has called me *hermana*—sister— a few times, mostly in greeting cards, tentatively, as if trying it out. Each time, it has felt like a gift, this word with its staggering connotations. But I've always felt too shy and unworthy to call her *hermana* back.

Throughout María's teen years, she longed for the close bond of sisterhood. As a little girl in her remote Quichua village, she'd had a thorny relationship with her older sister, who was prettier, fairer, plumper, and more even-tempered. María used to pummel her sister in a jealous rage over who got the biggest potato in the soup or the ripest berries from the bush. But from ages seven to fifteen, after María was taken from her family to be an unpaid servant, she yearned for a sister—someone to whisper with about her dread of her master's groping hands, her dreams of going to school, her major crush on MacGyver.

When María was on the verge of a dramatic escape from slavery, she contacted this older sister, whom she hadn't seen for eight years. María had often fantasized about meeting her again, but imagined her frozen in time, forever twelve years old, the perfect age for hysterical laughter and makeovers and secrets. This time, she resolved to offer her sister the biggest potato in the soup and the juiciest berries on the bush.

At their reunion, María felt gutted to see that her sister had grown into a twenty-year-old woman, engaged to be married. The window of time for sisterly silliness had vanished, never to be reclaimed. This was when it truly dawned on María that her childhood had been stolen. And this knowledge was so devastating that she very nearly chose to return to her state of slavery, despite the physical and sexual abuse, despite being denied education and dignity.

In the next few years, though, she managed to create a new, free life for herself, working hard to pay for food, lodging, and high school. She formed friendships with classmates, but was burdened with so much responsibility that she could never live out the warm and carefree sisterly bond she'd dreamed of.

As María told me her story, there were moments we cried together—when she described being strung up to the rafters by her neck as a five-year-old and whipped by her father; being beaten with handfuls of hangers by the mistress of the household; being sexually accosted by the master as a young teen. Yet her sadness seemed to plunge deepest when she described the realization that she'd never live out her dreams of sisterhood—laughing and crying together, dressing each other up, sharing memories, confiding fears.

This bewildered me. After all she'd been through, why was this sorrow so painful? It's hard to know why one particular loss can rip a soul's fabric . . . and perhaps harder to guess at the surprising ways it might one day stitch itself together.

Now that my ribs have been mercilessly swaddled, my makeover is nearly complete. Grinning, María hooks a necklace of dozens of gold-painted crystal bead strands around my neck, then holds up a hand mirror. The bright gold—stunning against María's warm skin and brown eyes—clashes with my fair complexion.

"You're sure indigenous women won't feel offended?" I ask, doubtful, staring at our reflection.

"It's fine, Laurita!" she insists, winding coral beads around my wrists, encasing my blond ponytail in a long ribbon. "They'll like it."

And she's right. Outside, beneath the palm trees and street lamps, Otavaleña women of all ages smile and titter, eyes bright. I'm an object of their amusement, but at least I'm not offending anyone. As for the men on the sidewalks, they don't even notice me. They're all staring at the TVs perched in markets and bakeries and *farmacias*, captivated by a championship soccer game. Sports announcers' amped-up voices compete with the trills of pan flute melodies floating from open doors.

The walk to *el centro* is a mile uphill, but feels longer with restricted lungs and thin mountain air. We're at 8,500 feet, cradled by Andean peaks, each a distinct silhouette poking at the moonlit clouds. The skirts of these mountains are laced with waterfalls and lakes, rich with folklore and ritual, and sacred to María and her people.

But at the moment, I'm less focused on the enchanting landscape, and dwelling more on my own squished torso. "Can't we just loosen this thing?" I ask, fiddling with the *faja*.

María smacks my fingers away. "Laurita! It might fall off."

Semi-suffocated, I gaze in awe at the Quichua women who bustle past, women who have worn these outfits all their lives. Many of them come from surrounding villages where they've pastured goats, cooked over wood fires, fed pigs, harvested potatoes, and navigated mountain trails much rougher than this gentle sidewalk slope . . . somehow managing to keep their blouses spotless.

"But Mari," I gasp, "how can you do it?"

"It's who I am."

During the eight years she worked as an unpaid child servant, María stopped wearing her native clothing, seeing it through the racist eyes of her *mestizo* oppressors—a symbol of poverty, filth, backwardness. The day she reunited with her sister, she put on her favorite *mestiza* clothes—an unfortunate safari-themed outfit from the late eighties—and carefully smoothed extra gel in her permed hair.

When her sister appeared in the traditional *anacos* and embroidered blouse and gold beads and ribbon-wrapped ponytail, María felt shocked. This woman looked like the indigenous people María had learned to scorn during her years with her *mestizo* masters. Her sister could have been from a different planet. The divide felt unbreachable.

After an awkward embrace, María served her lemonade, then sobbed her heart out.

Over the next couple years, María wore only *mestiza* clothes, spoke only Spanish, avoided her family, and hid her native roots. And then one day, she was asked to participate in a competition for the indigenous Queens of Sky, Corn, and Water. This involved wearing traditional clothing again and giving a speech in Quichua.

After a decade, she once again put on an embroidered lace blouse and heavy wrap-around *anacos*. In some ways, it felt uncomfortable. She worried about the *faja* coming unraveled. She felt like an imposter. But in another way, a deeper way, it felt perfect. And in these clothes that were familiar and strange at once, she glimpsed the possibility that there was something beautiful about her indigenous roots.

Inside the fluorescent lit, yellow-walled *pollería,* María and I have to wait at the counter to be seated, mouths watering amidst the scent of chicken roasting on spits. Service is slow. All the cooks' and waiters' eyes are glued to the soccer game onscreen. As my stomach growls, I glare, annoyed, at the TV—ubiquitous in small-town Latin American eateries, preventing people from communing, chatting . . . and serving food promptly.

I'm ravenous by the time our dinner comes— juicy chicken, cilantro-laced rice, rich potato soup, nutty lentils, fried plantains, local Pilsener-brand beer. I dig in, struggling to keep my lace sleeves out of the soup. It becomes quickly apparent that to make a dent in this steaming pile of food, I'll need more room in my abdominal area.

"Mari," I plead, "can't you loosen this *faja? ¿Por favorcito?*"

She frowns. "*Bueno,* Laurita, I'll do it, but before you stand up we'll have to tighten it again, O.K.?"

"O.K., O.K., *gracias!*"

She loosens the strip of fabric. Ahh. Sweet relief. My internal organs sigh, rearrange themselves back into normal positions. I devour the greasy, salty delight with abandon.

As the other customers and servers watch the game, transfixed, I munch chicken and gaze at María in wonder. I've long admired her spunk, her determination to overcome the obstacles in her life—poverty, abuse, racism, sexism, classism, enslavement—and not only survive, but thrive. And now the latest source of my admiration: how she manages to fit so many fried plantains beneath that tourniquet of a *faja.*

Now I can vividly imagine her sensations of wrapping herself in *anacos* after years of the baggy Western-style outfits of the late eighties. This native clothing isn't just an abstract symbol of her transformation, but a gut-restricting, chest-squeezing, rib-cracking reality.

When our bellies are full of chicken and local beer, we stretch and gather our things. I announce I'm going to the bathroom to wash the grease from my hands, so I won't sully the blouse. (How *does* she manage to keep her blouse snow-white, anyway?)

"Excuse me," I say, scooting out of the booth, handbag slung over my shoulder. I stand up and head to the *baños*.

"Laurita!" María calls out, alarmed.

But it's too late. The *faja* uncoils. The skirt falls to the floor, yards of fabric pooled at my feet. I am standing in my underwear, a not-nice pair, cool air grazing my naked thighs. I am smack in the middle of the crowded restaurant, exposed.

I flush hot magenta, frantically gather the fabric and *faja* to my waist. Sweating and prickling with embarrassment, I raise my eyes, prepared for a sea of faces, laughing and gaping.

But the only eyes on me belong to María—whose mouth has dropped open in a kind of amused horror—and a toddler girl in a high chair, cheeks smeared with potato. Every other face is gazing, oblivious, at the TV.

The blessed, beautiful TV.

After a stretched-out moment of shock, I stagger to the *baños*. And in the safety of the stall, I pull out the secret stash from my handbag: a loose T-shirt and sweat pants. My Plan B.

Carefully, I remove and fold up the long *faja* and *anacos* and the lacy blouse. I slip my comfy clothes over my not-nice underwear. I leave the golden beads around my neck and the coral strands around my wrists for a bit of dazzle. By the time I emerge from the bathroom, my blush has faded, my armpit sweat has dried, the soccer game has ended, and a relieved smile has sprouted on my face.

As we walk home, María teases me relentlessly. We replay my blooper and laugh and wipe our eyes. And despite lingering mortification, I realize that the wardrobe disaster of tonight will make our book a bit deeper, a bit richer. Not only has María let me into her mind and heart and skin, but her clothing, too.

Our relationship has deepened into something richer, too—silly and soulful, intimate and vulnerable, all woven together with tears and giggles.

Beneath the street lamp glow, María slings her arm around my shoulder. I lean into her, twirl my fingers around her ribbon-bound ponytail. "*Gracias, hermana.*"

She responds with a hip bump and a sparkling grin. "*De nada, hermana.*"

A few years later, our book is published, after a total of seven years of research and interviewing and storytelling and writing and revising. Nearly the same amount of time that María was enslaved. During those seven years, we have cried and laughed; we have confided to each other our deepest sorrows and fears; we have done makeovers and sleepovers and whispered secrets just before falling asleep; we have teased and joked; we have fought and made up; we have helped each other through painful times; we have driven each other crazy.

We have not yet pummeled each other over potatoes, but that could still happen some day.

≈≈≈≈≈≈

Laura Resau is the award-winning author of eight novels for young people, all set in places where she's lived or traveled, including Mexico, France, Guatemala, and Ecuador. Her most popular book with adults—The Queen of Water, co-written with María Virginia Farinango—gained a prized spot on Oprah's reading list for teens. Resau's acclaimed travel essays have appeared in anthologies by Travelers' Tales, Lonely Planet, and others. She lives in Colorado with her husband and young son, and donates a portion of her royalties to indigenous rights organizations in Latin America. For more about her writing, please visit www.Lauraresau.com.

JAMES MICHAEL DORSEY

❧ ❧ ❧

My Mexican Bus

An ongoing spiritual journey commences anew.

We all have a special place for solace and introspection; mine is a southbound bus in Baja California.

I only take this ride once a year to visit friends, but it has become both a pilgrimage and a ritual that occupies my thoughts for a far greater time. I seem to have an inbred need for this repetitive ride that would not have the same value should I do it more often. For me, the journey has always been as important as the destination, but in this case, they are both the same.

It begins in the Tijuana bus terminal, an aging, cavernous building and a time portal for my entrée to Old Mexico. When I step through those doors, I enter another era as well as a place. The concrete-and-glass blockhouse is a utilitarian monument to 1950s Mexican architecture and a reminder of how slowly time passes here. Inside, the smell of tortillas and *mole* mingles with the aroma of ammonia on linoleum floors. A feeling washes over me that does not translate easily into words, a feeling finely honed and nuanced over many years, somewhere between coming home and simple tranquility.

I pay my respects at the shrine to the Virgin of Guadalupe, whose statue stands a tearful guard next to the entrance to the public toilet. I drop a two-peso coin into the pay slot that lets me revolve the steel turnstile and open the door marked "Caballeros" over the grinning stencil of a mustachioed man giving me a thumbs-up. Inside, I am pleasantly surprised to find flush toilets complete with paper, but know they will probably be the last of their kind until I reach my final destination.

Outside in the main hall I walk past the *cambio,* a money exchange that has never been open in my presence, and then wait while the young girl behind the counter writes out my ticket by hand on a yellow legal pad with a dull pencil as she snaps her gum loudly.

Tijuana is an open city with no taxes and it is here that the *braceros* and *agriculturos* of the south come to stock up on the trappings of modern society, only recently available from the large new discount stores that line the border. The waiting hall is full of people lugging big screen TVs and assorted appliances on those tiny folding luggage rollers. One ancient grandmother has three crowded shopping bags on each arm that cause her to roll like a camel as she walks. I watch a mother wrap her children in blankets on the cold steel chairs and try to make out what the PA announcement is saying, but it is mostly garbled static.

With my fellow passengers, I walk through the metal detector that beeps loudly at each of us but fails to gain the attention of the bored-looking security guard. The folding knife I forgot to take out of my pocket will ride with me tonight.

Outside, as I stand in line to board, the tiny grandmother clutching a canvas bag in front of me is startled when I greet her in Spanish. She is so wide that it is an effort to board, but once in her seat, she pats the one next to her when I climb on. She offers me a bite of her churro, which I politely decline, then instinctively clutches my hand as the bus lurches from its stall. Her lips are moving below closed eyes and I think she is saying the Lord's Prayer. She is a child of the old world and clearly afraid of the journey ahead in this gigantic mechanized machine. She probably leaves the desert infrequently to visit a son or daughter and now must return. Her weathered face is a definitive map of the Mexican people: not Hispanic, nor Spanish, or even mestizo, but Mexican, a distinction often overlooked by racial generalization. I assure her in Spanish that all will be well and she nervously compliments me on my pronunciation.

Baja is not like mainland Mexico. It is older and set in its ways. On the world scale it is a tiny peninsula, but its deserts rival any on Earth and its jagged mountains appear shaped by an angry God, while tucked into its most remote corners are a people whose mode of living has not changed in centuries. They are the same people whose ancestors turned back armored Spanish conquistadors with bows and arrows. Away from Highway 1, horses and burros are the main mode of transport and doors of mud houses remain unlocked because there is no crime among neighbors. Cattle wander the highways with faces full of prickly *cholla* cactus and cougars and wolves roam in numbers across a vast lunar landscape. It is a separate reality from my own life and part of its allure is to realize that an imaginary line on a map is all it takes to divide such diverse cultures.

The noisy diesel coughs and sputters to life and we begin to inch our way past the gaudy neon and gridlocked traffic that is the Tijuana night. From my perch high above them I wonder about the lives in the countless cars below me, thinking any one of them could have been my own. What if I had born here? How would my life be different?

A big difference is obvious when our route takes us past the high concrete wall that forms part of the border. It is covered with graffiti and seems eerily similar to one that used to stand in Berlin. While people are not being shot for crossing this wall, it still makes me wish for a world where we need no barriers to separate us from our neighbors.

As we leave the city behind, the grandmother releases my hand and with a timid smile of apology, falls asleep with her head on my shoulder. She is going home now and is happy. A chunky moon slides from behind traveling clouds to reveal iridescent rolling surf, just before the highway turns inland on the way to Ensenada.

In the silent cloak of night, Mexico has always been more real to me. In this predominantly Catholic land, organized religion has merged with peasant superstition to create a belief system all its own, especially in the high mountains and remote deserts where I prefer to travel. This is the land of the *brujo*, witches, spirits, and demons, a land where people pray equally to Jesus in church and to syncretic images of Santeria in mud shacks. I have spent too much time in this place to dismiss anything metaphysical and recall a midnight encounter in a coffee shop, when a stranger swathed in black warned me of the full moon and then disappeared into a brightly lit and vacant street. I have yet to meet anyone in Baja who is not related to, or not had an encounter with, a witch of some sort. They are ubiquitous here.

South of Ensenada, we climb into the mountains of San Pedro de Martir. The temperature has fallen and I pull a fleece from my bag as the repetitive hum of the tires and familiar back-and-forth swaying on the switch-backed road triggers more memories.

Guillermo was on the lead horse when it reared up, and without any commands, trampled a rattlesnake to death. Its patterned skin eventually became a somewhat mutilated hat band. Later that day, while returning from a cave painted 6,000 years ago by the Cochimi people, we stopped at a *rancho* for beans and rice. I noticed what appeared to be a human skull on a shelf in the adobe. When I turned to ask the old patron about it, his face appeared weirdly contorted and I suddenly felt dizzy. The moment passed and when I looked again, the skull was a chunk of obsidian and the old man was smiling benignly. That revelatory moment ended any more questions on my part. Some things are just not meant to be understood.

The hours pass while my thoughts are elsewhere. Night in a foreign land is when I rethink my own life; what I should have done differently, what I can do better. What will I do next? The bus is silent except for random snoring and the hushed conversation between the middle-aged driver and his young girlfriend seated on the aisle floor next to him. We stop on an isolated piece of road where towering cacti stand like night sentinels in our headlights. The cargo door opens and a gentleman and young lady emerge to trade places with the driver and his friend, both girls giggling as they switch. Our new driver, refreshed in more ways than one, takes over.

I return to the night, and when the first purple streak of dawn slashes the sky we leave Highway 1 for the service road into Guerro Negro, gateway to Scammons' Lagoon. On the sides of the road we begin to see platforms topping telephone poles for the osprey to nest on and avoid electrocution. On the beach side, we roll past the enormous skeleton of a gray whale that announces this village as a major whale-watching destination.

Behind the bus station, the ever-present Virgin of Guadalupe, haloed by blinking Christmas lights, watches over the parking lot with outstretched hand. A faint whiff of marijuana comes to my nose and as I step inside, two ancient and gaunt *vaqueros* in straw cowboy hats are drinking coffee and passing a hand-rolled smoke. I buy a cold empanada so stale I toss it to a stray dog after one bite. Because it is close to the ocean, it is often bitterly cold in Guerro Negro at night. This evening I watch my breath rise in hazy clouds to disappear in the breeze. Above me, the Big Dipper sits low in the sky, the end of its handle pointing the way home for when I return. As we leave to continue south, the morning light begins to crawl over the horizon, mingling land and sky that slowly separates into a new day.

An hour's ride south, the desert floor widens and the road disappears into a cottony ground fog. The top of a distant volcano pokes through it and gigantic Cordon cacti slide in and out of sight in the haze, their upturned arms saluting as we roll past, a vast silent army, guardians of the land. We have reached the edge of the Viscaino biosphere, 5 million hectares of protected wilderness that cover a quarter of the Baja Peninsula. Suddenly, distant shadows become a herd of wild burros that cause us to brake hard enough to wake everyone, and we laugh as the driver must exit and physically shoo them off the road. Kestrels are hunting insects in the morning haze and the cacti appear to be stretching after the evening's sleep. Everyone crowds to one side and cell phones are snapping photos. The quiet night is gone. Across from me, a man in silver-tipped cowboy boots draws a long pull from a pocket flask then slumps back in his seat, his Stetson tilted low over his eyes.

The fog parts like a curtain and we pass low flat mesas full of sandstone caves carved by the eons. I know if I were to explore them I would find artifacts that hold stories from centuries ago. East of the mesas, rolling flat lands give rise to the Tres Virgines, three active volcanoes, named for the inhabitants of an old folktale. They sit in a perfect row, descending in height from the one nearest the highway, all mighty vents from the lungs of the planet. Archaeologists have speculated that when they last awoke, tens of thousands of years ago, they spewed molten lava up to 100 miles, all the way to the Pacific Ocean, from whose tidal waters on a clear day you can see the hazy outline of the tallest volcano.

Just north of San Ignacio we stop for a military checkpoint where a cardboard soldier holds a sign warning against drugs.

An officer with a clipboard climbs into the bus and struts up and down the center aisle, not really looking for anything; more an act of machismo than a search. Outside a sniffer dog scratches at the baggage compartment and after an amused soldier looks inside, we are waved on.

People are moving about the bus, stiff and sore after the long night. The driver puts a movie on the overhead screens and cranks the volume up to rock concert level. It is *Snakes on a Plane* with Samuel L. Jackson, a very bad B movie that makes me realize that a good movie is not about to be playing on a public bus in the rural deserts of Mexico.

We round a hairpin turn and from the tiny valley below us the adobe-tiled roofs of San Ignacio come into view through the date palms. It is a tired and sun-worn village whose main industry is cement brick and whose people appear to live in slow motion. The town sits astride an impossibly beautiful river full of egrets and herons that contribute to the town's casual aura. Two hours to the west, gray whales have annually migrated into the lagoon of the same name for centuries.

We pull into the dirt parking lot and I spot Jorge leaning against his van, waiting for me even though we are three hours late. He has one cowboy boot on the bumper above a "Jesus loves you" decal and his arm rests on the bullhorns mounted on the hood. He still wears the aviator shades I gave him two years ago. It is stifling hot under a van Gogh sun.

A stray dog barks at a swirling dust devil and I stare up at the familiar sign over the bus office.

I smile as I read, "*Bienvenido A San Ignacio.*"

I am back.

∼ ∼ ∼

James Michael Dorsey is an award-winning author, explorer, photographer, and lecturer who has traveled extensively in forty-five countries. He has spent the past two decades researching remote cultures around the world. He is a former contributing editor at Transitions Abroad *and frequent contributor to United Airlines'* Hemispheres *and* Perceptive Travel. *He has also written for* Colliers, The Christian Science Monitor, Los Angeles Times, BBC Wildlife, World & I, *and* Natural History, *plus several African magazines. He is a foreign correspondent for Camerapix International, a travel consultant to Brown + Hudson of London, and a correspondent for the World Explorers Bureau. He is also a fellow of the Explorers Club and former director of the Adventurers Club. His latest book is* Vanishing Tales from Ancient Trails. *His stories have appeared in nine travel anthologies. He is a nine-time Solas Award category winner and a contributor to* The Best Travel Writing, Volume 10.

❧ ❧ ❧

Yuan Fen

Big world, opposite sides, but still we meet.

This time, the Biotruck broke down near Bidor—a small, dusty Malaysian settlement lined with unremarkable storefronts. As I kicked around the parking lot of the mechanic shop, I asked myself: *Why can't the truck spring an oil leak at the Taj Mahal or Angkor Wat?*

The "Biotruck" was a twenty-two-year-old school bus my partner Andy salvaged from a scrapyard and converted into an RV. It ran on waste cooking oil. Everything in it—the lights, the sink, the countertop—was cobbled together from cast-offs. Our plan was to drive it around the world, but progress was slow. When you're traveling in a bus made of garbage, things go wrong on a regular basis. Breakdowns become a way of life.

I surveyed the lay of the land around the auto shop: a fruit stand, a hardware store, a hair salon. For the next few days I'd be exiled from the truck as it filled with eager mechanics, oily rags, and expletives. The most helpful thing I could do was to keep out of the way.

Bidor appeared to be the Middle of Nowhere. Of course, the last time I'd thought that (during a breakdown in the Malaysian port town of Galang Patah), we ended up on a

Dionysian jag with influential journalists and local politicians celebrating us—and the Biotruck—with champagne.

I needed to give Bidor a chance.

What's interesting about breakdowns isn't what goes wrong, but the question of how to get rolling again. A disintegrated fuel filter can throw you at the mercy of strangers. Who will help you? You invariably meet people you would never have met otherwise, and often walk away with the sorts of strong friendships that get forged under duress.

In this case, the truck had quit abruptly on the highway and Andy had to guide it onto the shoulder. While he poked around under the hood, I spread a blanket on the roadside grass and, setting up our laundry hamper as a backrest, resumed reading the literary megalith that is *Shantaram*. The day dimmed, the mosquitos bit, and I started to worry that we might have to spend the night right there. Thankfully, two laughing Chinese mechanics from Kim Lim's Towing happened to drive by, and stopped to give us a hitch. That's how we got to Bidor.

I am fairly useless in breakdown situations. It's not that I lack the brain power to figure it out, or that I'm too girly to get my hands dirty. It's just that I'm completely uninterested. Car parts, to me, are *so boring*. Thankfully, Andy feels otherwise. *"It's like having a conversation with the engine,"* he explained.

Days passed while he carried on heated chats with the fuel filter and the injector pump. I filled the blank hours drinking tea and submitting myself to inane distractions—like having my hair flat-ironed—just so I could wait out the brutal Malaysian heat in the air-conditioned salon.

It felt wrong. While poor Andy was covered in grease, I was strolling around the parking lot all day with great hair. So I went over to a fruit shop, deciding that I would bring refreshment to the oily crew. I selected a few mangos, bananas, and a watermelon. I knew the counter space in the Biotruck

would be covered in wrenches, so employing a clumsy mix
of English and charades, I asked the owner for a knife and
a cutting board. I sat down and chopped the fruit on a mat
near the register, balancing a plate on my knees while runnels
of watermelon juice ran down my arm. The owner's son set
a box by my feet to catch the peels, her husband came over to
watch and soon, cutting up the fruit became a family effort.

Mr. and Mrs. Fatt owned the fruit shop. The morning after
our collective fruit-slicing session, they idled their car up to
our bus and asked us to breakfast. We sat at an open-air Chinese market, poked breakfast dumplings with chopsticks, and
did our best to make conversation. We must have done well
enough, because they took us out to dinner again that night.

We got on with them well. They were fun loving. Mr. Fatt
liked to tease, and in return his wife delivered regular impish punches to his arm. During the next few days, while the
Biotruck was in surgery at Kim Lim's shop, we started hanging out at their house: watching TV, using their shower and
internet connection. They showed us a nearby waterfall, and
we waited out one long hot afternoon in its mist. Before long,
Mr. and Mrs. Fatt began to feel like family, and that dusty
block of Bidor storefronts started to feel like home.

At last the Biotruck was repaired. On our last night,
they took us out to dinner. While we sipped from our beers,
Mr. Fatt pulled out a pen and a napkin. He scribbled out a
single Chinese character and drew a big circle.

"Yuan fen," he said, pointing to the Chinese symbol. Then
he retraced the circle. *"Big world, opposite sides, but still we
meet. This friendship is a special privilege."*

Much later, I would look up the meaning of *yuan fen*. I
began to love the word for the way it filled a gap in the English language. It explained a phenomenon that I had often
experienced, but lacked the verbal tools to articulate. I think
"chemistry" might be the closest word we have.

Simply put, *yuan fen* is the binding force that brings people together in a relationship. The amount of *yuan fen* you share with someone determines the level of closeness you will achieve. It's not just about proximity; you can live next door to someone all your life and never get to know them. This just means you have thin *yuan fen*. On the other hand, you can fall madly in love with someone, but just can't stay together. "Have fate without destiny," is the Chinese proverb used to describe this tragic condition.

The meaning can get more complicated. Some believe that *yuan fen* is tied to past lives and karma. As another Chinese proverb goes: *It takes hundreds of reincarnations to bring two persons to ride in the same boat; it takes a thousand to bring two persons to share the same pillow.*

But for me, it is enough that *yuan fen* explains how sometimes people who meet get along or don't get along, why friends become friends, why lovers become lovers, and why relationships sometimes break apart. It puts a word to why there are people I've lived near for so long, yet consistently failed to maneuver the conversation past a "hello" and yet managed to make a heart connection halfway around the world.

Yuan fen explains how Andy and I should break down, find Kim Lim's shop, and intersect with Mr. and Mrs. Fatt—people who don't speak our language, live thousands of miles away, and run a fruit stand in a dusty little "nowhere" town called Bidor.

Christina Ammon has penned stories for Orion Magazine, Hemispheres, *the* San Francisco Chronicle, Condé Nast, *and numerous travel anthologies. She is the recipient of an Oregon Literary Arts Fellowship for nonfiction and organizes the Deep Travel writing tours in Morocco and Nepal. When not traveling, Christina Ammon lives in Ruch, Oregon where she writes, sips wine, and paraglides. For travel tales and workshop information, visit her blog at www.vanabonds.com.*

≈ ≈ ≈

Warsaw Redux

Tracing personal history from an
uncommon Cold War birthplace.

In summer, Warsaw smells of linden trees. The remembered scent greeted me promptly, as even the street leading in from the airport is lush with leaves. They help soften
the blow of gray apartment blocks.

Jurek parked in front of one such building on a tree-
lined boulevard in the neighborhood of Mokotów. We took
the small elevator up to the third floor, where his wife Monika greeted me warmly. In the kitchen, supper was laid out
on the table and the windows were open to a view of the
prison. Gazing out I thought, as I always do when taking
in that scene: What a strange place for one's wife to have
been born.

April 6, 1952. The previous year Halina Matra had been
accused of espionage on behalf of the Polish government-
in-exile and, though pregnant, sentenced to ten years in
Mokotów Prison. That summer her sister came to take the
three-month-old baby away. Little Hania looked so sickly
that, on the tram, outraged mothers hurled abuse at her aunt.
Halina was released after five years, during a period of de-
Stalinization, but those five years took a heavy toll.

I learned some of this when I met Hania in London in the summer of '76, and more when I came to Warsaw two years later—a few days before her mother died. One of the last things to make her laugh was the story of my going to the store to buy water and coming back with a bottle of clear vinegar. More successful at job hunting, I found work as an English teacher. After six months my visa expired, and when I requested an extension I was asked to become an informer. (My own small, sour taste of the system.) I refused, which meant quitting my job and leaving the country. But, thanks to the birth of Solidarity, I was able to return in the fall of 1980. Hania and I were married that October in the Old Town, and I stayed for two years—teaching English, learning Polish, and gathering material for my first book.

In the morning, the guard gazed out from his corner tower. Over breakfast I told Jurek, who is Hania's cousin, of my desire to visit the prison. Hania had gotten in touch with a retired professor who had written a book about female political prisoners, and had been a prisoner herself. Jurek, to my surprise, thought that a visit wouldn't be impossible. But more immediately, he said, there was an event in the park next to the Hotel Bristol, as today marked the twenty-second anniversary of the first, free, postwar elections. And, like the scent of linden trees, the Polish passion for remembrance came back to me.

Le Méridien Bristol, Warsaw's most elegant hotel, sits, appropriately, on its stateliest street. In the early '80s I had used Krakowskie Przedmieście—with its reconstituted grandeur—as a refuge from the drab, dilapidated city beyond. Leveled by the Nazis, Warsaw was rebuilt by the Communists—about as horrible a fate as any city could have. Though the Old Town, and my favorite street, were painstakingly made to look their former selves.

On recent visits, having seen more cities, I had begun to think of Krakowskie Przedmieście as possibly the world's most perfect street. It is infinitely cozier than Fifth Avenue, and much more varied than the regimented Champs-Élysées. In the space of only a few blocks it contains all the classic elements of a great urban boulevard: shops, galleries, bookstores, restaurants, cafes, gracious apartment houses, baroque and neoclassical churches, historic palaces (including the president's), a grand hotel, a fine university, diminutive parks, and heroic statuary, honoring, among others, a prince, a poet, and an astronomer. Krakowskie Przedmieście is more than a thoroughfare; it is a capital, and a culture, distilled to their essence.

On this bright June afternoon it looked better than ever. (The nostalgia that normally accompanies a return to a former home is magnificently tempered when that home was formerly Communist.) I walked with summery crowds past sidewalk cafes in a soothing but puzzling calm—until I realized that there was no traffic. The perfect street had found the perfect solution (at least for the weekend).

The park next to the Bristol was furnished with poster boards, and tables of books, devoted to the distant late twentieth century. Mock voting stations had been set up in honor of the anniversary; I grabbed a ballot that asked if fans should be allowed to attend an upcoming soccer tournament. It was cheering evidence that the national delight in absurdity—an essential in the past for keeping one's sanity—had not disappeared. I checked "*Nie*" and dropped my ballet into the box.

A small bookstore behind the hotel sold postcards with black-and-white scenes from the Polish People's Republic. There were now guidebooks devoted to walking tours of old Communist-era landmarks and I found it encouraging that enough time had passed for Poles to acknowledge (if not embrace) the vestiges of that time. One postcard showed three peasants in overcoats, each holding a piglet. I bought it to send to Hania, who, because of work, had been unable to come.

Heading toward the Old Town, I came across a bench with a button at one end. I pushed the button and unleashed the Grand Polonaise Brillante, Op. 22. The writing on the bench, in Polish and English, informed me that it had been from the building across the street, in 1830, that Fryderyk Chopin had left Warsaw on a stagecoach to Vienna, "never to return."

Krakowskie Przedmieście—its treasures now with musical accompaniment—began its descent into Plac Zamkowy (Castle Square). Protestors clamored around King Sigismund's column, speaking through megaphones and waving Syrian flags. Asking around, I learned that almost all of them had come to Poland as students and decided to stay. They provided a new twist on an old theme—"*Niech żyje Syria!*" they chanted, "Long live Syria!"—and proof of Warsaw's international status.

Noemi sat at a sidewalk café on Plac Konstytucji, a monumental, Stalinist-era square now softened by umbrellas. Even its reliefs of heroic workers and teachers had taken on a kind of period charm now that the ideology behind them had been sent packing.

Noemi was the daughter of friends of a friend, a pretty young woman with dark hair and brown eyes and almost unaccented English. She had recently graduated from Jacek Kuroń High School, a private institution named for one of Solidarity's leading lights. There had been 16 students in her graduating class. Now she was looking for a summer job, not abroad—as generations of Poles, like Hania, had done—but in her hometown.

"I used to hate Warsaw," she said, with that universal teenage belief in the superiority of elsewhere. "Then I went to Ottawa. The grass," she said with disgust, "was cut so perfectly."

She reflected for a moment, then continued. "Warsaw might be a mess, people may be angry, but they say what they think." I thought of the mothers berating Hania's aunt on the tram. "They don't care what people think of them."

She sipped her strawberry smoothie, sitting in an armchair that looked as if it were on loan from a prewar apartment. She told me, as if revealing something shocking: "Young people don't read. I read and I'm a weirdo." When I asked her about the Copernicus Science Center, she spoke matter-of-factly about the exhibit that indicates which sexual position is best for use inside a small Polish Fiat.

Then, before heading off on her job search, she invited me home to meet her parents. "Polish hospitality," she said smiling.

But I had a full plate. The following day I met Kasia, the daughter of friends of mine who lived in Philadelphia. The country's robust economy has brought back quite a few Poles who had immigrated; in this family's case it was the children—both Kasia and her sister—not the parents, who had returned (at least for a while).

We walked down Próżna Street, past the last brick buildings of the old Jewish Ghetto. We crossed Plac Grzybowski, whose unruly grass made me think of Noemi. We visited Nożyk Synagogue, the only one in Warsaw to survive the war.

Kasia had started an organization, Forum for Social Diversity, whose challenging mission was to make tolerance in Polish society mainstream. With her American upbringing, she was accustomed to being with people from different countries, cultures, religions; this type of experience was new to most Poles, who lived in a predominantly Catholic and ethnically monotone country that traditionally produced immigrants but now, with its healthy economy on a continent in crisis, was receiving them. She had recently been working with the Ministry of Internal Affairs as it attempted to implement a strategy on immigration.

We stopped for lunch at Chłodna 25. The café had a familiar look: mismatched furniture, T-shirted staff, laptops-in-residence. Yet its renunciation of slickness was perhaps more crucial here because, as Kasia said, "Warsaw is still in a transition period." Foreign chains continued to move in, threatening the existence of places like this. Kasia mentioned that the cafe often hosted events: readings, discussions, exhibits. "It's a model," she said, "for those who do socially conscious businesses."

After lunch, we met two of my friends for a tour of Praga. Joasia was an artist who had recently moved from Krakow to be with Jason, a translator originally from Austin, Texas. Praga is a working-class neighborhood on the other side of the Vistula River, long famous for drunks and now popular with artists.

The tram rumbled east across the Poniatowski Bridge. Joasia told me that she sometimes felt homesick for Krakow, its beauty and compactness, but that she was enjoying the clean air of Warsaw. "And there are a lot more things happening here."

We changed trams, ending up eventually at Fabryka Soho, a former factory now housing offices, studios, and exhibition spaces. A bus—Jason had the routes down pat—took us to Fabryka Wódek, an old distillery now peppered with galleries and studios. At one point we passed the gates of the old Bazar Różyckiego where Hania and I and many Varsovians used to hunt for Western goods—food, clothing, household items—unavailable in the shops.

We wandered ignored down supposedly mean streets, ducking occasionally into Dickensian courtyards. One had been turned into a bar—with trees in huge pots—and christened Sen Pszczół (Bees' Dream.) Tonight it was showing the multimedia works of student artists. Their professor gave a short speech, then kissed the hands of all of the females.

"In Krakow," Joasia said impressed, "students kiss professors' hands."

The next morning I went to see Barbara Otwinowska, the professor with whom Hania had been corresponding. She lived on the eleventh floor of an eyesore at the edge of the Old Town. Her apartment was a cramped space lined with bookshelves and hung with oil paintings, as well as a large mirror in an ornate gold frame. Like the apartments of many older Varsovians, it was a rich representation of a rudely circumscribed life.

The professor showed me a copy of her book on female political prisoners. Walking past the prison a few days earlier I had stopped to read the plaque on the wall. Warsaw is a city of plaques, the majority commemorating victims of war and totalitarianism. They are ubiquitous, everyday reminders— often brightened with flowers—of the immense suffering that has been inflicted on this place. And they make one appreciate, in a way, the charmless (if leafy) neighborhoods outside the center. For if all of Warsaw looked like Krakowskie Przedmieście—if the city possessed the unbroken beauty of Paris—it would be difficult to believe in its brave and tortured past. The gray apartment blocks are their own kind of memorial.

The large plaque on the prison wall carried the names of the people who had died inside during "the years of Communist terror . . . 1945-1955." The date of its unveiling was 1992.

Now I sat at the professor's book-piled table, eating lemon sorbet while she read the letter I had brought from Hania. When she finished, she said that she knew a man at the Ministry of Justice who might be able to get us into the prison.

Jurek and Monika were leaving for vacation, so I moved to a hotel on Krakowskie Przedmieście—exchanging a view of a guard tower for one of fairytale rooftops. Downstairs there was a notice of a book reading—my hotel was Dom Literatury (Literature House)—starting shortly in the Museum of Literature on the Old Town Market Square.

Tour groups scuffed the cobblestones of Świętojańska Street. Because it was rebuilt, the Old Town is sometimes criticized for being Disneyesque. Such complaints usually come from people who have never seen it deserted on a winter's night. It is an exquisitely detailed, faithfully rendered, and now well-worn replica of the original. It is long past its days as the commercial heart of the city, and so has the feel more of an attraction than of a vibrant urban center. But it is far from being what one might call plastic.

In a crowded room overlooking the square, Jacek Moskwa spoke about his biography of Pope John Paul II. The beloved actress Maja Komorowska read dramatic excerpts. The filmmaker Krzysztof Zanussi listened in the back. It was like an old Catholic intelligentsia meeting.

Czesław Bielecki arrived for the reception. A renowned and often reviled architect, and former mayoral candidate, he had also been a resident—in '68, and again in the '80s—of Mokotów Prison. When told that I was writing an article about his city, he announced in characteristically hyperbolic fashion: "Warsaw is the ugliest capital in Europe."

"I would agree with that," Filip said quietly when I fed him the line. "But it's got its own charms."

We were having breakfast at Charlotte, a bright café on Plac Zbawiciela next door to the English Language College where I used to teach. I had seen it a few days earlier, when I had visited the school and met with Jolanta, the daughter of the headmaster who had hired me in 1978. Back then the school had 2,000 students; today, according to Jolanta, it has 350. Language schools now dot the city, while in the '70s and

'80s the English Language College was the only private school teaching English, and the only place Poles could learn to speak it with a New York Jewish accent. (On Fridays I played tapes of Woody Allen's old stand-up routines.)

I knew Filip's father, a photographer who had grown up in England and moved to Poland in the 1970s, a propitious time for photojournalists in Eastern Europe. In fact, in 1981 he took the iconic photograph of martial law: a tank parked in the snow in front of the Moscow Cinema which was advertising the film *Apocalypse Now*.

His son had gone into the writing side of journalism, and was now a magazine editor. He had not only studied but worked abroad, and he spoke English with a British accent. I asked him why he lived in Warsaw.

"It's an easy life," he said. "It's much more comfortable than in New York or London. And it's cheaper. You can afford so much more. You can go out every night." The words of a man with a good job in publishing; pensioners were a lot less sanguine.

Filip admitted that Krakow had better nightlife. In Warsaw, he said, you always went to the same places: Powiśle, for instance, the converted ticket hall under the Poniatowski Bridge. "Practically every night you end up here on Plac Zbawiciela." Upstairs from Charlotte was the club Plan B, though it was hard for me to think of my old school's square (really a circle) as constituting "the scene."

On his way to the office—it was now after ten—Filip dropped me at the Copernicus Science Center on the banks of the Vistula. Inside, crowds of excited children pulled at contraptions and excavated for artifacts and listened to the voice of an electronic poet (based on a character in a Stanisław Lem novel). The place had more of the air of a funhouse than of a museum. After some searching, I found the interior of a small car built into a wall; taking a seat, and pressing buttons,

I heard forthright answers to questions about human repro-
duction. Jurek had told me that the government wanted to
get more young people studying hard sciences, as subjects like
sociology had become popular. And it struck me that it was
not only the museum's interactive aspect that was novel, but
its focus on the future.

In the evening, back in the city center, I walked into the
whirl that is U Kucharzy (Chez the Chefs). The name was
appropriate, because the restaurant is housed in the former
kitchen of the Europejski Hotel. I knew the place well; Hania
and I had eaten a sad dinner there on December 25th, 1978—
her first Christmas without a mother.

The owner, Adam Gessler, stood overseeing the action in
jacket and tie. He had gone beyond the concept of the open
kitchen by placing cooking stations out in the dining rooms,
and then having the chefs deliver their own food.

"It's not that important that people see the cooks," Gessler
told me, deftly stepping out of the way of an oncoming cart,
"but that the cooks see the people. Usually, they're cooking
for a wall."

Under his jacket, sweat darkened his shirt. "You can feel the
energy," he said enthusiastically, as more chefs-turned-servers
barreled past, "of all the people who worked here for the last
150 years." In Warsaw, even restaurants respect the past.

Next door, giving onto Krakowskie Przedmieście, stood
another Gessler establishment: Przekąski Zakąski (Snacks &
Bites). A curved bar faced a room emptied of tables and over-
heated with young people. A silver-haired barman—in black
vest, white shirt, and black bow tie—poured shots of vodka
and handed across dishes of kielbasa and herring. He had an
assured, unhurried, almost courtly manner; I watched as he
greeted regulars, shaking the men's hands, kissing the wom-
en's. There has been a refreshing return to national cuisine: a
rash of pierogi restaurants after the obligatory influx of sushi.

But this place—open twenty-four hours—managed to do something more: It took Polish standards and made them hip.

Friday morning I sat with Professor Otwinowska in the waiting room of Mokotów Prison. (Now officially named Areszt Śledczy Warszawa-Mokotów.) After a few minutes the man from the ministry arrived—our liaison—and when I said "Nice to meet you" he replied: "We've already met. I was one of your students. I remember very well. You told a funny story about buying vinegar."

Tomasz led us through the gate, where we relinquished our IDs and cell phones, and into the prison yard. The professor, elegant in her sunhat, clung to my arm as we entered the first building.

Two prisoners were rousted from their cell so we could have a look inside. The professor measured its width by spreading her arms, declaring it bigger than the one she had lived in. And, of course, she had had no TV.

There was the sobering air of any correctional facility, but here it was thickened by the historical chords. I thought of all the interrogations, hunger strikes, acts of torture, and executions that had taken place within these walls. All the lives lost, the productive years wasted. (A waste that seemed all the more senseless when seen against the prospering normalcy outside.) I thought of all the courageous citizens treated as criminals, the mothers separated from their babies. The babies separated from their mothers.

Our tour ended in the director's office. Bogdan Kornatowski was a tall, handsome, well-built man. He presented each of us with a small etching on glass of the old prison building. He talked with the professor about upcoming events. Then, unexpectedly, he turned his gaze to me.

"What I am about to say may sound a bit strange," he began, then paused, searching for the right words. "Perhaps even ugly. But please tell your wife that she has best wishes from the director of the prison."

⇜ ⇜ ⇜

Thomas Swick is the author of a travel memoir, Unquiet Days: At Home in Poland, *and a collection of travel stories,* A Way to See the World: From Texas to Transylvania with a Maverick Traveler. *His most recent book,* The Joys of Travel: And Stories That Illuminate Them, *explores, through personal essays and nonfiction narratives (including "Warsaw Redux"), what he considers the seven fundamental pleasures of travel.*

OLGA PAVLINOVA OLENICH

❧ ❧ ❧

When the Journey's Over

An angel appears in the night
on the train from Venice to Nice.

When the journey's over,
there'll be time enough to sleep.
—A. E. Housman

I left Venice in the night, which is the best time to leave Venice because the city's luminous and melancholic beauty continues to ripple through your mind like the long shimmering reflections of lights on the lagoon. You can fall asleep without really feeling you have left, and you are saved the worst agitation of parting by this prolonged dream of Venice. But, as it turned out, I was not to sleep nor to dream on the night I left and I was not to be the romantic traveller swathed in her silk scarf, dreaming her diaphanous dreams in the corner of the first class carriage of the night train to Nice.

At Padua a young woman hauled her backpack into the carriage and dumped it at my feet as she turned around to say something to a bulky shadow in the corridor. The bulk shifted. The dim corridor light appeared at his shoulder and I could see the hunched figure of a man, hunched because he was shouldering a large plastic shopping bag stuffed to overflowing (all his worldly possessions, as it turned out) and hunched because of some inner defeat, some blackness that followed him into the carriage. I felt uneasy. I looked at the girl for reassurance and she was obliging, overly so. She did not stop talking. Words bubbled out of her impossibly small mouth like water from some secret spring that is the unlikely source of a great river. She loved Italy. She loved France. She loved the world. She loved God. Didn't I? She didn't give me a chance to answer, which was possibly a good thing. She was a pilgrim and she was overwhelmed with the messianic desire to make herself heard above the indifferent noises of the speeding train and through the heavy darkness of the carriage. She stopped only to make signs at her silent traveling companion who got the message and wearily put his shoulder to her backpack, heaving it painfully into the rack above my seat.

"I picked him up at Padua," she explained breezily, as if the man was an inanimate souvenir she'd acquired at one of the booths outside the Giotto-frescoed Capella degli Scrovegni. "I can't work out what language he speaks. I've tried everything, but he seems happy enough to tag along. It's handy for the luggage." She smiled. Then she went on at length about the miracles of Lourdes and the sightings at Fatima and the *Black Madonna* of ... I didn't quite catch the location of the *Black Madonna* because I found myself wishing, uncharitably, that the slick Italian ticket inspector would do his rounds and send them to second class where they obviously belonged.

Where they obviously belonged! My own line of thinking appalled me. Only a few days ago I had declared adamantly that the worst people traveled first class. I had an international rail pass, which made me a first-class traveler and, since my first trip from Switzerland to France, I had seen enough of the petulant first class to tempt me back to second class, where, by the way, I belonged, despite what the ticket said. But the sight of the fabulously comfortable first-class seats weakened my resolve time and time again, especially at night when the prospect of comfort fell in so easily with the prospect of sleep. So here I was again, in first class and, appallingly quickly, making myself a first-class passenger with all the misguided arrogance and ignorant intolerance I had observed in my first-class fellow travelers.

However, when the slick conductor insinuated himself into the carriage to check the tickets of my new companions, I woke up to myself and pleaded their case. The carriage was empty, I said. I didn't mind, I said, convinced, out of a sense of guilt that I could listen to some more about the *Black Madonna*. But the man who had come in with the girl was already on his feet, frightened and defeated. It seemed to me that he was ready to run. I felt that something was required of me, as the girl also got up, perturbed perhaps by her friend's alarm. I was soothing. I suggested that they leave their luggage with me, at least while they looked for a seat in the crowded second class. It was summer and the height of the season. The rest of the train was full. The girl took up my offer quickly. The man hesitated, looked at me with sad eyes, and then nodded. They left. The conductor smiled at me triumphantly. I turned to the window where the lights and yellowish facades of earth-bound Italian cities swam in the darkness and made me think of Venice again.

At Milan I was disturbed by a great commotion, the sort of Italian commotion you get used to after a while in Italy. Loud voices, dramatic exclamations, flights of curses and any number of Madonnas. Madonna this and Madonna that!

Someone wasn't happy. The door of the carriage crashed open and the light went on. I blinked to see a bad-tempered Adonis who stood in the doorway insolently waiting to be admired and feared. While I am enchanted with Italy and the Italians, there is a type that leaves me cold. This is the type whose sultry droop of the eyelid is just that bit too sultry, whose mink eyelashes are that much too thick and long, whose crushed-grape mouth is that much too full-lipped, and whose expression is entirely self-absorbed. I suddenly felt very cold. Behind Adonis, in the narrow corridor, a jostling, wiggling, giggling group of black girls (*Black Madonnas?* The thought was tempting.) Or at least they were dressed like girls. Les Girls. Hot volatile stuff. Pink mini, spangled top, midriff as black as night. Lime green shorts, gelato bra, hair as high as a cloud. Amid screams and curses and whistles and laughter, he sent them packing to the second class. There was no sign of the ticket inspector. There was no longer any hint of Venice in the night.

The Adonis closed the door, switched off the light and took up a position opposite me, stretching his legs across the carriage to the other seat and smiled, insolently, waiting for a sign of nerves or perhaps even fear. I wanted to grab my handbag on the seat beside me and leave the carriage, but I would not give him the satisfaction. Instead, I continued to look out of the window into the warm summer night but my breathing was shallow and I was alert to any movement in the carriage. It was unpleasant. I cursed the inspector and my first-class ticket and the pride that would not let me make a run for it. Then the door opened. It was the pilgrim's traveling companion, the silent man. He'd come for their luggage, his and the pilgrim's. I felt relieved. His bulk made light work of Adonis whose legs came down to the floor in a flash. I heard the newcomer utter his first words, a guttural curse. "Bloody Italian!" he muttered in Russian. I didn't quite make the connection. It was three A.M. I hadn't slept but the darkness and the motion of the train had given me the occasional sense of being asleep and dreaming. I was momentarily confused and then he said it again. "Bloody Italian!" In Russian. In my language, or should I say, the language of my parents. Before I could make myself known to him as this new person, this person who could understand him, he had taken up the seat next to mine, making it very clear that he was not going to leave me alone with Adonis. I was grateful.

It didn't take long for the Adonis to make his exit. He saved face by studying his showy watch for a long time, as if he was worried he'd miss some appointment. Then he sighed loudly and stood up stretching. The smell of some expensive spice-laden aftershave lotion flooded the carriage as he slithered out. My companion smiled at me. It was a weary smile but a smile nonetheless.

"Thanks," I said in Russian. For a moment he was confused.

"Thanks," I said again and followed up by telling him who I was. He was still confused.

"Are you a dream?" he asked.

"No," I said.

"Then you must be an angel." This made me laugh. No one had ever mistaken me for an angel. I told him this. He told me his story.

He was from Moldova. He had been a music teacher, but times were so tough that he'd been reduced to playing his fiddle in the streets. His wife, also educated, was unemployed. His child was sick.

"All children are sick in Moldova now," he said ominously as the train lurched, giving his statement an edge of unreality, like something in the theatre or in a dream. Even I was beginning to wonder if we were in a dream, the desperate man and the holidaymaker thrown into the same dark carriage of someone's imagination. He was on his way to Lisbon where he told me many of his compatriots had gone in search of work.

Of course, they were "illegals." He'd paid "some people" $4,000 that his family and friends had managed to put together after selling their instruments, their furniture, their wedding rings. The "some people" gave him a visa that had him down as a sports trainer and then smuggled him across borders in a truck along with several other single men. "We did not speak to each other," he said sadly. "We might have been able to help each other but it's a dangerous business and it's better if you don't speak." He was left with a railway ticket, no money and no help in some back room of a dive in Padua. He thought he was going to die. He hadn't eaten or slept in days. After forty-eight hours he was kicked out of the room and he made his way, somehow, to the station where he met the pilgrim. The pilgrim! I suddenly saw her in a different light. Thank God for the pilgrim! His words were beginning to slur. I could see he was exhausted. I gave him some fruit that I had in my bag and ordered him to eat though, as he said, he was beyond the point of hunger. "You are an angel," he kept saying, not as a compliment to me but as a way of explanation. It was, I had to admit, an amazing thing that he had chanced upon me here, in the first-class carriage of the night train to Nice, the smart train of European travelers, the Riviera train, the romantic train from Venice. I told him to stretch out and go to sleep.

"You are safe," I repeated more than once, "You are safe and I will watch over you." Like an angel. I grimaced at the thought. He gave me his passport and his rail ticket.

He was worried about the inspector.

"I'll sort him out," I said.

"You have got to be an angel," he murmured and fell asleep instantly, the dead sleep of total exhaustion. While he slept I wrestled with a whole battalion of thoughts. How to help this man? The inspector was easy. If necessary, I'd pay the difference. But what about afterward? What about getting him safely to Lisbon? I switched on the small light above my seat and studied his ticket because I suddenly had a terrible thought that he'd been duped again by "those people." I compared the ticket to my own. It looked legitimate enough. I could see that there were two more changes of train he had to make after Nice. I remembered the pilgrim saying she was on her way to Spain. I wondered if I could count on her. I rummaged in my bag and found a pen and a rather decent envelope containing the account from a hotel in Singapore. I screwed up the account and threw it back into my bag. And then I wrote on the envelope, first in English and then in French, a "please can you help this traveler" set of directions that I figured he could show to people if he got into trouble on his journey to Lisbon. This feverish burst of activity made me feel better, as if I had somehow managed, by my inadequate scribbling, to stave off the strange sense of panic and gloom that had suddenly filled my night. I took a look at the "illegal" who was dead to the world and I switched off the light.

The train was skirting the coast. In rapid succession the window was black or filled with the lights of some coastal town. Occasionally there was the sea, blue-black in the night, chopping between the two colors, flecked with lights whose source was invisible but might have been the moon. At one point the train seemed to move through a beach party like an invisible guest. I saw people dancing on well-lit sand, I heard loud music and voices, and I saw the shore dotted with figures of partygoers who'd been hard at it all night. Summer nights on the Riviera. It must have been five o'clock in the morning and, like the people on the beach, I had not slept. When the light began to stream into the carriage, the Moldovan woke with a deep shudder. He looked around confused for a moment but he recognized me and remembered who I was.

"An angel!" he exclaimed and gave a real smile.

"Like hell!" I said and we both laughed. There wasn't much time left until Nice. I gave him the envelope, which, in the light of day, revealed itself as a fragile and shabby piece of armor against the world. Nevertheless, I translated it for him. After his sleep, he was a different person, quick on the uptake, humorous and almost optimistic. He told me that his friends would be waiting for him in Lisbon.

"Are you sure?" I asked.

"You can always rely on friends," he said. And I didn't doubt that someone would be waiting for him in Lisbon, no matter when he arrived. My own family, after all, had been refugees in some distant past that had never been thrown in quite the same relief as it was now. I felt I had to help him. I did not consider the implications of his being an "illegal." Up close, like this, you don't worry about the status of a person. Legal. Illegal. Here was a man in a state of desperation. The worry was to get him to Lisbon. I left him in charge of the luggage and went in search of the pilgrim. I found her sprawled on the floor of a carriage full of backpackers. It was a cheerful unruly scene. Normal. I wondered why I'd ever gone into first-class. The pilgrim followed me into the corridor where I told her his story.

"Oh!" she sighed, full of compassion, her tiny mouth forming a perfect circle.

"He's a good man, you have nothing to fear from him," I said. She nodded.

"A good Christian man." I was shameless. She was convinced.

"I will look after him until Spain and then I will put him on the train to Lisbon," she said with righteous zeal. I was very encouraging. Together, we made our way to first class, our mission clear and our mutual admiration at a high point. The trolley came around. I bought everyone breakfast. We were cheerful. I acted as an interpreter, establishing some communication between the pilgrim and her charge that I thought would make their ongoing journey easier, or at least their silences more comfortable.

In the station at Nice, we parted ways. I gave him some American dollars. Dollars speak all languages. He gave me a telephone number of a relative in St. Petersburg so that I could ring to say I'd seen him and so that I could find out if he made it to Lisbon. Presumably, word would get back to his wife in Moldova. I watched him hoisting his plastic bag and the pilgrim's large backpack over his broad shoulders. The sun was already hot and the platform was crowded with holidaymakers. My own train to Les Arcs Draguignan and the village in Provence where I was staying with a friend was already at the station. I pushed my way through the crowd moving farther and farther away from the point where I had said goodbye to the music teacher, farther and farther away from the point where my dreams of Venice had collided with his flight. I looked for a second-class carriage and threw myself in with the holiday throng.

≈≈ ≈≈ ≈≈

Olga Pavlinova Olenich is a widely published Australian writer who lives in Melbourne.

~~ ~~ ~~

Sacrifices, Desires, New Moon

In Brazil, things are often not as simple as they seem.

S tanding on the balcony in my wrap-around bathrobe, naked underneath, I ponder jumping the twenty feet to the ground. I really don't like this idea because I can't see in the tarry blackness of the new-moon night, and I remember seeing a flagstone patio somewhere around this end of the house. I might hit that stone and break both legs, and then I certainly would not be able to escape. Even if I land on the grass—so lush and green here in Brazil during the rainy season—the movement would alert Denilda's four dogs and they would set off again.

Yes, the dogs . . . but now after being jolted awake only a few minutes ago my foggy brain stumbles onto the notion that the dogs are *not* barking, which is an impossibility considering all the commotion in the house. They must have killed them. *If they killed the dogs, then these guys mean business.* She was talking to me now, the survival voice, ordering me around.

At this point the adrenaline kicks in and the synapses of my brain start firing like a Formula 1 engine—because I realize another fact: the invaders know that the cook and her husband, who always sleep downstairs in their little room by the laundry, left yesterday for their hometown. After all the madness of Carnival, Denilda had given the servants the weekend off and we are alone in the house . . . a fact the man in the black ski mask surely knows. *This is an inside job, and you are screwed.*

I try the French doors, the only exit off the balcony, and they are bolted from the inside. I'm hoping the man will just get what he came for and leave. But this line of reasoning is cut short because at the other end of the balcony I see a flashlight beam swing an arc across the night air and come to rest a few inches from my bare feet. I flatten myself up against the house hoping he won't see me, my arms outstretched against the white stucco wall like Jesus hanging on the cross. The flashlight beam moves back inside, but now through the windows I can see it moving down the hall toward me, scanning the empty rooms. Any second he is going to open this door to the balcony and stare me in the face. Quickly I weigh the options of jumping to the ground versus being shot or kidnapped . . . and who knows what horrors await me then? I determine that anything is better than having them take me, and this is when the voice tells me: *Hang from the balcony, in the darkness he won't see you.*

I throw first one leg then the other over the railing, feeling the rough wood chafe against my naked thigh, then lower myself till my weight is suspended by my hands gripping the cool cement floor as I dangle above the ground. But once I'm underneath the balcony I spy a wooden pole holding it up, grab it and shinny down. As soon as my feet hit the moist grass, I start running. I consider hiding in the jungle till they're gone. *Don't go there—it's full of snakes.* My wobbly legs threatening to give way, I move onto that wretched dirt road, running down the mountain at midnight, over the rocks, the burrs, the branches, the cow manure squishing between my toes, expecting to hear shouting or gunshots any minute, for who knows if they have a lookout stationed at the entrance to the estate. I won't notice the damage to my bare feet until days later but strangely, in that instant, another thought leaps to mind: *You came to Brazil to get a story. Well by God, you've got one. Now all you have to do is live to tell it.*

This particular story had begun two years prior, back in California at a time when I was desperately trying to finish a biography I'd been working on for ten years. I told a friend that as a reward to myself I intended to take a long vacation to Latin America to relax when I finished the book. As if the universe were listening, the following week I found a brown paper package covered with foreign stamps stuffed into my mailbox. I opened it and hurriedly skimmed the cover letter, which invited me to come to Brazil to write the life story of a woman named Denilda Lizardo dos Santos, all expenses paid. The pitch included a binder of photos of her estate on top of a mountain above Paraty, with breathtaking views of the Atlantic coast in the distance. This is where I'd be staying.

I researched Denilda and the man who had sent me the package, Jiri Havrda, a Czech documentary filmmaker; he had been friends with Deni for thirty years. Like many of her acquaintances, he had long encouraged her to write the story of her life, one filled to the brim with outrageous incidents of fortune and mayhem. Jiri, experienced in organizing large projects as a producer, volunteered to bring together the elements to put the book project in motion, including finding an author and a translator since Deni spoke no English. Having read *Desert Flower*, a book I'd written, Jiri determined I was the right woman for the job and he'd composed a very professional pitch designed to lure me to South America.

My collaborators sent me 200 pages of notes Denilda had put down—a record of her life's events. She had the rather remarkable pedigree of having been a political dissident,

maid, refugee, television game show personality, cargo boat
cook, exotic dancer, laundress, factory worker, jewelry maker,
shepherd, trafficker of leftist guerrillas, fashion model, dish-
washer, La Scala Opera slave, restaurateur, chorus girl, inn-
keeper, and Michael Jackson impersonator. Who could resist
this assignment?

When I landed in Rio de Janeiro, waiting for me was Deni
herself, a tall muscular *negra brasileira* with a blinding white
smile. Also waiting, with a look of nervous anticipation, was
Fernanda, who would serve as our translator while I inter-
viewed Deni. She was very pale, of Italian descent, and had
the bulging, luminous black eyes and dramatic mannerisms
of a telenovella star. They loaded my two bags into a hired
car and the driver remained stoic and silent while the women
chattered on like multilingual magpies. "Cachy . . ." Fernanda
opened the questioning, demonstrating what I'd learn was
Brazilians' common inability to pronounce Cathy. "We are
dying to find out your zodiac sign!"

Four hours later we pulled into the UNESCO heritage site
of Paraty, a picturesque colonial village of white stucco buildings and palm trees on the southern coast of Brazil, a resort
town popular with Italian and French tourists. I later learned
that before I arrived Denilda had been sauntering down Paraty's cobblestone streets bragging about the "famous American
writer" who was coming to research her life story. In a town of
35,000 this type of news travels far and wide and fast.

A mud-splattered Toyota pickup pulled up next to us and
I noticed with some alarm that our driver was now taking my
red suitcases and tossing them in the back of the 4x4. Next he
grabbed my backpack containing $5,000 worth of electronics
equipment. "Wait!" I hollered just before he launched it onto
the truck bed. "What are you doing?"

"Cachy, we are getting in this vehicle," said Fernanda.

"Buy why?"

She and Deni grinned. "You'll see!"

A young white guy with crystalline blue eyes sat behind the wheel of the Toyota, his biceps bulging out of his t-shirt. He adjusted his baseball cap in the rearview mirror, then slid his hand down his jeans. I had no idea at this point in the journey that I would later be seeing him with those jeans off. "This is Cellino, my white son," Deni said. They both laughed since he was actually the caretaker but it was clear they had an easy and affectionate relationship.

I sat in the back seat of the cab as we left the city. Soon we were chugging in low gear up a rutted dirt road the color of rust. My head bounced on my shoulders as we pitched in and out of gulleys, waded through streams, past waterfalls, whined over boulders, and circled around sleeping cattle. "This . . . is . . . the . . . worst . . . road . . . I . . . have . . . ever . . . seen!" I sputtered and my words strobed with the motion of the truck. "And . . . that . . . includes . . . India . . . and . . . Africa!"

The lurching stopped at the top of the mountain and I hopped out of the cab, caught my breath, and spun around to see the view: thick clumps of forest, blue ridges of distant mountain ranges, horses grazing on the green velvet hillsides, a gorge which fell away sharply hundreds of feet, and off in the distance sailboats bobbing in the harbor of Paraty. Beyond that the Atlantic Ocean. Overhead turkey vultures floated on the thermals, their wings spread majestically. I twirled around— turning and turning—taking it all in.

This magnificent estate called Casinha Branca would be my home for the next couple of months; it was a somewhat homespun affair having been constructed by a local contractor who hauled the building materials up that awful road on the back of a mule. The design was based on a fantasy that had incubated within Denilda since her mother listened to a song called "Casinha Branca," a tune expressing the desire to be in a green place, in a white house with a balcony, and watch the sunrise—which I did from the balcony of my suite overlooking the Atlantic.

I quickly settled into the idyllic rhythm of life in the wilderness, waking up early to be greeted by the fresh morning air coming through the open French doors of my room on the second floor. I'd walk out to the balcony and admire the view, the hillside sloping quickly down to Paraty and the sea beyond. About a half mile down the rusty ribbon of road in the distance I could see the little shack where Cellino, the caretaker, lived. There were no other houses around to disturb the tranquility, only the cacophony of tropical birds chattering, greeting the dawn.

I'd head downstairs where Benedetta the cook would have my breakfast set out, papayas or mangoes she'd just plucked from the trees outside, along with homemade bread, cheese, and tea. Fernanda lived in town so till she arrived I was alone here with Brazilians who understood no English. Deni communicated in a language her friends called *Denildese*—her mishmash of Portuguese, Italian, and Spanish. Embarrassingly monolingual, I understood none of these but I noticed early on that Deni and I were able to communicate in an odd telepathic way . . . no words required.

After breakfast I'd go upstairs and sit at the desk in my room and write until I heard Deni calling, "Cachy! *Almoço está pronto!*" Then I'd go downstairs to find the twenty-five-foot-long table on the deck laden with a succulent spread of pork or chicken raised here on the farm and vegetables fresh from the garden. I'd shovel it in as if this were my last meal before being shot at sunrise while my companion chattered on in Denildese and I answered in English. When Fernanda arrived we'd get down to business with the interviewing so I could piece together Deni's life for the page.

One afternoon I spotted an odd little doll hanging upside-down beneath the stairs to the second floor. It was the figure of a man, with a bottle of cachaça strapped to his back and a tiny cigarette in his mouth. I froze, sensing that this was no mere child's toy. "Deni . . ." I pointed, "what is this?"

She smiled that infectious grin of hers and said something I couldn't understand. Fernanda explained: "That's the magic charm she created to bring you to Brazil to write her story. Like all smokers he desperately wants a cigarette, but she won't light it until her wish is fulfilled." Like Catholicism in Italy, Macumba—Brazilian voodoo—is an undercurrent running through the country's daily life. In São Paulo you can walk down the street and stumble upon a chicken slaughtered at the crossroads on the night of the new moon—the proper time for sacrifices to attain your desires. The larger the desire, the bigger the sacrifice offered to the gods.

After a couple of hours of interviewing each day we'd stop and get down to the serious business of drinking caparinhis in the pool, then move on to my samba lessons—all orchestrated to the sexy rumbling voice of Seu Jorge which had now replaced birdsong as the dominant soundtrack of life at Casinha Branca. Some nights Deni would call Cellino on her cell phone and summon him to drive us into Paraty where we'd join the Europeans drinking beer at one of the beach cafes. Everyone seemed to know Denilda. Her estate was legendary—someplace up there on top of the mountain, the locals knew—though few had been there.

Our routine here at the house was interrupted when we began traveling to see the settings of Deni's life as research for the book. In this pursuit we ventured into the favelas of Rio, the green mountains of Minas Gerais, and drifted down the Amazon from Belem to Manaus. For our trips by car we had a fourth musketeer who joined our entourage, Arturo, an

American who lived in Paraty. Although he'd been in Brazil for years, the 6'4" ex-Marine hadn't lost any of his Staten Island accent and I'd smile every time he opened his mouth.

When Carnival season arrives all day-to-day business in Brazil ceases like someone's thrown a circuit breaker. At Cashinha Branca the holiday transformed the estate into a beehive of activity, starting with the arrival of Denilda's husband, Paolo, a psychiatrist who lives most of the year in Italy. Their bicontinental marriage was an endless source of curiosity for me but I liked Paolo instantly, especially that he spoke some English. Two more visitors came from Italy, along with a German woman we'd met on the Amazon, and for five days we indulged in the type of bacchanalia which has made Brazil famous—everything from dancing in the blocos of Paraty by the light of flaming torches, to watching the parades at the Sambadrome in Rio till 8 a.m., to rolling in the volcanic mud of Jabaquara Beach. But by the end of Carnival I was destroyed, and when the guests left, Deni gave the servants the weekend off. There were long good-byes and kisses on both cheeks—and promises that we would visit the Italians soon to trace Denilda's past life in Italy; she'd fled there thirty years ago as a refugee after the Death Squads had killed her brother in Rio. When the military dictatorship and her fear of violence ended, Deni had returned to her homeland.

Carnival finished on Friday and on that muggy Saturday night, I bolted my door, climbed naked under the mosquito netting, and finished reading Peter Robb's *Death in Brazil*—a true tale of political intrigues that includes a home invasion where the servants conspire in the plot to execute PC Farias. In another incident a Brazilian congressman dealt with one of his enemies by cutting off the victim's arms and legs with a chainsaw, and hammering nails into his head. I closed the book, turned off the light, and fell into a deep dreamless sleep.

"Cachy! Cachy wake up!" Denilda is screaming in English, punctuated by the splintering sound of knuckles pounding on my door. How long this has been going on I can't fathom because it's as if I'm swimming up from the bottom of the ocean trying to regain consciousness. I hear the locked knob rattling. "Cachy!"

Still nude, I open my door just a crack. All the lights are ablaze in the hallway and I see Deni with tears pouring down her black face, then I realize her husband is standing next to her, his large blue eyes open wide but otherwise calm. Somebody must have died, I decide. I try to imagine who.

"Paolo, what's happening, what's going on?"

"Cathy, there's a man in the house and he wants you to come out."

"What?"

He repeats his line calmly, slowly, in his best psychiatrist's voice: "There's a man in the house and he wants you to come out." While I'm pondering what on earth this can mean, I see a sudden movement in the hall and look up to see a man standing about ten feet behind Paolo, dressed all in black. He wears a black ski mask; underneath it are a ghostly pale face and brown eyes wide with an expression of terror, pupils dilated. His chest is heaving with rapid breaths. He has both arms outstretched holding a Magnum semi-automatic pointed at my head.

My first impulse is to laugh. This is a joke, right? They've gotten high and had one of their friends dress up like a robber. It's a scene we've witnessed hundreds of times in films—the costume, the pose—so that it has the illusion of unreality. I glance back at Denilda's tortured face and my dazed brain realizes this is not a joke.

"O.K., let me get my bathrobe." I push the door shut, go back into my room and switch on the light to find my robe. It's a cotton blue pinstripe, purchased especially for the tropical climate of my languid Latin American assignment. I wrap it around me and tie the belt.

Now a voice from inside me starts giving me orders. This instinct had steered me through dire consequences in the past, taking command of the situation. She left no room to argue: *Just like in the book—they are going to kill all of you. But if they're going to shoot you, they'll have to shoot you in the back. Make a run for it.*

With this I walk outside to the balcony facing the front of the house where the hillside falls away to a drop of about twenty feet below. Around the corner of the building is another balcony with a sheer drop between the two. I scramble over to it and as I maneuver over the railings I fight the bathrobe twisting around my trembling legs. Once I land safely on the other balcony I run as far as I can until I reach the end and wait hiding, hoping the man in the ski mask will get what he came for and go away. I have a sickening feeling, however, that what he came for is *me*.

From some locked vault in my brain drifts up the advice of an article I'd read years ago: *If someone tries to kidnap you, don't go with them thinking you'll escape later. Make your stand right there.* I am now fully awake and realizing the circumstances, all evidence pointing to the fact that this is an inside job, someone who knows the layout of the place. Someone who knows that Benedetta and her husband wouldn't be sleeping downstairs in their little twin bed tonight. When I see the black ski mask peer around the side of the house looking for me I know the time for debating my course of action is over. I'd rather risk breaking my neck than be taken hostage, so I shinny down from the balcony and begin to run.

I have no idea how many men are with the intruder or if they have a lookout or if they will soon stand on the balcony and shoot at the pale blue bathrobe streaking down the mountain road. Certainly there is no one around to hear the gunfire. I reach the large steel gate that Deni closes across the road at night. I try to open it but a chain with a padlock prevents that. In my happy-go-lucky existence here I have never pondered the need for these security measures. Moving to the side of the gate I realize I will have to climb over the barbed wire fence which comes up above my waist— which will be quite the challenge barefoot in my robe. The possibility to do real damage to myself flits through my mind, straddling the barbed wire and having it rip into my genitals. I manage to get over it without injury, and run down the road to the caretaker's house where I knock softly.

Cellino opens the door a crack and I can see that he is standing there nude with a small hand towel covering his private parts. "Let me in," I hiss.

"*Por* Cachy?" Only later do I think about how absurd all this must seem to him, a woman in a bathrobe showing up at his door in the middle of the night demanding to be let in. But at the time I was not interested in propriety. I press my way in and try to explain what's happening.

"*Homens com* . . ." here I pause because I have no idea what the word for gun is in Portuguese. "*Homens com* guns at Casinha Branca." I take my finger and point, thumb up, to my head. "Deni and Paolo." I'm anticipating he'll leap into action to rescue his black mother. Instead he collapses onto a sofa; the little towel draped across his groin slips to the floor, and he goes into a trance. Then he begins softly whimpering and shaking his head as tears stream down his cheeks.

Across the room his young blond wife wears a black slip; she's watching this scene intently but does not speak. "Cellino, *chame a polícia!*" I cry. I take a hold of both his sweaty shoulders and begin to shake him—trying to snap him out of it—but he continues in his trance, making little noises like a mewling kitten. The thought pops into my head to slap this man as hard as I can like I've seen in the movies. Perhaps the wife senses this is what I'm ready to do, understands in that way of women when physical danger is imminent.

"Cachy!" she calls out and holds up a Blackberry and begins to dial. As the woman thumbs the buttons of her phone I turn loose of her husband and for the first time look around. Their tiny house consists solely of that one room which is modestly furnished except for a lavish big screen TV. They must have been watching a movie when I arrived because now I stare at the screen where a man is charging in and assuming the all-too-familiar stance: both arms rigid pointing a handgun straight into the camera—straight at me. I grab the remote and turn it off.

"What is happening?" I demand of the wife who is still punching buttons on her Blackberry. How many digits to dial the cops in this place? Is she calling Uranus?

She holds the phone out toward me and shrugs, indicating that it won't work.

"We need to get dressed."

"¿Por?" she frowns at me like I'm making an unreasonable and ridiculous demand.

"Do you have some clothes I can wear?" She gives me a long-suffering look and shrugs again, then walks over to her closet where she slides one item at a time down the rod studying her wardrobe. At last she hands me a hanger sporting a red sequin party dress. For a few seconds I stare at her, my gaze going back and forth from her emotionless face to the garment extended to me—no doubt her best dress. "No. *Pantalones. Sapatos.*" At this moment the voice starts talking to me again: *These people are idiots and you are going to have to leave them and save yourself. You've got to take charge of this situation.* I push the petite blonde out of the way and grab some gym shorts and a tank top, both of which are about three sizes too small. Then I stick my feet into her tiny flip-flops.

I turn my attention back to Cellino now who has a cell phone of his own, the one I've seen him talk on dozens of times. He's put on some shorts and a t-shirt and is finally trying to dial someone, but indicating the call won't go through. In some of my travels in the past I'd experienced situations where the signal was too weak for a phone call but would transmit a text. "Text Arturo and tell him to go the police." Cellino nods and begins punching the buttons of his phone. We wait, but there's no reply.

The minutes drag on with both husband and wife trying to dial out but nothing happens. Then suddenly Cellino's cell phone rings and he stares at it. "Denilda!" He says something in Portuguese which I take to mean: "Should I answer it?" I nod thinking this is the stupid question of the century. He puts the phone to his ear then shrugs as if to say no one was there.

At this point I freeze. For a half hour these two have been claiming they can't get a signal to call the police and now Cellino's phone rings, so clearly it's working. For the first time the horrible thought occurs to me: *Maybe they're in on it. No one in the world knows where you are right now . . . they can kill you and drag you out into the jungle and in a couple of days those vultures will have devoured you. You'll be gone without a trace.*

I point back and forth between Cellino and myself. "You and I, *moto para polícia.*" I pantomime holding onto the handlebars of his dirt bike and turning the throttle.

He shakes his head emphatically. "Ah *não.*"

"That or I will walk," and here I wiggle my index and middle finger back and forth to mimic walking. *Really? Are you going to hike miles down this mountain on a new moon night—through the streams and waterfalls and snakes and masked bandits? In a pair of flip-flops?* The voice of survival is fierce, and she has guided me through many a crisis in the past. This time though I answer her: *If I don't, those guys are going to kill Deni and Paolo then I'll have to live with it for the rest of my life.*

Before this debate can go any further we hear shouting outside. Cellino motions for us to stay put while he investigates. The wife and I lock the door behind him and I press against it, my heart thudding inside my ribs. Then he calls for us to come out. I fling the door open and immediately a flashlight is in my face, blinding me. I see the outline of a man holding an assault rifle and there are other figures in the dark around him. *You walked into their trap and you're not going to escape this time. It's over.*

"Are you O.K.?" says a deep resonate male voice in English. "Yes, I'm O.K.," I reply weakly. He takes the flashlight away from my face and as my eyes adjust to the dark I scan his clothes: camo fatigues with no insignia, no badges. Are these the good guys or the bad guys? I have no idea. But he's movie star handsome and in that moment I fall in love with him in a way that's absolutely primal. That swooning when the Mounties rush in is not just for the melodramas. I later learn that my rescuer's name is Juliano from the Paraty police.

"Good. We have to go up to the big house now and see what's happening up there." He turns away with a look of resignation that I will not forget in this lifetime—it said: "I may die in a few moments." Now the nausea overtakes me, imagining Denilda and Paolo lying in a pool of blood. As the three men move away the last one in line runs his eyes over me, my breasts bulging out of the doll-sized tank top and several inches of bare ass hanging out of the shorts.

In a few minutes Deni and Paolo come running down the mountain—very much alive—and we run into each other's arms to lock in a group hug. The intruders had shut them in the laundry room then quickly cleaned out the house of cash and computers. They took all my electronics, stowing them in a sack before running off into the jungle. We later learned that from their camp they'd been watching us with binoculars as we danced around the pool and drank caparinhis . . . waiting for their moment. The police believed that one of their motives was to kidnap the "famous American writer"—a popular money-making activity in South America amongst the criminal class. Listen up, illiterate kidnappers: "famous American writer" does not necessarily equal "rich American writer."

Later I learned that my computer was recovered from Cellino's uncle's house; Deni mailed it back to me in California. The caretaker resigned shortly after the robbery and moved away. While Cellino was never arrested to my knowledge, the man in the ski mask was shot and killed by law enforcement during another hold up.

And yet the caretaker really *did* text Arturo—one of the many unsolved riddles surrounding this whole story. Arturo received the text and went straight to the police station where he informed them: "There are robbers up at Casinha Branca."

"If they made it all the way up there then this is going to be a fucked-up job," they said as they began grabbing automatic weapons off the rack and slamming in ammo clips. While they put on bulletproof vests they said to our driver, "You've got to go up there with us because we don't know how to get there."

"I can go, but give me a weapon. I was a U.S. Marine in Afghanistan."

With that they set off in a car, which promptly got stuck on the awful road. They abandoned it and hiked the rest of the way up, stopping at Cellino's house first.

The next morning after the gunmen invaded Casinha Branca, I tell Denilda: "You have two choices. Either we go to Italy and finish the book there, or I get on the first plane back to the States and that's the end of this project."

With that the entire entourage packs up and heads to Milan, where we begin tracing Deni's wild life throughout

Italy; I stay on alone when she returns to Brazil. Sleeping on a friend's couch in Rome, I lie awake each endless evening reliving the whole incident, trying to sort out the mystery of it all. A recurring thought nags: Why couldn't I see anything when I was trying to jump off the balcony. It was so dark. . . . *It was the night of the new moon,* came the answer. *The proper time for sacrifices to attain your desires.*

≈ ≈ ≈

Cathleen Miller circled the globe to interview the sources for Champion of Choice, *her biography of U.N. leader Nafis Sadik. Miller's previous work includes the international bestseller* Desert Flower, *which has been translated into fifty-five languages and adapted as a feature film. She is also the author of a memoir,* The Birdhouse Chronicles. *A winner of the Society of American Travel Writers gold award, her travel essays have appeared in the* Washington Post, Chicago Tribune, San Francisco Chronicle, *and* Los Angeles Times. *She teaches creative writing at San José State University.*

ANDREW LEES

❧ ❧ ❧

Mowtown

The author enjoys a first visit to Detroit:
ear worms, Henry Ford's vision for the Motor
City, and the destructive force of lawn mowers.

An obsession with polished aspirational black music
finally carried me to Detroit. I had come to redis-
cover the heartbreak of first love and unearth a few last Okeh
Records "cover ups." Poking my nose against a high window
in the MGM Grand Hotel, I survey this strung-out city constructed on the lands of the People of the Three Fires. Michigan Central looms in front of me, the morose emblem of the
city's mutation in death. Through the perforations in its evis-
cerated carcass I see smoke signals rising up from the Poletown Incinerator. No train has left the station since the 353 to
Chicago on January 5, 1988.

A Sunday afternoon in "The D" does not differ too much
from a run-of-the-mill Monday morning. A few beaten-up
jalopies and bedraggled trucks glide downriver on the blis-
tered freeways. Traffic flow is now glacial only on the Ambas-
sador Bridge. Above Bagley Street, where Henry Ford had
his first garage, the People Carrier skirts around the Notown
hub connecting the city's new casinos with its historic glass
dollhouses. An overcast sky casts an ashen grayness over a

dismal spectacle of relentless devastation. Closer to the river, the beleaguered skyscraper garrison of the RenCen is encircled by an enclave of empty neglect. Since I arrived four days ago I have not heard a police siren, the squealing of tires, or even the expected gun boom. Unshaven and with only out-of-town mod preconceptions to comfort me, I set off from the chrome boomerang tower of the MGM for the river. Beyond the brightly colored cantinas of Mexicantown at the end of West Grand Boulevard I arrive at the sea wall bordered by corroded rail tracks. Above me a wedge of honking Canada geese flies in from Baffin Island to graze on the edgelands. A convoy of trucks waits at the border to enter the Great White North from the bridge. Two fishing skiffs are returning from Lake St Clair with catches of walleyes and small mouth bass. Far out in the river a black woman and a white man are swimming in synchrony. There is a pastoral stillness that reminds me of Liverpool, Otterspool Promenade, the garden suburbs of Wavertree, and the parkland estate of Grassendale.

In Corktown, close to Slow's Bar-B-Q and the McShane bus, a burnt-out gray-hooded schizophrenic is drinking from a paper bag. On Michigan Avenue a dude on a Detroit bike gives me the finger and shouts "Hey dog what's a cocksucking whitey doin' down here?" My Saint Cosmas and Damian medallion left in the hotel safe cannot protect me now from this unexpected fear of blackness, but a favorite Tamla brainworm "Baby I can't let you go, /I realize I hurt you so/Our love, surely can we mend it/It's just a little misunderstanding," helps to shore me.

With a rerun of The Contours clanging in my ears I keep going in search of authenticity. Art Deco stacks tower above me like colossal tombstones. On a clapboard, a few blocks from Campus Martius Park next to a coffee shop, a joker has written "Free Coffee with Purchase of Wurlitzer building."

A brown teddy bear fastened to a street sign nearby marks a homicide. The last big box store remains boarded up and the nearest Apple shop is twenty miles away in a strip mall. Nigga is still the code name for Detroit. I am trying to find a friendly dog who likes Motown in this burnt-out forest.

After my journey to the end of the night a curtain of dark thinking descends. Strangers are not welcome here any more and music is linked with violence. I enter the Greektown Casino where an unhealthy candlelight and total absence of clocks confronts me. Solitary jaded smokers man a flashing conveyor belt of gears, brakes, and levers. Round the clock *Insertpushpullthehandle* has replaced *Pickuppushinturnreverse* shifts. The money-obsessed automations scoop up Detroit's last profits.

Back at the MGM Grand, and still searching for common ground, I hire Thomas Bell of Speedlight to take me for a spin in his Ford Cherokee. Thomas is massive, bearded, and wears a slate blue suit with matching bow tie and pocket square. He doesn't say much but when he speaks I pay careful attention. From behind his shades and royal blue tam o' shanter he informs me that laughter not music or fighting is his secret. When I ask him where it all went wrong for Detroit he chuckles defensively, "Kilpatrick was a bad dude that stoled from the 313 but it ain't his fault." Before we set off for Gratiot Avenue I ask him to drop me off in Midtown at the Detroit Institute of Fine Arts, the fifth largest gallery in the United States and home of the city's crown jewels.

I mount the stone steps and make my way through the deserted Italian Renaissance marbled hallways to Diego Rivera's Detroit Industry murals. The almost life-size workers on the North Wall are portrayed as vital cogs in the Highland Park wheels. In a panel in the upper corner, to the right of the Toltec guardians and above the glowing furnace, a Christmas parody catches my eye. A glorious infant is being comforted by a nurse who resembles the actress Jean Harlow, as he is being vaccinated by a doctor doubling as Joseph. Behind the Holy Family, three Magi scientists beaver away in a chemicals laboratory. The machines are depicted with all their high-powered efficiency but are matched by the moral power of Ford's dedicated and inventive craftsmen.

Henry Ford's gimmick of five dollars a day pay had allowed thousands of desperate men to start all over again and make something of themselves. As a young boy in Greenfield he had been described by a neighbour as, "the laziest little bugger on the face of the Earth," and his momentous achievements had been inspired by a desire to eliminate the drudgery of farm labor. At their first meeting at Fairlane the wealthiest indus-trialist in the world and the Marxist painter found more in common than they could possibly have imagined. Both men were renegades, united by their passion for mechanical preci-sion and technological beauty. Many years later in his mem-oirs Rivera enthused about the meeting:

> In my ears I heard the wonderful symphony, which came from his factories where metals were shaped into tools for men's service. It was a new music, waiting for the composer with genius enough to give it communicable form.

Rivera and his wife Frida Kahlo had arrived at Michi-gan Central from New York in April 1932 during the Great Depression and just four weeks after 4,000 starving men had marched carrying banners from Fort Street to the heavily guarded Rouge plant. Its seven silver chimneys loomed in front of the wretched workers like a colossal church organ surrounded by smoldering mounds of coal. When Harry Ben-nett, the fascist bully and ex-boxer who was in charge of Ford's Internal Security, arrived in his car he was pelted with stones and knocked unconscious. Vomit gas, wooden clubs, and jets of icy water failed to disperse the angry crowd and in a panic the Dearborn police and Ford security guards began firing their machine guns from the bridge. Four of Ford's protesting workers were shot dead on the battlefield and others seriously wounded. Rivera bitterly regretted the failure of the labor movement to defend itself against the dark forces of capitalism but tactfully omitted the struggle from his masterpiece.

I am still thinking of Henry Ford and his influence on the trajectory of this melodramatic city as Thomas drives us north up the Automotive Heritage Trail past the Wayne State University Medical School campus and the old General Motors building in Cadillac Place. Loyalty, hard work, patriotism, and family orientation were virtues Ford associated with rural agrarian life. To him city dwellers were brave pioneers who had been forced to adventure into a terrifying uncharted waste. The soul could never be nourished in the predatory city. Detroit was now crowded with people and covered over with pavements making it impossible for the soil to exercise its natural function. In his column in *The Dearborn Independent* he declared that the city as the pinnacle of civilization was finished:

> Plainly, so it seems to some of us, that the ultimate solution will be the abolition of the City, its abandonment as a blunder . . . We shall solve the City Problem by leaving the City.

By the time of Ford's death in 1947, Detroit was an industrial powerhouse with a population of almost 2 million people and had risen to become the fourth largest city in the United States. It was the shining city on the hill, an innovation crossroads where highways converged on a river that connected to the Great Lakes and the sea. Detroit's car companies dominated the global market and produced four out of every five cars manufactured in America. The Ford Motor Company employed 100,000 workers, many of them black, who embossed, flanged, welded, stamp-pressed, blanked, and bent bearings six days a week. Phantom flashes of light came from the Rouge's scorching foundries, steam hammers tortured slabs of near-molten steel, and its acrid fumes sulphured the sun. The river was the color of pig iron and its polluted water became the poor man's paint stripper. Detroit was in the vanguard of America's machine age and an "arsenal of democracy." Its hard-working, well-paid workers braved the factories' pungent smells and the deafening ring of metal on metal and took a pride in their work. But there was a price to pay for the gains in productivity achieved by division of labor and vertical integration. Ford's workers had been permanently thickened and dispossessed of their creative individuality.

We pass a large gang of bikers on Harley-Davidsons heading downtown. A constellation of temples with enchanting names like The Chapel of St. Theresa of the Little Flower and Sweetest Heart of Mary stand forlornly among the tares. Inside crutches and calipers stacked in the Lady Chapels acknowledge former miracles. Other churches like the Martyrs of Uganda lie abandoned, stripped of their copper and stained glass. A deserted convalescent home has been flagged with an amended red spray slogan,

Not

"God has ^ left Detroit"

Malevolent dragon's vapor rises from the manholes by the side of the road. Piety Hill, as Woodward was once called, now seems to be in the grip of a diabolical curse. In his article, "The Modern City—A Pestiferous Growth," Henry Ford wrote:

> The modern city is a classic illustration of what ensues when we fail to mix the arts. The three great arts are Agriculture, Manufacture and Transportation.

The self-acclaimed founder of the modern age had begun to see himself as a liberator and educator of men. In

his enlightened vision for America there would be no skyscraper columns or fetid tenement courts contaminating the
landscape:

> The mingling of the arts would restore economic balance and
> racial sanity.

Beyond the four parallel historic streets of Edison-Boston and
the Cathedral of the Most Blessed Sacrament on Woodward I
get my first view of the sadness of the Motortown ruins. Here
on Manchester, the sons of slaves from the Jim Crow South,
the rednecks from Appalachia, and the unemployed from
every corner of Europe had once worked for The Ford Motor
Company and created a vibrant city. A chain-link fence, a
shuttered row of no-go, taped-up warehouses and the down-
market Model T Plaza shopping strip is now all that is left of
the genteel tree-lined streets of Highland Park. The decom-
posing eight-story-high ceilinged structure where the Model
Ts rolled out directly onto Detroit's streets now houses the
Ford archives.

"Mustang Sally" by Wilson Pickett is playing on WOM-
SEE radio. Fifteen minutes down the road we arrive at the
Model T heritage site on Piquette with its museum of vintage
cars and Henry Ford's secret office. A few months earlier an
urban explorer in search of hidden treasure had found a mum-
mified corpse in one of the rotting hulks. Nothing remains of
Regal and Cadillac but the vacant Fisher Body and Autocar
Service buildings are still here. Dereliction vigilante teams are
clearing the adjoining charred Studebaker/E-M-F plant for
food production.

Thomas, who has not said a word since I got back in the
car, comes out with "Berry Gordy produced music like Henry
Ford shaped metal." I reply, "Without Tamla where would
the Beatles have been?" Gordy modeled his Hits Factory on
Fordism and later wrote:

At the plant, cars started out as just a frame, pulled along on conveyor belts until they emerged at the end of the line, brand spank-
ing new cars rolling off the line. I wanted the same concept for my
company, only with artists and songs and records. I wanted a place
where a kid off the street could walk in one door an unknown and
come out another a recording artist—a star.

Tamla Motown became the sound track for the assembly
line encapsulated in an unrecorded vowel. Its blaring horns,
clinking chains and pounding jackhammers made it the perfect car radio music. The Funk Brothers and the Andantes
had the whirring beat of the Rouge in their veins and their
black brothers were dancing in the street. The River Rouge
plant had subjugated the skill of each worker to produce an
end product far greater than the sum of its component parts.
Gordy's trick was to create a brand that retained artistic
individuality.

By the early 1970s "white flight" had reached epidemic
levels and the packs of "jits" (young mothafuckas that don't
know shit according to Thomas's definition) left behind in the
fragmented hoods were killing for fun. Escalating oil prices
had started to make gas-guzzling cars with V-8 engines less
attractive, even for Americans, and Gordy had moved to Los
Angeles, the last home of the pink Cadillac. Whenever a new
challenge reared its head, the Ford Motor Company seemed
to be incapable of changing tack, falling back on outdated "if
it ain't broke don't fix it" practices. The "City of Champions"
had become decadent, seedy, overgrown and dangerous. Its
streetlights had gone out, red traffic signals were now just
for information, and its overworked and underfunded police
were slow to respond even to homicides. As its outmoded
manufacturing base suffered a lingering death, so did its elm
trees. Even when it came to tree planting, Detroit was a one-
horse town. The world had entered a new era of information
technology and the "D," devoid of artificial intelligence, had
become a negligible irrelevance.

Into this vacuum rode Juan Atkins, Kevin Saunderson, and Derrick May, three black adolescents with a futuristic robotic musical manifesto. Cast adrift in the leafy suburban metropolis, they rejected disco and employed analog synthesizers and sequencers, a Roland TR-909 drum machine, robotic vocal tics, and a prominent black hole bass to create sonic grooves. Their music—conceived in garages and played at suburban parties—was a way of subverting the assembly line, the alienating effect of mechanization and the inexorable march of corporate plutocracy.

Machine Soul turned anger and rage into a rare beauty and brought a glowing future out of a chilling past. A dreamy otherness kept a generation of forgotten young Eastsiders sane. The self-centered, the conformists, and the broken-hearted were banned from Techno Boulevard's fast-moving underground dance floors. The new music's repetitive cadences and sophisticated minimalist melodies were the ideal soundtrack for cosmic car journeys on the virtual autobahn. Electronic technology had unleashed a liberating defiant dream world and blown away the last vestiges of Tamla Motown. Detroit Techno was out of sight on the edge of forever. It was what Ford and Rivera had dreamed of, euphony created by machine and man for the benefit of the human race.

On East Grand Boulevard, directly in front of us, lies the trussed concrete steel corpse of the Packard automotive plant, a lawless square mile of overgrown wasteland ringed by snarls of marooned sleepers, where scrappers, vampires, packs of feral dogs, and crazed graffiti artists roam amongst the bonfires. One or two small auto repair shops hang on here in the crumbling heart of the Rust Belt. Thomas points to a shack with an aerial perched on a drooping corrugated roof, the home of Alan Hill, a blessed sixty-eight-year-old automobile worker who tinkers with scrap in the rubble. Watching

Detroit rot has left deep retinal scars for those with no alternative but to stay behind.

Among the gray freeways and vacant lots Thomas helps me search for the old Ukrainian, African-American, and Arab communities, the tragic former world of three seasons and the ghost of Dodge Main. The gates of Chevrolet Gear and Axle are chained up but I can see through the shattered glass windows the floor where the cast iron wheels spun and the giant presses drew breath in the choking heat. Close by is the Greater Detroit Resource Recovery Facility, the largest solid waste incinerator in the United States, disposing of the city's shit and venting a death stench of polysyllabic chlorinated carbons on Poletown. A row of plug-in Chevy Volt hybrid cars is waiting to be transported downriver outside the fenced off General Motors Assembly. Back in profit, the Big Three, like Berry Gordy before them, have finally decoupled from the bankrupt D. Only the Chrysler Jefferson North Assembly plant owned by Fiat remains totally within the city boundaries.

Down "Gra-shit" (Gratiot) Boulevard near McNichols, secreted away between the party stores, fast food joints and beauty parlors, Thomas pulls up and points out a middle-aged black man with a torn face, sitting on a crate in a parking lot under a solitary tree. Next to him is a sign saying "WHAT IT DEW lawnmower repair and sales." Behind him two hangers-on wait like vultures for easy pickings. "That guy works six days a week every summer, charges a flat $45 fee and usually has the job done in an hour. On a good day he gets through twelve machines but bro, does he put up with some shit." As we move on a car pulls up and two men get out asking for temporary work.

Eight Mile Road is six lanes wide and runs east to west for eighteen miles. It is lined with cemeteries, bungalows, strip clubs, and a few run down businesses. Off the main drag many of the wooden single-story houses are derelict and boarded up. Others have bed sheets as curtains and there are several fly tips. There are cavities where deserted properties have been torched on Devil's Night. In one of the bereft zones, someone has painted on the side of a bombed-out crack house, "Baltimore Murder Capital of the World." Nearby some youths are playing golf on a plot where knee-high grass sprouts through the asphalt. Most of the residential streets are empty in the afternoon but a gas station back on Eight Mile has several prowlers hanging around near the barred grille. This irregular pattern occurs mile after mile. Cocooned in the Cherokee I start to think Detroit has got its due deserves for its inequality and segregation of diversity.

A man with Savanna Syndrome is mowing the lawn of a deserted house. The viridescent postage stamps help to keep up appearances and impose shape and meaning on a broken city. In Indian Village there is talk of the dangers of close cropping and the best way to avoid white clover and crab grass infestation. A cutting-edge monoculture preoccupied with cylinder and rotary mowers has grown up in some of the abandoned districts and many private places now smell of freshly mown grass.

Not far from the cultivated sectors wildflowers grow in abundance, as though nothing has ever disturbed the pristine pastoral verdure. There are a few sugar maples and a solitary Tree of Heaven that has taken root in a crevice of crud. A pheasant rooster flies over a fence from an allotment planted with vegetables. Swathes of switchgrass, alive with the chirruping of grasshoppers and foraging black Californian squirrels, grace a brownfield frontier. Thomas tells me coyotes have been seen wandering through this forty square miles of non-human wildness and beavers and salmon have returned to the Detroit River.

We keep going up Woodward out into the cornfields and hanging gardens of Michigan. As we cruise through the all white suburb of Warren I hum Aretha Franklin's "Freeway of Love."

Twenty miles out and still on a four-lane highway we wind through wooded parkland past vast stretches of manicured grass. Independence Township and Romeo resemble hillbilly rifle camps where wolverines and northern bears are known to prowl. Birmingham has a fresh, raw expensive look with stylishly decorated mansions and fancy drive-in restaurants. There is an odor of new money and plenty of Pashmina Princesses in Bloomfield Hills. This verdant terrain dotted with ornamental lakes provides the denizens with security and exclusivity.

Automobile manufacturing had been good for Ford's white employees. They had been well paid and well represented by the United Automobile Workers Union. Many had been able to cast aside their blue-collar immigrant heritage and enter the ranks of Michigan's middle class. A fair few had followed their boss's lead and settled in rural log cabin and red barn communities with schoolhouses, general stores and chapels buried amidst the pastures. Unfortunately Detroit's new high society ended up dragging the hard drive of the city behind it down Telegraph Road and into the garden suburbs. Sterile business parks and struggling enclosed shopping malls sprawl all over. In the rush hour, the feeder roads coming off the Chrysler and Edsel freeways are choked with commuter traffic. Although haunted by an irrational sentimentality for the old neighborhoods, most return to their "Paris of the West" only on special occasions—and always with extreme caution—to watch the Red Wings at The Joe, to buy potted chrysanthemums at Eastern Market, or to disinter their distant ancestors from the desolate boneyards. For most of Metropolitan Detroit, downtown might just as well be an Indian reservation.

A few neophyte techies, condemned by their anxious and sentimental parents to grow up in these alien dormitories, have discarded their bourgeois utopias that left no trace and followed the Belleville Three back to "Gra-shit." Chided by Eminem's rap "Ain't seen a mile road south of Ten" and encouraged by "Isms," peach orbs, *Alice in Wonderland* chessboards, and the illuminated orange-topped Qube building, they try to reclaim the streets through which I tramped this morning with Thomas. I read that two metrosexuals are selling psychedelic Fordite swirls created from a concretion of automobile paint enamel. There is the zero-emission Element One racecar, Baxter the Rethink Robot, and the driverless car. Twitter has arrived at the M@dison building.

On the way back to the MGM Grand we make a sightseeing stop at American Jewelry and Loan. Outside on the forecourt a man in a cowboy hat is talking up the virtues of his beaten-up Lincoln in an attempt to raise enough money for a Honda ride-on mower. Thomas tells me that Les Gold now has more pawned grass cutters than plasma televisions or vintage guitars. The lawn is a divine American sacrament, but here in no-man's land I have started to associate it with bad karma and the pugnacious Harry Bennett.

Ford's missing art has arrived in Detroit and his advice that failure is the opportunity to begin again, only more intelligently, is the new vibe. A wrecking ball has brought the last smokestack down and Detroiters can now see the killing moon and an endless horizon. Healthy lines of broccoli, rows of okra, and patches of Napa cabbage flourish in black soil allotments and redress my jet lag. The hub is going back to the farm. A creeping green quilt tended by an army of guerrilla gardeners is spreading over the corroding carapace of bulldozed gray steel. Brambles are spilling over a Firestone

tire and a few birches nourished by decomposed textbooks
are growing through the open skylight of the Detroit Public
Schools Roosevelt Warehouse. There are lasagna beds composed of alternating layers of brown and green on a junk-mail
base ripe with pumpkins. A new and different natural world
has infiltrated the ruins. Peasant markets feed the growing
number of locavores. Beautiful hydroponic "grass" farms and
orchard paradises brimming with forbidden fruit fill the void.
The grass roots of a higher consciousness are sprouting in the
gaps exposed by ferric disintegration. Watched over by angels
in the arrivals hall of Michigan Central you can now buy a rail
ticket to the open sea. The river tells me that Detroit is changing into the redemptive Composite City.

✎ ✎ ✎

*Andrew Lees is a writer and Professor of Neurology at Univer-
sity College London. Recent books include* Liverpool, The Hur-
ricane Port, The Silent Plague, William Richard Gowers
Exploring the Victorian Brain *and* Mentored by a Madman:
The William Burroughs Experiment. *He has also published
essays in the* Dublin Review of Books, Scottish Review of
Books, *and* Tears in the Fence.

PETER WORTSMAN

⭒ ⭒ ⭒

I Am a French
Irregular Verb

*Speak in French when you can't think
of the English for a thing . . .*
—Lewis Carroll, *Through the Looking Glass*

Forgotten is the pain of memorizing all those irregular French verbs, the torment of rounding the mouth just right and skewing the glottal apparatus so as to emit a fair approximation of the proper nasal inflections. The Gallic syllables are honey on my tongue, a mastered password that lets me pass, if not as a native, then as a presumed Luxembourger, French Swiss or Belgian, or perhaps an Alsatian, a useful trick for traveling incognito in these troubled times.

In my own private atlas of the heart, the Old World is divided down the middle by an imaginary Maginot Line, a border which, I readily admit, bears little, if any, relation to today's geopolitical reality, but which bisects Europe along a tenuous fault line riddled with psychic land mines along which the phantasms of inherited memory stand guard. While the European Union dropped its national borders, according to the Schengen Agreement of 1995, the dividing line on my internalized roadmap has a serrated edge that roughly runs along the Rhine.

On one side they speak German, a loaded language, burdened for me, as the son of German-speaking Jewish refugees,
with contradictory associations, since it is both my mother
tongue (the language I spoke with my mother) and the guttural
grunt of asphyxiation. On the other side they speak *Liberté,
Egalité, Fraternité* (Liberty, Equality, Fraternity). The French
have a sense of humor about their national slogan. I recently
saw it parodied with a wink in graffiti spray painted on the
side of an official government building as: *"Liberté, Égalité,
Béyoncé."* Simplistic though my distinction may be—and I am
full well aware of the historic inconsistencies and discrepancies,
of the vagaries of collaboration and resistance—in Germany
my throat tightens and stomach twitches with apprehension,
while in France I breathe easy, eat well, and fall in love.

In the harried but hopeful expression of every African street
peddler of counterfeit Louis Vuitton handbags, inflated
plastic flying saucers, creepy crawly, sticky fingered little
figurines that shimmy down windows and walls, and other
innocuous knickknacks knocked off in China and hawked
on the streets of Montmartre and the Parvis de Notre Dame,
I see the face of my late beloved father, who, as a young
man, an illegal alien struggling to make ends meet, lived off
the doughnuts he whipped up illegally in his garret room
on the Île Saint Louis to peddle to tourists at the *Exposition Internationale des Arts et Techniques dans la Vie Moderne*
(International Exposition Dedicated to Art and Technology
in Modern Life), better known as Paris Expo 1937, where
the pavilions of Nazi Germany and the Soviet Union, situated within winking distance directly across from each
other at the fairgrounds, represented the opposing forces of
a world order soon to dissolve around him.

These greasy Viennese treats flavored with zest of lemon
rind were called *Gebackene Mäuse* (Baked Mice), a name

derived from the tiny tails sprouted from the globs of dough congealed in boiling oil, which name and notion sent us children into peals of laughter every time our father fried us up a batch. And so, for me, the Île Saint-Louis, that mouse-shaped lump of land where mimes, magicians, musicians, pickpockets and puppeteers play the crowd—a pauper's paradise in my father's day, more recently co-opted by sheikhs and erstwhile Russian apparatchiks-turned-insider traders—and where the exclusive ice cream-confectioner Berthillon dispenses exquisite scoops—will forever be associated with sweetness.

I am a French irregular verb. My father sowed the insidious seeds of French syntax in me early on. It was his grownup pleasure and my childhood chore to have me practice French pronunciation almost as soon as I learned to mouth and mimic English. My ears were receptive, but my mind was lazy. I failed to grasp why these nasally linked syllables mattered so much. French declensions wouldn't help much on the baseball mound. Rolling the lips into a hollow circle to shape a proper *Bon jour* wouldn't buy me a bubble gum or a pretzel stick at Jimmy's Luncheonette. My father lost patience and slapped me when I mispronounced. I protested. But resistance was futile.

In junior high I was always the best in French, but when at the parent-teacher conferences, my father challenged the "very good" as opposed to an "excellent" that Mr. Banks, my junior high school French teacher, circled on my report card, Mr. Banks shrugged: "Not even Charles De Gaulle deserves an excellent in my book!"

My high school French teacher, Miss Lorenzo, a skinny, tight-lipped, mouse-haired, prematurely old matron of indeterminate age who must surely have learned her French at a convent school, unwittingly took us to see the movie *Viva Maria!* by Louis Malle, wanting to expose us to things French, but when Brigitte Bardot proceeded to perform a striptease on the silver screen, a scandalized Miss Lorenzo promptly shuffled us ogling adolescent boys out of the cinema in disgust. That and reading *"Le Dormeur du Val,"* a poem by Arthur Rimbaud about a soldier found lying in a field, who, only after the poet discovers a red hole in his head, we realize is dead, are my most vivid memories of French class.

But I do recall having to assume all kinds of contorted positions, the painful polar opposite of stances featured in the *Kama Sutra* (which I would discover in college), pressed body to body on the subway in the morning rush hour, my wrist thrust into the overhanging strap, hand gripping a French grammar, memorizing my noun declensions and my irregular verbs. And once, arriving late for a first period French exam, on account of a delay on the Canarsie Line (now known as the L Train), I remember passing the gauntlet of pigeons positioned on the overhead ledge of the school, when one let drop its hot liquid payload that landed on my forehead and ran down my left cheek. I wiped myself with a handkerchief in disgust, still muttering French irregular verbs to myself, bravely marched into class, inured but able, and scored a perfect 100 on the test, and have retained a hostility to pigeons ever since.

And so I graduated high school with the gold medal in French, a tri-color ribbon dangling from the fake gold pin which Miss Lorenzo proudly pinned to my graduation gown, kissing me on both cheeks, the closest I will surely ever come to nomination to the *Légion d'Honneur*—which somehow stirred up the memory of the striptease scene in *Viva Maria!*, though Miss Lorenzo was definitely no Brigitte Bardot— and which medal I recently rediscovered upon rummaging through old papers and possessions in a desk drawer. (I wonder if wearing the medal and fluttering tri-color ribbon while waiting in line to board an Air France flight might impress the ground crew and merit consideration for preferred seating?)

I started off college as a French major, the favorite of Professor Rothschild, a somewhat more erudite and intellectual, albeit equally tight-lipped and stoic, replica of Miss Lorenzo, until I fell from grace. In the final exam she asked for an analysis of one of the works covered in class. I had underlined racy excerpts from *Les Fleurs du Mal* (The Flowers of Evil), by Charles Baudelaire:

> *"C'est l'Ennui! L'oeil chargé d'un pleur involontaire,*
> *Il rêve d'échafauds en fumant son houka.*
> *Tu le connais, lecteur, ce monstre délicat,*
> *—hypocrite lecteur,—mon semblable,—mon frère!"*

> "It's BOREDOM. Tears have glued its eyes together.
> You know it well, my Reader. This obscene
> beast chain-smokes yawning for the guillotine—
> you—hypocrite Reader—my double—my brother!"[1]

And having taken the scholarly initiative, laudable I thought, of furthermore reading the poet's *Les Paradis Artificiels*, his treatise on the effects of opium and hashish, and in the undergraduate Romantic mood of the moment, taking what I thought to be his message to heart and mind, smoked a pipe of hash before class and boldly confessed to the fact in perfect French in my blue exam booklet, Professor Rothschild took my bravado as a personal affront and gave me an F. Whereupon I switched my major to English, but kept my fondness for Coleridge's opium-induced dream poems to myself.

But French profoundly infiltrated my private life. My father would never, alas, live to meet Claudie, whom I met at a party in a state of total intoxication, true to Baudelaire's poetic dictum:

> *pour ne pas être les esclaves martyrisés du temps, enivrez-vous, enivrez-*
> *vous sans cesse de vin, de poésie, de vertu, à votre guise.*

> (so as not to be the martyred slaves of time, get drunk, keep getting
> drunk on wine, on poetry, on virtue, as you please.)

---

1   English adaptation by the poet Robert Lowell

I managed to charm her in the warp and woof of my slightly
slurred irregular French verbs and perfectly declined French
nouns; intoxicated state notwithstanding, my sentences held
together and actually made seductive sense.[2]
Nor did my father ever live to see the French seeds he
planted in my thankless mind bear fruit in the form of our
hybrid Franco-American, perfectly bilingual, perfectly cheeky
offspring, our daughter Aurélie and son Jacques, walking, talking bundles of Gall, with a twinkle of insouciance, an ironic
smile, and emulating Albert Camus, Simone de Beauvoir,
Serge Gainsbourg, and countless French rebels with or without
a cause, with a cigarette forever riding the lower lip, who correct my gender errors and my wife's occasional English faux
pas, and in the way all children do, remind me of my many
faults. *Merci, Papa!*

It's only *natural!* we Americans maintain to affirm those truths
we hold to be self-evident. *C'est bien normal, ça!* (It's normal!)
the French insist, to substantiate the naked facts at the tip of the
nose. There is perhaps a certain irony that we Americans should
harp on the natural in our Brave New World of artificiality, the
home of artificial flavoring and coloring, plastic, MSG, processed
foods, fracking, McDonald's "Happy Meals" and Monsanto's
genetically engineered blockbuster crops. "All natural ingre-
dients," as per the required marketing etiquette, can be found
on the box or flap of most American packaged, i.e. processed
foods. Our seemingly limitless "natural resources" are there to

---

2   Still fond of a drop of spirit on select occasions, years later I
identified with a soused breed of spider that lives down under the
Chateau de Cognac, in the pit of the former dungeon known as
"le Paradis" (Paradise), where the oldest casks of spirit are left to age
in a snow-white coat of fungus. Its state revealed in the asymmetrical weave of its web, the spider feeds on insect larvae and watches
over the precious stash with a certain sloppy majesty.

be drained dry. *It's only natural* in a country with an elected Congress inclined to gloss over environmental protection.

As for the French norm, consider the following definition found on the website About.com:

> "*Normal* is a semi-false cognate. While it can mean 'normal,' it is often used in a more figurative sense, as in 'usual' or 'expected.' For example, the weather is supposed to be clear and sunny all week, but there's a freak rainstorm. One might say:
>
> *Ce n'est pas normal*—'That's not right, not what was supposed to happen.'"

French schoolteachers earn their stripes at various *Écoles Normales* (Normal Schools). The French inculcate the norm early on in untutored little savages, and the upper echelon of professors are graduated from one of a handful of *Écoles Normales Superieurs* (Superior Normal Schools), whose graduates, the elite *normaliens*, comprise a select pedagogical club of sorts of which my wife is a member (roughly equivalent to the privileged spawns of the Ivy League, only in France, they pay you to attend) who ascend to leadership positions in which they, in turn, set the new norms. An ordinary person, particularly an American, can sometimes be made to suffer a sense of abnormal ignorance in the company of *normaliens*. It is only normal, I suppose, that, as an American, I should be held personally accountable for all artificial flavoring and coloring, plastic, MSG, processed foods, fracking, McDonald's "Happy Meals" and Monsanto's genetically engineered crops, just as I hold the French personally responsible for the dissemination of smelly cheese. Naturally, I protest my innocence. But such protestation of innocence is further proof of a shamefully abnormal ignorance of the norm.

Just as geography makes the French hexagon a natural bridge between the sun-drenched Mediterranean and the chilly gray North Sea, so, too, are the French, in custom and manner, a hybrid of Latin looseness and Teutonic rigidity. But the formidable bulwark against linguistic corruption upheld by the stiff-lipped members of the Académie Française, the solemn brotherhood of guardians of the language, who collectively comprise a veritable dictionary-dyke in a valiant, albeit vain, attempt to keep the sacred tongue from springing holes, is sabotaged by an unstoppable influx of Americanisms and a seemingly bottomless well of argot and colorful idiomatic expressions, some mentionable in good company, some not.

Loose-tongued on a drop of wine, the poetry comes pouring out. The popular French expression for twilight, for instance, *"entre chien et loup"* (literally: between dog and wolf) perfectly captures the visual drama at the tenuous border between day and night when daylight drops its muzzle of civility and darkness bares its fangs. How Chaplinesque, or rather Jacques-Tatiesque, are the Gallic takes on "to be lost": *"marcher à côté de ses pompes"* (literally, to walk beside one's clodhoppers); and "to be sleepy": *"ne pas avoir les yeux en face des trous"* (literally, not to have your eyes lined up with their slits). How perfectly bobo (Bohemian-Bourgeois) is the inverted, self-mocking snobbery of the tongue-in-cheek term for tap water, *"Château de la Pompe"* (literally: Château Water Fountain). How anti-clerical and positively blasphemous the French equivalent expression for "not in a million years": *"à la Saint Glin Glin"* (literally, when Saint Glin Glin wills it).

But French curses, insults, and idiomatic expressions really let it all hang out with true poetic license. The anodyne Anglo-Saxon nitpicker becomes a *"sodomiseur de lépidoptère"* (sodomite of Lepidoptera), or better yet, *"un enculeur de mouches"* (fly butt-fucker). The French equivalent of the English "looking for a needle in a haystack" is: *"chercher un pet dans une bain à jacuzzi"* (fishing for a fart in a Jacuzzi). More lustfully vulgar still, the French for "Step on it!" is: "*Il faux pas tortiller le cul pour chier droit!*" (Don't wriggle your ass to shit straight!) Or the ultimate scatological French standby for "really having to go take a dump": "*avoir le cigarre au bou des lèvres*" (to have a cigar at the tip of your lips). And since we've dropped our *culottes*, so to speak, what coarse Anglo-Saxon expression could possibly match the sheer lyric license of the Gallic take on "she's got the hots for you": "*Elle a la moule qui baille*" (literally: Her mussel is yawning for you).

And then there's the division of creation by sex. How curious for an American accustomed to a neuter world in which all else outside the "I" is a swathe of "it," to fathom that everything around you is gendered to the French eye. The logic is often perplexing. So the perennially gray sky (*le ciel*) overhead is a moody old masculine. But the rain (*la pluie*) falls in female tears. The building (*le bâtiment*) you pass on the street is a strapping buck, but the house (*la maison*) is a sleek lady, to which only a privileged few are given the pass code, inviting or forbidding entry. The person (*la personne*) you meet, man or woman, is a female a priori, as is the conglomerate crowd (*la foule*). Bread (*le pain*), most typically in the elongated shape of *la baguette*, is male, as is wine (*le vin*) and cheese (*le fromage*), the two other staples of the French diet. But the table (*la table*) at which you eat at is a woman. The truck (*le camion*) is a lumbering porter bearing *his* load. But the car (*la voiture*) is a woman that carries destinies in *her* metal womb. The same gender divide holds true for French states of mind. Joy (*la joie*) is a she, as is sadness (*la tristesse*). It is as if the world around us, in its stark duality, comprised infinite models or mirrors, constantly instructing us not only in how to behave, how to walk, talk and dress, but also how to think (*la pensée*), thought being female, and dream (*le rêve*), reverie being male. The gender of the French noun, furthermore, affects the adjectives that decorate and adorn it as a kind of costume jewelry and the verbs that manipulate, or rather are manipulated by it.

And what about those gender-bending homonyms, like manly liver (*le foie*) and feminine time—as in how many times—(*la fois*), or the manly mold you bake with (*le moule*) vs. the feminine mussel you buy at market and simmer in white wine (*la moule*)!

In France I walk around in a constant state of hermaphrodite grammatical confusion, my male body (*le corps*) enveloped by my female skin (*la peau*), ignorant of the distinction that every French schoolchild has categorized in the filing cabinet of a male mind (*un esprit*) lodged in the female head (*la tête*).

Speaking of gender, every Parisian, and particularly every *Parisienne* is a walking billboard advertising the ever-present possibility of seduction that a walk down a Paris street just might entail. Mick Jagger may not have managed to find "satisfaction" in London, but if Serge Gainsbourg, the patron saint of '69, with his big nose, stick-out ears and droopy eyes, could bed down BB (Brigitte Bardot), surely you could too—or so the tantalizing legend would have us believe.

My attachment to French gender difference is up close and personal. At the Tuileries Gardens one memorable 14th of July, I danced a dizzying *valse musette* with Claudie, the perky petite brunette who would become my wife, faking the steps, though she later convinced me to take dancing lessons for our wedding. I remember exactly the outfit she had on, the cinched yellow polka dot top beneath which her belly button peaked forth, and a short, white, tri-layered skirt that flared up in enticing cascades of cotton, baring leg well above the knee, and her perky brown ponytail that sashayed like the tail of a proud thoroughbred as we whirled about. I remember the rhythmic rippling notes of the accordion played by

Aimable Pluchart, better known by his first name Aimable, the legendary French bandleader, already of advanced age back then, but no less lithe and supple, beaming and swaying as he played, hovering above the dusty dance floor on a prefab stage like a puppeteer directing our clip-clop with the invisible strings of his music, unabashedly fondling his instrument, as my fingers replayed the melody down the keyboard of Claudie's spine. We swirled in an ocean of bodies, a whirlpool of humanity, when an older man, a fleet-footed hoofer, brashly reached out, plucked my fiancé out of my arms, and spun her round like he was a planet and she was the sun. Whereupon I boiled over with a cocktail of contradictory emotions, burning with jealousy, glowing with pride, seething with heretofore untapped erotic fury whipped up into a virtual frenzy by the ever-accelerating pace of the music. And when at last, after what seemed at the time like an eternity but could only have been a matter of minutes at most, he returned her to my waiting arms with a bow and a wink that betokened both gratitude and regret, my jealousy melted into boundless love leaping from my eyes (*mes yeux*), those masculine orbs, to my beating heart (*mon coeur*), that dumb male muscle, encased in my head (*ma tête*), that feminine lockbox of mind and emotion, for granting me this moment of beatitude.

※ ※ ※

Peter Wortsman's travel memoir, Ghost Dance in Berlin, *won a 2014 Independent Publishers Book Award (IPPY). An excerpt was previously selected as the Grand Prize winner in the 2012 Solas Awards for Best Travel Story of the Year. A writer in multiple modes, including fiction, drama, prose poetry, and translation, his other recent books include a novel,* Cold Earth Wanderers, *and an anthology which he selected, translated, and edited,* Tales of the German Imagination. *Forthcoming are a book of short fiction*, Footprints in Wet Cement*, and a translation*, Konundrum, Selected Prose of Franz Kafka. *He was a Holtzbrinck Fellow in 2010 at the American Academy in Berlin. This story first appeared in the 2016 issue of the* Catamaran Literary Reader, *Santa Cruz.*

K. M. CHURCHILL

≈ ≈ ≈

A Love Song

Walking on the edge of myth in Ireland.

S now rarely fell in Ireland. When it did the dusting was
so light it looked like confectionary sugar had been
sprinkled all over the green ivy and winter-blooming roses.
So I knew our first winter storm in Union Hall, a tiny fishing village on Glandore Bay in the remote southwestern tip of
County Cork—where I'd moved with Francis, my Irish chef
husband, and our two young children to open a restaurant—
would be nothing like the New England blizzards I was used
to. The joyous, drunken raucousness of the Irish holiday season was upon us and, even with the storm clouds spreading
out against the sky, our seaside village seemed festive rather
than pensive.

Pensioners made their way slowly along Main Street.
Stopping every few feet to chat with passersby, "Are ye
well?" They marveled at windows, trimmed with shiny
silver, gold and green tinsel roping, displaying ceramic or
hand-carved manger scenes: Mary and St. Joseph, along
with shepherd boys, flocks of sheep, donkeys, camels, and
the Magi journeying. Sometimes there would be a little
drummer boy or an angel with a trumpet. All carefully
positioned facing a tiny crib, empty but for a bedding of

hay, where the baby Jesus would be placed on Christmas morning. And a gold star, the Star of Bethlehem, dangling from a wire above the scene.

So it must have been a few weeks after our second child had been baptized—first by my mother-in-law using a bottle of Holy Water she kept in her handbag, then by an angry priest in a ceremony at St. Brigid's Catholic Church on the outskirts of town, across from the blue Virgin Mary grotto and the winding laneway that lead up to the village witch's cottage.

The storm came slowly. Brooding out over the Atlantic before blowing into town. The fishermen were the first to know. Securing their boats in Union Hall's snug harbor, they made their way to pubs to recount mariner's tales over pints. Stories of boats trapped in raging storms. Winds that shrieked and howled. And giant waves that swept the ocean ashore and the shore out to sea, before tucking men's boats into bed at the bottom of it.

A couple of *auld ones*, sitting at the back, took their turn among the men. Shaking their heads in disbelief and wonder they spoke slowly, as though they had all the time in the world, about what *they'd* seen and heard: the otherworldly roar of a voiceful wave at the mouth of Glandore Bay. Not just any wave mind you, but Tonn Clíodhna, an ancient thunderous wave foretelling death and disaster. "T'was nothin' less than Tonn Clíodhna I tell ye!" When the old men finished speaking no one said anything. Each man sat quietly staring down into his pint. Until someone called to the bartender for "another round."

When I'd lived in Dublin, years before the children were born, I'd take the train from Connelly Station and head north. The raised tracks ran through neighborhoods I had never seen before. Row after row of "attached" houses became wastelands, then fields and pastures, then sandy beaches. After half an hour, the train arrived at its final destination, Howth Railway Station, where I'd disembark and walk out along the harbor road.

Sometimes, if I was hungry, I'd stop by The Waterside & the Wheelhouse pub for a plate of fish and chips and a half pint of lager. Like a local I'd sprinkle the chips with salt and vinegar and eat them while staring out the window at a small island that lay like a voluptuous woman reclining in the sea. Once I'd asked the plump waitress who brought my lunch what it was called.

"Ireland's Eye," she said, holding my plate of hot food aloft while answering. Then, with the quiet pride of a good student, she repeated it in Irish, "Inis Mac Neasáin."

"Anyone live there?"

"Ah no. Birds and seals is all. Though there's a ferry goes out soes you can picnic and walk about."

She leaned in to set my plate down and I could see that her wavy auburn hair was streaked with gray.

"Then, of course, there's the murder cave."

"The murder cave?"

She lowered her voice. "Sure didn't a man kill his wife out there in 1852? And didn't they find that poor woman's body lying stone cold in a sea cave? He swore he hadn't done it. Said she'd accidentally drowned and been washed ashore. But no one believed him." She stood up then and, putting her hands on her ample hips, looked around to see if there was anyone else needing her attention. There wasn't. "Sure I could get you the ferry schedule if you'd like," she suggested, smiling down at me.

I declined the offer and, when I'd eaten my fill, I paid and said goodbye. Then I went outside and followed the green arrows pointing toward the cliff walk.

The climb from the harbor road was slow but not steep. On one side, the green cliffs of Howth's Head fell gradually away into the sea. On the other, a sloping wild heath bloomed bright with yellow gorse bushes. A well-worn path trimmed the cliffs closely. At times too closely so that it slipped off the edge and I could see where others had plotted a new path, a little bit higher up, on the grassy verge.

Cliffs fringe the whole of Ireland. In the northeast there's the Giant's Causeway where 40,000 smooth, hexagon-shaped rocks jut up out of the seabed. It's a place of pilgrimage for school children: in Irish mythology the Causeway is the remnants of a land bridge built to Scotland by the gentle giant Finn MacCool. In modern science, it's a unique volcanic geological formation formed 60 million years ago. Like the school children, I preferred the first explanation. Either way it is a UNESCO protected World Heritage site, meaning that its significance transcends all national boundaries and belongs not just to the people of Ireland, but to the peoples of the world.

So too do the Skellig Rocks, sharp black cliffs off the southwes coast of County Kerry that for centuries have been a site of pilgrimage for Catholic penitents who have clamored aboard tiny boats, then bobbed up and down on the cold and unforgiving Atlantic Ocean to reach the Blue Cove. And from there pick their way up the steep stone-cut steps leading to St. Fionan's abandoned beehive monastery that sits alone and abandoned atop the jagged cliffs.

So harsh and barren and isolated a place is Skellig that when Irish playwright George Bernard Shaw visited, he wrote to a friend that it was, "an incredible, impossible, mad place . . . I tell you, the thing does not belong to any world that you and I have lived and worked in: it is part of our dream world." And that was the problem exactly, I thought, the thing about Ireland that both enchanted and confounded me—it *did* seem to be part of a dream world; myth and reality mingled so often that sometimes it was difficult to tell the difference between the two.

Not a soul did I meet on the cliffs and when I crested the hill just beyond the summit I sat down in the grass. It was quiet, but for the cries of gulls and the wind whistling in my ears. A breeze blowing up the hill came in salty gusts, tickling my nose and tugging at my hair. I stretched my legs out in front of me and my toes appeared to touch the green, green Irish Sea that was glittering all the way to the horizon. From my hillside perch I could see the haunted Baily Lighthouse standing tall and sure on a high craggy tip of land reaching out into Howth Harbor. Looking southward I saw the whole of Dublin Bay, with its fleet of fat white ferryboats sailing to and from the U.K. and France, and beyond that too, all the way to the hazy purple Wicklow Mountains. What I could not see were the dark open-mouthed caves in the cliffs far below me, nor the bones of the smugglers who had died there, nor the lichen-covered, storm-tossed ships that lay silky green and sunken at the bottom of the sea.

News of the winter storm spread swiftly. We all knew it was coming, long before it was announced on RTÉ, Radio Telefís Eireann, the national news station. When I'd walked with my two-year-old son, Isaac, up to Fuller's shop to buy half a pound of salted butter, a loaf of brown soda bread, and some smoked salmon for lunch, Mrs. Fuller asked me if I'd heard about it. I hadn't. By the time we'd walked back home and I'd found Francis in the kitchen to tell him, he'd already heard it from Tom, the young Irishman mending our wall in the back garden.

"There's a big storm coming, Daddy!" Isaac shouted as we came in through the restaurant's side door. "Missus Fuller says so!"

"I know!" Francis said, lifting his son up and sitting him down on top of the box freezer next to his baby brother who was already asleep there in his infant car seat. "Isn't it exciting?"

Francis handed Isaac a slice of green apple he'd been about to sauté with pine nuts and currants to add to the duck stuffing.

Isaac took a big bite and nodded "yes." Then he looked down at his brother and gently poked his cheek to see if he might wake up. He didn't.

The restaurant phone rang.

"You remember to pick up peat and coal yesterday?" I asked, reaching over to re-tie the red silk ribbon that hung from the handle of the baby's car seat. The ribbon was a practical precaution; red for protection and strung with small silver jingle bells to frighten away "baby stealing fairies." (A notion I had no intention of arguing with.)

"Yep, there's three bales of briquettes and a big bag of coal in the boot of the car. I'll bring them down later."

The phone rang again but it did not wake the baby.

"How many on the books?" I asked, swinging Isaac back up onto my hip and picking up our small bag of groceries to bring upstairs to our apartment.

"We've got three deuces and a four-top at six," Francis said, giving the soup du jour a quick stir then turning down the heat, "a six-top at half seven, a three-top and four deuces at half eight and we just picked up a five-top—three adults, two kids—at six forty five. Oh, and they'll be needing a high chair."

The phone rang again and he slid a sauté pan off the burner, wiped his hands and came out from behind the line to answer it. (*House Rule—never let the restaurant phone ring more than three times before picking up.*)

"We're off then." I said, heading out the door with Isaac. "I'll let you know when lunch is ready."

"Better check for flashlight batteries and storm candles!" Francis called after us as he picked up the phone. I waved my hand so that he'd know I'd heard him.

As the day wore on the wind, pushing whitecaps into the harbor, made the boats bob wildly at their moorings. In the pubs the fishermen's voices got louder and their tales grew taller.

Until, as was so often the case in Ireland, the past and the present mingled—the borders of each obscured by drink.

By late afternoon what had been a soft mist turned into light rain. When I passed by Hayes' Pub, on my way back from another run to the shop before service, I could see a fire blazing in the grate and I heard a *bodhrán* drum and a couple of fiddles warming up. Across the street, both Casey's Bar and Maloney's pub were packed with people. Their windows fogged over with the damp heat of the bodies pressed inside.

I wondered if no one seemed worried about the storm because all the men were safe ashore. Even the older villagers, who were sensible and thoughtful folk, did not seem concerned. I knew that most houses had open fireplaces with "back boilers"—a clever system that used ordinary hearth fires to heat the house's hot water tank and sometimes the central heating too—and I found myself questioning the wisdom of having replaced ours with a more efficient gas-fueled system for the restaurant when we'd moved in.

I tried to take solace in knowing that the colorful buildings huddled together on Main Street had been built with outer walls three feet thick to withstand the weather. Those closest to the harbor had their backs to the sea and the others, like ours, their backs to the hillside. For hundreds of years, I reminded myself, these houses had endured Atlantic gales and still they stood, resilient and cheerfully candy colored.

On the hillsides across the harbor, windows that had been dark turned yellow and in the village earth-scented peat smoke, puffing up chimneys, drifted down and slid along the streets like low lying fog or wispy ghosts. I was pleased to see that the white fairy lights, which I'd wrapped around the potted bay trees on either side of the front door of the restaurant, looked bright and festive in the gathering gloom. I ducked up the alleyway and in through the side door.

The kitchen was warm and smelled of roasting garlic and freshly baked rosemary bread. Francis, wearing a long apron and his chef whites, was just finishing his *mise en place* for service. He looked up when I came in but didn't stop speed-slicing vegetables with his Nakiri knife (one of his many impressive kitchen tricks that made me nervous).

"Did they have everything?" he asked.

"They did."

I set the bags of groceries down on the counter. Overhead I could hear the pitter-patter of a toddler's feet running fast toward the bathroom.

"Brilliant! Thanks." Francis said. Then he smiled at me, his beautiful blue eyes holding my gaze for too long, while he julienned more vegetables into thin matchstick strips without looking down at his hands.

"Stop it!" I said. Then, trying not to laugh I turned my back to him and began unpacking the bags.

I'd walked many cliff paths in Ireland before falling in love. Some were easy to get to, but not the one that enchanted me the most. To get there from Dublin I had to take a train into the west and hitchhike from the station. When my last ride deposited me on an empty country road at the foot of sloping farmers fields, "For the love o'Jaysus mind yerself!" I'd climb up and up through tall green pastures—keeping an eye out for roaming bulls—until I reached the top, where the land dropped away, and I stepped out onto the wet grassy path that edged the Cliffs of Moher for almost five miles. Running all the way along the western edge of County Clare, from Nags Head to O'Brien's Tower where the magnificent sheer gray cliffs rose up to their full dramatic height, 700 feet above the Atlantic's white-and-black blown waves. So spectacular and shocking are they that Hollywood director Rob Reiner came here, to the far west of Ireland, to film "The Cliffs of Insanity" for his cult classic film, *The Princess Bride*.

The precipitous drops at the boundaries of Ireland are magnetic; they pull some and repel others. On the Cliffs of Moher there was no gentle slope to sit on. The cold Atlantic did not glitter and the shrieking call of thousands of seabirds was as sharp and loud as the wind. Still I was drawn to them. From the highest point I would find myself searching the horizon for a glimpse of the New England beach where years before I'd sat, digging my feet deep into the cool soft sand, and staring longingly across the sea towards Europe. But America was too far away and I could not see it.

On days when the wind blew too strong to walk along the cliffs, I would climb up as far as I could. Then, standing in a farmer's field, I'd close my eyes, lift my chin, and lean into the wind. I would lean into it the way, in a few years' time, I would lean into love—with my arms out stretched like wings and only the tips of my toes still touching the land. And I would stay like that, hovering, until the wind shifted and dropped me to the ground.

Sometimes, when I was feeling brave, I'd lie flat on the ground, below the wind, and inch forward on my belly until I could see over the cliff's grassy lip to where kittiwakes and razorbills nested in the vertical rock face. Where nimble wild goats climbed out along slender shale and sandstone ledges. The birds were beautiful, the way they took to the air, but watching the goats walking along the precipice frightened me. People jumped from cliffs like these. I'd heard about women mostly, some with children in their arms, some with babies in their bellies.

There were myths that swirled about these cliffs. My favorite was about a beautiful mermaid, the Mermaid of Moher, who was tricked into marriage with a local fisherman when he stole her magic cloak so she could not escape. She stayed land bound, with her husband and children, until one day she found the cloak that he'd kept hidden from her. Then, without a word, she put it on, left her family and slipped forever back into the sea.

Years later, after my sons were born, the entry to the cliffs near the sleek new visitor center had been blocked with warning signs, memorial plaques, and bouquets of wilting flowers. And folks began to agree that now only crazy people climbed past the barrier to walk the ancient way—crazy people and intrepid tourists. But I still wandered the cliff edge as I always had. And, in the throes of motherhood myself, I would imagine the mermaid riding seaward on the waves and wonder, could her children could hear her singing?

By six o'clock the rain was coming down in big wet drops and the wind blew it hard against the restaurant's plate-glass windows. Inside the dining room was humming, the tables filled with people, each in their own candlelit world of convivial conversation, secret glances, or awkward silences. Sometimes a laugh or guffaw, "Ah, gw'on!" escaped into the room and the other diners, smiling, turned to look.

Our restaurant was at its best on nights like this. When it was dark and cold and wet outside so that you only wanted to be indoors where it was warm and lit and welcoming. Where you could sit by the fire and order crocks of spicy seafood stew and pints of foamy stout. When the burgundy walls glowed with pretty colored light cast by stained-glass wall lamps and the slate floor disappeared into shadows as the firelight, picking out their bright patterns, turned the carpets into floating soft stepping-stones across the dining room.

As soon as one table was cleared and reset, it was seated again. A steady stream of customers jostled with each other at the door to get their names on the wait list so they could nip across the road into Maloney's Pub for a pint while they waited. When a table became available, one of the busgirls dashed across the wet street, jumping over puddles, and made her way through the crowded pub shouting out the name of the next party on the list.

"Now, would ye say that the venison is a tough piece of meat? Would ye say it was tough, like?" the old man at Table 10 was asking.

"Oh no," I said. "The chef has slow cooked and marinated it so it's quite tender."

"Is it a good size chop though?" he asked, lifting up his hard hands and miming in the air for me the size he thought the chop should be. "How big would ye say it t'was, now?"

"I don't know about you, Pat," his sturdy wife interrupted, "but I can't say I'd fancy any of that now; t'would be like eating Bambi!" She laughed. Then, snapping closed her menu, ordered.

"Right so, first I'll have the leek soup. Then I'll have the roast chicken," she said, settling back into her chair. Then, as though confirming with herself that she'd made the best possible choice, "Yes," she said, "that t'would be lovely."

I thanked her, tucked the menu under my arm and turned back to her husband.

"And for you sir?"

Overhead I heard a thud, the sound of something falling, then a pause and then a toddler's howl. The man pushed the open menu across the table towards me and tapped at the page with a short square forefinger.

"What sort of potatoes did ye say those were again?"

I made an executive decision. I promised to bring him the traditional three types of potatoes with his main course no matter which entrée he chose— *at no extra charge!* When he finally decided, settling on a filet, well done (which I knew would annoy the chef), I went into the kitchen with the order ticket and called it out to Francis, whose head was bent in concentration over dishes he was plating. His hands paused mid-air when I said, "filet, well done," but only for a moment. Then I handed over the ticket, dashed out the side door and ran, through the wind and the rain, up the back steps to our apartment to check that all was well with the children.

By 9:00 the wind was gusting in short sharp bursts and rainwater was flowing like a stream down Main Street. I was on my way to Table 12, balancing a potentially lethal tray of flaming Sambuca shots with three lucky espresso beans in each, when the lights flickered. Then went out. A collective gasp swept round the room. Outside it was pitch black; the electricity had gone out throughout the village. Tabletop candles made small pockets of flickering light around the dining room and the fire threw quivering shadows across the walls.

Then the wind came. Prowling down the street. Snarling, it knocked over the bay trees and rattled the front door; trying to get in. When it couldn't, it groaned and pressed itself up against the plate glass windows, almost as though it were peering in, looking for someone—the couples sitting by the windows leaned back. So physical was its presence that I fancied I might have been able to decipher a face, were it not for the rain and the darkness in which it hid.

In the void beyond the wind we all heard a rumbling. A dreadful low lament, like wailing, coming closer and closer. An impossible sound—roaring like a dragon off the bay. I felt goose bumps rising on my arms and the back of my neck prickled. "Tonn Clíodhna!" I heard someone whisper. And in the dark and the silence, we all listened hard to what we did not want to hear.

There are many versions of the story of Tonn Clíodhna or Cleena's Wave. The one I'd heard was that Cleena, queen of the South Munster fairies, was a banshee, a woman from the fairy hills, and a foreigner. She'd come to Ireland from fairyland, fallen in love, and drowned while sleeping on the strand near Glandore Harbor. In death her mournful voice became a wave, one of the legendary Three Waves of Erin: Tonn Tuaithe in County Derry, Tonn Rudraidhe in County Down, and Tonn Clíodhna in County Cork. A mythic, haunting, anguished wave whose loud woeful sound had for centuries forewarned local inhabitants of impending death and tragedy.

And death *did* seem to come easily and often in the west of Ireland. Coastal churchyards were dotted with worn gray tombstones and mossy Celtic crosses that read: "Captain," "Mariner," "Drowned with Son," and "Lost at Sea." In the waters off our village alone eighteen ships had slipped below the rocky waves. Beneath the charming blue of Bantry Bay thirty boats lay sunken in their graves. And beyond the craggy cliffs of Baltimore lay the rotting bones of forty-four more.

Fishermen, drunk or sober, drowned in the harbor or at sea. Farm accidents snuffed out children's bright spark. Grandfathers died from "the cigarettes," and lonely people from "the drink." It seemed that barely a month went by when we did not shut the restaurant's outer wooden doors and draw closed the curtains—the windows all up and down Main Street shuttered tight like the eyes of the dead—to show respect for slow, black funeral corteges passing on their way to and from St. Brigid's church.

Across the street, I saw the lights flutter then come on in Maloney's Pub. Then ours did too. The Van Morrison CD started playing again, picking up where it had left off, and then, as quickly as it had come the wind moved on, whirling and whooping down Main Street, and was gone. Leaving behind just the wet black night.

In the dining room, everyone was quiet. Then it was as though the façade of adulthood slipped away and we were children again—grown men and women sputtering and laughing: relieved and a little bit embarrassed at having been so frightened.

When the last customer left, Francis and I wrestled the battered bay trees inside. Then pulled closed the double doors and slid the old cast iron lock into place. Upstairs, we gathered up the children and carried them into our bed. Where we hid under piles of feather duvets.

Outside the storm raged on and I slept fitfully, listening to the wind calling. *Is that Cleena or my child crying?* I drifted in and out of dreams. *What was it the poet from Michigan said? Something about measuring spoons . . . indeed, ridiculous!*

n the middle of the night, when the baby woke to be fed, the rain was still crashing against the house in waves and the wind rubbing its back upon the windowpanes. With all of us in one big bed and the baby drowsing at my breast, it felt to me as though we were adrift, a family lost at sea. And in many respects we were, an urban fledgling family adrift in the wild Irish countryside.

I lay awake thinking of a story I'd heard about two Dutch tourists being swept off the Cliffs of Moher. A strong gust of wind swirled up and over the precipice, raced across the fields, flattened the grasses, and with nothing to stop it, scooped up the tourists and flew off with them. Up and up they went, soaring like sea birds out over the edge of the land, the wind swinging the Dutchman up and down on currents of air high above the crashing Atlantic. Then, unexpectedly, dropped them into the sea.

In the morning, it was not the wind, but human voices that awakened me. The clamor and bang of men tossing empty metal kegs onto the sidewalk across the street. Isaac was awake too and together we climbed down from the bed and went hand in hand out the back door to see what the storm had wrought.

Outside it was wet and cold. The green grass and trees and dripping ivy leaves glistened in the sun and overhead a soft breeze sent white clouds sailing across a sea blue sky. I rolled the bottom of my flannel pajamas and walked to the top of the garden where I could see down into the village where the pink and blue and pale yellow houses were still standing, the smooth water on the bay sparkling.

There would be time to put the kettle on for tea so I lingered, breathing deep the briny air and stretching—swinging my arms as though I were swimming. I watched my son rummaging. In the garden there was red-brown seaweed. Isaac picked it up to show me. And when I turned to go back inside I was surprised to see, beside our kitchen door, bright red winter roses full blooming in the sun.

≈ ≈ ≈

K. M. Churchill is a writer, world traveler, and award-winning restaurateur. Her work has appeared in Harvard University's Charles River Review *and the cookbook anthology,* Newbury-port: Portrait of a Restaurant *and online at Nowhere Magazine. She is a member of AWP, the Association of Writers & Writing Programs, and is currently working on her food/travel memoir,* Salmon Cakes and Saints: Three Years, Two Toddlers and One Restaurant in Ireland. *She now lives with her husband and two teenage sons on the seacoast of New Hampshire.*

❧ ❧ ❧

The Train to Harare

Reflecting on Africa, circa 1988-1998.

In Africa, we are all children. Everything is new, and everything is old. The sapling sprouting among the creepers is new; the forest, old. Though the baby in the *kaross* sling is new, his tribe is old. The dawn's breeze swirls the dust over the Magadigadi Pans and is gone, but the ancient dust remains, the scorched powder of a continent's bones.

The heat of the Kalahari, thick and mighty across this sweep of gasping desert, has a life force of its own. Like an animal, it waits, resting, through the African night. But with the day it stirs, and grows with the sun, gathering power like a sky-borne fist. It stalks you as you move, watches for weakness. If you stumble, it will thrash you. Show frailty, and it will murder you. Still, this is Africa, and there are many ways to die. This is known, but no one knows Africa.

From the Gabarone railway station, Sunday morning, late October, the sky grades from ink to plum to, in the east, vermillion. Botswana is well into the dry season. Hundreds of miles north, in the Okavango Delta, the hippo drags the smooth barrel of his belly through the mud-strewn grass, along the swampy troughs that lead from pool to pool, stream to stream, all of them shrinking. He, like the elephant and the antelope, follows the receding water, still taking life from the rains that came but now have fled.

But that is north, up where the rivers spilling out of Angola form that broad, fecund, swampy paradise on the skirts of the Kalahari. Here in the south, across the border from Johannesburg, all is parched. The heat grips its human victims, threatens to grind their strength to sand against the desert's stones. Threatens to, but doesn't. For the Africans are at one with the heat, as though with that animal that could kill you and eat you but doesn't because you are one with it. As strong as the heat is, the Africans are stronger.

It was 1988, and I was in Botswana absorbing the hospitality of friends who worked there. It was one of many such trips I would take—and still take—moving, exploring, untangling the twisted shoelaces of my life. I had been up with Dan to the Delta, seen the hippos and the marabou storks and the *tsessebe*, the malachite kingfisher and the bat-eared fox and the mud-encrusted, blunt-brained Cape buffalo, black-eyed and brutish.

Dan had taken a break from his duties with the State Department, and we'd gone from Maun by bush plane into the center of "the Swamp." We bought provisions at the trading post of a mad Australian who lived full-time in this back-of-beyond, and belonged there. At the post we'd found a guide, and the three of us set off—Dan, Kamanga, and I—covering the hilly grasslands by foot and the waterways by *mokoro*, Kamanga's dug-out canoe. We'd tramped and camped in the open, swam in ponds that the crocodiles had surrendered, and followed elephant spoor within sight of a lion's kill. Three boys in the wild woods, pure and without purpose. On the best of nights, the horizon danced around us under the blue-white branches of a forest of lightning.

Now it was over. I was back in the bake room of Gabarone, on the platform with my pack, waiting for a train. I was leaving Botswana. The train would take me north-northeast along the border, up to Francistown on the Bulawayo line, then on to Harare. From there I would fly to Sydney, and on to my new job back in New Zealand.

But, for now, I stood in the rising, ticking heat. Dan had dropped me off on his way to the embassy—even on Sunday morning, he had work to do. Our trip to the Delta had cost him some valuable desk time, and now he had to make it up. So I waited in the station's shadows and tried to comprehend Africa.

The wild Africa of storybook, the vibrant, frightening terra incognita on whose verge Burton, Speke, and Stanley stood, staring and trembling with excitement, has long since passed into history. That Africa, the biologic, ecologic, uncategorizable cosmic diversity of forms and species has died, in its skin as well as its heart. The Africa we think we know, or at least recognize today, began much later.

In the 1930s and 1940s, confrontation blossomed around the world between geographic sovereignty and imperialist politics. European powers adjusted to new political equations, and Britain surrendered its jewel, India. The culture of Empire was dying. But the stakes were high here, conflicting interests not so easily moralized or recalculated. Opposing wheels of change churned against each other through the 1940s and 1950s, and ideologies, greed, lust for power, old scores, and the myriad promises of what the end of colonialism would bring all combined to set Africa at large—and African countries individually—on a violent path to self-determination. To this dream called *independence*.

The now-terrible irony is that the exploitation and suppression of Africa, honed by European and Arab interests over centuries, found, in the surge to independence, willing collaborators among black African opportunists and outside con-men and -women. As freedom-hungry Africans threw themselves headlong into their passion for self rule, they too often acquiesced to the charisma of leaders and movements with agendas geared toward tribal and/or individual supremacy. Amin, Obote, Mobutu, Arap Moi, Kabila, Mugabe—the litany of abusers and consequent abuse reads long and sorrowful. Assassination, coups, backdoor deals, cults, civil war, ethnic cleansing, genocide. If Conrad was right, and there is darkness here, it was and is in the hearts of those who led Africa to its current state of decline.

The old black-and-brass steam locomotive snarls and squeals into the station, setting loose in the enervating heat a score of Botswana Railways personnel to scamper or drag themselves from desk to door, from baggage to cart, from cargo storage to track-side dock. Passenger carriages roll in behind the engine, conductors step down, and with no special ceremony, I hump my pack onboard and find compartment C-10.

Botswana Railways wears its livery with pride, only a year into its own independence from National Railways of Zimbabwe. The tan-and-green paint is holding up, as is the serviceable gray leather-and-fabric upholstery on the seats in my compartment. It isn't my compartment, but one I share with two others, both black Africans. He is a minister, in clerical dress, on his way from Johannesburg to Selebi Phikwe. She is traveling to Francistown "on family business." They are both solicitous of my welfare, and we speak of the heat.

Botswana is one of the success stories of independence in Africa. It has no coast, land-locked between South Africa to the south, Namibia and the Caprivi Strip to the west and north, and Zimbabwe and other countries to the east. It has vast expanses of desert, mineral wealth that escaped early detection, and a small native people. The Bushmen of the Kalahari are short and sinewy, not designed by their God for the heavy manual labor that slave-traders to Arabia and the New World were dealing in. So, Botswana was never the exploitation target for outsiders and corrupt Africans that its neighbors were, and it has moved into the current century with a reasonable promise of survival and success.

The train rolls along its narrow-gauge tracks, headed north-northeast, due in Francistown that afternoon. For a century, Francistown had been an outpost for frontier survival, gold mining, and the cross-border trade with Rhodesia. It saw, over that time, uncounted tons of legal, if blood-stained, elephant ivory pass through the hands of the merchants and agents in this sun-seared, tin-roofed settlement. Now, 1988, ivory export is illegal, but rumor claims that hasn't extinguished the trade. Poachers and smugglers move the contraband by other means—bribes, mislabeled goods, trucks by night. But the sins of Francistown aren't my concern. I am a vagabond.

I have traveled by rail in many countries prior to this, through Europe, Great Britain, the Americas, and New Zealand. But, as Botswana's wilderness rolls past the carriage window, I can make only one comparison to these scenes of the great Kalahari. Only once have I seen so inviting a stretch of uninviting country. Twelve years ago, I crossed Australia by train. West of Adelaide, spanning thousands of square miles of sand, saltbush, and desiccation, is the Nullarbor Plain, flat as a page and hot as a griddle. You get a hero's welcome in Perth just for traversing that God-forsaken desolation. Yet, as in Botswana, a certain comfort can be found in its near-emptiness. Knowing that life is actually being sustained, albeit tenuously, by some few hardy species in such waterless terrain makes the place seem less unkind than it appears. And it appears very unkind indeed. For in these deserts, life seems a stranger to the day. At dawn, the disc of the sun slices through the seam between sky and land, and, until it sets on the other side of Earth, your views are of sweeping, barren tracts that appear unmarked by man. The sandscape's reaches are so vast, yet within range of one's eye, that, as a mere human speck, you feel like a grain of soil on Nature's ground. And blessed to be so.

Evidence from anthropology and archeology shows that Africa, before the white man's maps, was a galaxy of clans, tribes, and native nations. It is now beyond modern conception to grasp how diverse and generally functional it was, and today it is too complex to list the factors of change that have brought much of Africa to its knees. If a single statistic could show what is squeezing the continent's breath from its body, it would be one given to me by a fifth-generation Anglo-African. He was a farmer from Kenya with a graduate degree in rangeland management from Cornell University. As near as he could estimate from available research, the black population of Kenya circa 1900 was 350,000; in 1998, it was 35 million. Are these figures true? The first one may be unreliable, but the second one is close. And then consider Rwanda: 2 million people in the 1950s; forty years later, 9 million. These facts alone paint a broad-brush sketch of what faces Africa. Kenya as it stands cannot possibly provide the work and food needed for 35 million people. Add to these at least another dozen African countries in similar or worse condition, and the scope of the calamity takes shape in one's mind.

With bursts of steam and whistle, we arrive in Francistown. Around and through the station pulses the street bazaar. Food vendors, trays and baskets on their heads, sashay along the tracks and carriage-sides, selling fruits of all colors, sausage sandwiches, corn snacks, and fizzy drinks. Sweet and spicy food aromas mix with the oil smells of the train. Hawkers sell handicrafts and trinkets—bangles and beads, fabrics and hats, buffalo horn napkin rings. It is momentary commerce, and the traders will survive the day, if not much richer for it.

The black-garbed minister left us at Selebi Phikwe. Now the African lady, tightly wrapped in her banana-flower prints, and with business in Francistown, also disembarks. As do I, changing to a NRZ train, bound for Harare on the line through Bulawayo.

Some socio-economic process about which I can only guess has given National Railway of Zimbabwe very different rolling stock from Botswana Railways. Or, at least, this stock is different. The BR wagons were of painted steel and "sensible" upholstery, evidently designed, assembled, and finished as utilitarian conveyances for people used to the serviceable basics as a way of life. But the NRZ carriage I enter is a traveling Edwardian parlor—walnut wainscoting, carpeted floors, purple mohair and velour upholstery, burgundy velvet curtains, copper washbasins. It is generations old, pre-WWII, perhaps pre-WWI, and was built and outfitted, probably in Britain, for well-to-do African travelers. Then it served exclusively white families; the men, women, and children who had followed on from Cecil Rhodes in the colonization and wealth-gathering of British East Africa. They and their successors had turned Rhodesia, later Zimbabwe, into a farming economy unsurpassed in Africa. Hence the luxury trains, though they were no longer white only, and no longer luxurious.

From Francistown to Bulawayo, I share my compartment with a new passenger, a Zimbabwean man. A large man. A black man. A large, well-dressed (except for his shoes, which were tatty), black man on his way home to Bulawayo. These attributes, as I list them, may seem obvious, irrelevant, or pedantic. If so, consider this, as well: He is carrying 20 kilograms of rice in a burlap sack.

What does all this mean, all this description? I say these things about this man because, in Africa, nothing is superfluous. I tell you he is black and a Zimbabwean so you know that he comes from the historical majority in that country, and has historical reasons to support the current (and still current) dictator of their republic ("leader" would be a poor choice of words, though that black president and his party, only eight years before, wrested Rhodesia-Zimbabwe from its legacy of white rule and white control).

I tell you our man is well dressed because this shows he isn't part of the poor majority of his country. I tell you he is large, because that means well-fed and powerful, things that tend to go hand-in-hand in Africa. The shoes are a different thing. Good Western-style shoes are not for sale in the bazaars and shops here, and good ones get old and show their age and may not be easily repaired or replaced, despite one's station in life. So if his shoes are broken, it means that Botswana, and certainly Africa, is possibly as far afield as this man, this well-fed, well-placed, native African man, has been.

Why is all this relevant? And what about the rice? I'll let him tell you, remembering this was 1988: "While on business in Botswana, I bought this rice. It is becoming difficult to find in our country now, and very dear. It is a disgrace. The farms in Zimbabwe were once the finest in Africa. Everything was here"—he gestures at the expanses of arable land rocking past the carriage windows—"and it was cheap for us. Now we must go to Botswana to buy rice. *Botswana!*" He uses the voice of disgust and derision to refer to his neighbor to the west. It is unimaginable to him that poor, desert-filled, humble Botswana could sell him rice cheaper than his own proud country, that it makes some kind of economic sense for him to haul twenty kilos of uncooked rice back from Botswana to his home in Bulawayo.

I have heard rumors of this embarrassment. From living, working, and traveling in its former colonies and Great Britain itself, I have tried to keep current with the affairs of the Commonwealth. Though it is my first time in the country, indeed in Africa, I have heard that Zimbabwe is gradually slipping away from its once prosperous, well-fed position in the agriculture and economics of East Africa, indeed of all of Africa.

"And not only rice. Corn, too, and cornmeal. Melons. Meat. All of it is becoming scarce and expensive." What can I say to this man? This is Africa and he is an African. This is Zimbabwe and he is a Zimbabwean. I am a foreigner, a stranger with no more advice or comfort to give this patriot and his bag of rice and his marketplace anxiety than a surprised landlubber, watching and listening to the report of a sinking ship, could give to one of the sailors onboard. So, I ask the fool's question.

"Is the government doing anything about it?"

"Oh, yes," he says, "our government will face this. Our government will take us out of this crisis." He has been watching his country slide past the window in the setting sun. Now he looks at me with conviction on his face, but fear in his eyes. "Robert Mugabe and his people—we can trust them. He will fix this. Mr. Mugabe will save us."

A decade passes before I return to Africa. Now it is 1998, again October, and Michael, another friend with the State Department, is running the reconstruction and rehabilitation of our embassy in Nairobi. In August, more than two hundred people were murdered by Al Qaeda fanatics in the suicide bombing of a bank and the American Embassy. Twelve of the dead were Americans; the rest were Kenyans going about their daily business.

Michael has taken me to the site of the bombing. Nairobi's Ground Zero. The embassy building, now a perforated block of scorched concrete, squats windowless on a busy corner of the city. Plans to relocate it, or at least redevelop its security, had been delayed and delayed in Washington. Beside it, an eight-story commercial building, the location of the bank, is caved in like a dollhouse that's been dropped from a great height.

Nearly all the deaths were there. The bombers, blocked from entering the embassy compound, but on a mission for their cause, detonated the weapon anyway and orphaned hundreds of children in a few seconds. Once again, zealotry triumphed over human reason and compassion. Once again, Africa was chosen as a battleground for ideologies, and innocents paid the price in blood and lives.

From Nairobi, I travel south trough Zambia and, once again, into Zimbabwe, where Robert Mugabe is in his eighteenth year of uninterrupted power. Lounging on a hotel patio, I pick up a copy of the *Sunday Mail*. Like most of the country's newspapers, it is government-controlled because, after twenty-five years of "independence" and "self-determination," the Zimbabwean on the street, according to national policy, is not yet ready for free access to the news. The headline story is of a manhunt: a local shaman and his client are on the run from police for having removed and eaten the heart of a twelve-year-old virgin in an effort to cure the client of AIDS.

The traveler, the Zimbabwean man on the train, with the small cargo of rice for his family, comes back to my thoughts. I recall his unshakable faith in Mugabe to lead his country into the light, and I ask myself if there is an ungovernable terrain between Africa and its future.

    ∾ ∾ ∾

Lance Mason was raised by working parents, products of the Great Depression. His first job was in his brother-in-law's gas station in Oxnard, California. During school vacations, he picked lemons, packed lima beans, laid fiberglass, sold hotdogs, and spliced cable for the local phone company where his mother worked. He studied at UCSB and Loyola University, where he earned a BS, and then at UCLA for his graduate degree. He has taught at UCLA, the National University in Natal, Brazil, and Otago University,

Dunedin, New Zealand. In addition to overseas teaching, Mason has lived, worked, or traveled in more than sixty countries during a dozen trips around the world. His first publication was a piece in Voices of Survival *(appearing alongside writers as diverse as William. F. Buckley, Jr., Joan Baez, Indira Ghandi, Arthur C. Clarke, and Carl Sagan). His work has appeared in* upstreet, City Works, Sea Spray, The Packing House Review, New Borders, Askew, The Santa Barbara Independent, *and* Solo Novo, *as well as several professional journals.*

≈ ≈ ≈

We'll Always
Have Paris

Sharing the City of Light with
New Yorker writer Adam Gopnik.

The night I met Adam Gopnik, his train from New York to Wilmington, Delaware was delayed. A soft breeze moved across the parking lot as I leaned into the car's headrest; I was sweating even though the door was open.

As of that spring evening in 2011, Gopnik had written for *The New Yorker* for twenty-five years. He was an intellectual, a man of letters, so brilliantly capable of casual erudition combined with self-deprecating humor and just a dash of name-dropping, that I could only hope for myself that I would bask in his genius for just one evening without saying anything silly. I discreetly checked my armpits.

Gopnik would be speaking the next day at a University of Delaware memorial for the poet W.D. Snodgrass. My darling husband Matt, knowing of my starry-eyed crush on Gopnik's work, and perhaps the man himself, had finagled his way into being the faculty member to pick the writer up and take him out to dinner. I had no official role in this welcoming committee or particular reason to be there other than

a persistent admiration that had endured since I first encountered Gopnik's essay about John James Audubon in the *Best
American Essays of 1992.*

My copy of *Paris to the Moon*, Gopnik's book about the five
years he spent in Paris with his family in the late 1990s, sat
safely on the seat next to me, but although it was a favorite of
mine I was not tempted to pick it up and skim it. How embarrassing would it be, how *jejune* would I seem, I thought, if he
and Matt suddenly appeared and I had my nose buried in his
book? Instead I stared at the flat gray sky, at my lap, at the
expanse of cracked sidewalk and parked cars, and rehearsed
what I might say when I met him. I wanted so much to con-
nect, to show him that that I understood his love for Paris,
about which he wrote beautifully, longingly.

"Your writing is important to me. I've read every word
you've written for *The New Yorker*." Ugh.

"I love Paris too, just the same way you do. I wrote about
it on my blog—I even mentioned your book!" Double ugh.

He's here, Matt's text read, and so I had time to prepare
myself, deciding at the last minute that instead of sitting in the
car, I would lean up against it. As they walked toward me, I saw
Gopnik tilt his head as if to ask a question. He approached, smiling, looking a bit rumpled, shorter than I expected, but much
like the photo on his book jacket. To my relief, I didn't do anything foolish but simply stuck out my hand and said my name
and "nice to meet you." But he was looking intently at my face.

"Have we met before?" he asked, and I laughed spontane-
ously. Oh no, I was sure we hadn't, for I would without question remember such a meeting. No, we had never connected,
unless you counted the fact that it was his words that kept
Paris alive for me.

Loving Paris is not the most original thing I've ever done. But
like so many people, like Gopnik himself, I came to this love

independent of experience and then had it confirmed by reality. He wrote of falling in love with Paris by means of a cardboard French policeman, an advertisement for Air France that his mother procured somewhere and placed in his room for decoration when he was eight years old. "My head was filled with pictures of Paris," he wrote in *Paris to the Moon*, "and I wanted to be in them."

Paris became a dream for me in the fifth grade, when once a week for thirty minutes I reveled in the gorgeousness of ordinary words—*fille* for girl, *papillon* for butterfly, *lundi* for Monday—as my teacher wrote them in spidery print on a sheet of poster paper. Somehow learning French for me became almost instantly about going to Paris, home of Madeline and of the boy with the red balloon. Like Gopnik, I wanted to be in those pictures.

No one else in my family had any particular interest in visiting Paris and so it became a personal mission. How carefully I studied my favorite subject, even when I was bedeviled by the subjunctive or when the summer reading for my advanced high-school course was a Beaumarchais play I could barely understand. I chose the college I attended based on its study abroad program and even lived for a semester in a building on campus called Le Chateau, whose design was inspired by a pavilion at the Palace of Fontainebleau.

And then, finally, in August 1990, at the end of the summer I turned twenty, I arrived in Paris for the school year. Riding the bus from Orly Airport to the Gare Montparnasse, I gazed at the haughty lion sitting in the middle of the Denfert Rochereau traffic circle and thought, as I often would riding past, that he waited just for me.

Although Gopnik served as *The New Yorker*'s French cultural critic and journalist when he lived in Paris, covering everything from elections to strikes to fashion shows, he says in the first chapter of *Paris to the Moon* that his life in Paris was primarily domestic. He describes visiting the park, playing pinball in a café with his son Luke, watching an old couple in one of his favorite bistros eat dinner in the company of their blind dog.

My favorite things about the city were similarly quotidian. Even now I see my younger self, almost but not quite an adult, purchasing a ham-and-cheese crepe seasoned always with a generous amount of black pepper and wrapped in wax paper. I would have made this purchase from the storefront window near the Alliance Française where some of my classes were held. Clutching my warm treat, I'd make a right turn on the Rue du Fleurus past the stone façade of Gertrude Stein's house with its black wrought-iron window ornaments. Angled and narrow, the street showed no sign of what lay at the end, but I walked confidently, a stray string of melted Gruyere sticking to my glove, until I reached the gold-tipped fence and slipped into the Jardin de Luxembourg where I would pass by the carousel and puppet theater without stopping, gravel crunching beneath my feet, headed for the fountain at the garden's center to wile away hours on a small folding garden chair as if it were my own private realm.

Before I left Paris in May of 1991, it was in the Jardin that I took my last stroll, snapping photos of the statues including an angel with large swooping wings, her podium surrounded by electric orange flowers. This picture would hang on my dorm room bulletin board, representing Paris, where, I was convinced in the easy optimism of youth and inexperience, I would simply will myself back to work and live once I graduated from college.

When this fantasy proved to be just that and no trip to Paris was forthcoming for almost twenty years, it was often Gopnik's writing, first in *The New Yorker* and later in his book, that took me back. As I got older and eventually had babies, my favorite parts of this favorite book were the tales of Gopnik roaming the city with Luke.

I especially enjoyed the stories of how Luke as a toddler was fascinated with the carousel in the Jardin de Luxembourg and its old-fashioned game where riders capture rings on a stick as they ride. As Gopnik points out, this game is the origin of the American myth of "going for the brass ring," but the French rings here are small and made of tin, making the game quite challenging. Gopnik and Luke returned to the carousel routinely until in the book's last pages Luke, now a brave six-year-old, rides the carousel and grabs the rings under the eyes of his proud and melancholy father who mourns his family's imminent departure for New York. For Gopnik this game, this ride—whose only purpose and prize was the experience itself—represented all that he loved about the beauty and charm of Paris, as seen through the eyes of his child.

When I finally returned to Paris in 2008 with my sons Tommy and Teddy—six and three respectively—in tow, I didn't even wait twenty-four hours to introduce them to the Jardin, which has a large playground next to the carousel where the boys played for hours. It was the end of June, the sunlight dappled the ground, and rarely had the world ever felt so good and right as it did while my children climbed and ran near the place where my own younger feet had strolled.

I eventually lured them on my pilgrimage to the merry-go-round and its slightly seedy charm. Tommy chose a worn wooden elephant for his ride. A leather belt encircled his waist to hold him safely on the animal and in his right hand he clutched a thick and worn wooden stick. This he used to grab rings off an old-fashioned contraption specially designed for that purpose and held up for each child by a bored attendant who again and again resisted the urge I would have felt to move the ring just out of reach at the last minute.

With intent focus Tommy managed to fill his stick with the small metal rings, one at a time, with each circumnavigation of the ride. This was no small feat for a first-timer. I knew this because Gopnik told me so, and like him, I delighted in my son's success. "I was unreasonably pleased," he wrote, "and then felt a little guilty about my own pleasure. It seemed so American, so competitive."

Tommy was so triumphant to have captured almost all of the rings that he lost his head and as the carousel slowed to a stop, turned his stick to face the ground, where they all slid into the dirt. For a suspended moment we all sighed, but then the breeze in the plane trees, the sound of children calling to each other from the nearby playground, the scent of coffee and age, the essential perfection of the moment took over. It was a perfection borne of layers of experience: my own long sojourns in the Jardin, the pleasure of experiencing something I had read about and loved, and the very real happiness of the day, of Paris, of sharing a place so dear with my family.

Gopnik wrote of the Eiffel Tower, which in Luke's company he saw lit up for the millennium, "Here we are at the end of the century and *that's* what we have to get excited about, same old *belle époque, fin de siècle* stuff, champagne and the Eiffel Tower? That exhausted stuff, that dead stuff. Only it isn't dead, or even really sick, or, in a certain sense, even old. It's here right now, we're looking at it right now. Luke is young and in Paris right now, and in that sense the sparkling tower is the same age he is. He's going to take it with him through life, not as part of the lost glory of the French past but as part of what happened to him when he was a kid."

I understood the pleasure of being in a moment, a pleasure brought on partly by all the previous pleasurable moments that have been lived there, and by all the moments to come. When I visited the carousel and watched Tommy I replicated Gopnik's pleasure; this enhanced my own joy. That this was so seemed both very French and very Gopnikian.

And so of course, on that spring evening nearly three years later with only a few hours over dinner to convey it, I wanted Adam Gopnik to know how much his book meant to me, how it had brought me to many places I wanted to go. I wanted him to know that I too understood the revivifying effect of bringing children to a city that's sometimes accused of being a museum, a dusty relic.

And I had no idea how to tell him.

So instead I listened in the car on the way to the restaurant as he talked about eating at Ina's house (Ina Garten!) and mentioned his friend and colleague Malcolm (Malcolm Gladwell!). He was charming, comfortable in his own skin, well aware that he was the most interesting person in the vehicle. He insisted that we choose the wine at the restaurant, but then gave in to our protestations and selected a handsome bottle of Bordeaux.

There was no way I was going to call myself a writer in front of a man who referred to *The New Yorker* in conversation as "The Magazine," but I hoped somehow to figure out a way to mention my modest travel blog, The Mother of all Trips, and to share that one of the very first stories I published there was of our visit to the carousel.

As soon as we had finished ordering our wine, he looked at me again with that same curious expression, and said, "Mara, I hate to be a bore, but I'm sure I've seen you before. Have you ever been in Paris?"

"Well, yes."

"You have two blond little boys, right?"

"Yes," again (I was feeling very odd at this point).

"That's it! I saw you at the carousel at the Jardin de Luxembourg a few years ago."

And so the moment I had been seeking arrived unbidden. He and I looked at each other in utter recognition. Of course, he had seen me before, as I in turn had seen him in the pages of his book. He went on.

"I was there with my family—it's an annual tradition for us when we visit Paris in the summer.

"I remember that year especially because it was the last time Luke would ride—his legs were getting too long. I remember watching you and your family. I could tell you were American."

When Adam Gopnik finished describing our chance encounter, he looked almost bashful, "I remember wondering if you had read my book. I almost came over and asked if that was why you were there, but you and your family looked so happy I didn't want to disturb you."

Later, I asked him to sign my book and he wrote on the title page, *For Mara—A friend from Paris unknown!*

I wrote about our two-week trip to Paris on my website. I talked about Teddy's infatuation with the Eiffel Tower, his wonder that it appeared so often in the landscape. I shared the perfect days we spent exploring Marie Antoinette's folly in Versailles and Monet's garden in Giverny, where Tommy made his own sketch of the famous Japanese Bridge. Although this wasn't the first time I traveled with children—far from it, for Matt and I spent thirteen months on the road with Tommy when he was a toddler—it was the *naissance* of my online travel-writing life, begun with such joy and optimism and meaning and a shared love of one of my favorite places in the world. And without question, the most significant moment was the one when Tommy triumphantly filled his stick with all the rings. A moment I had unwittingly shared with the man who inspired it.

⁓ℓ ⁓ℓ ⁓ℓ

Mara Gorman is an award-winning freelance writer and family travel blogger at The Mother of all Trips. The blog's name was inspired by a thirteen-month adventure across six states, three countries, and two continents that she took with her husband and toddler. Since that first extended trip, Mara has logged thousands of miles of travel with her children across North America and Europe. Mara is the author of The Family Traveler's Handbook *and her lifestyle and travel articles have appeared in a variety of* USA Today *special-interest publications and on websites such as* AOL Travel. *This story originally appeared in November 2015 on* BBC.com/Travel. *She is an avid skier, loves museums and cultural travel, and has never met an ice cream that she didn't like. She also believes in serving global causes, especially those that help women and children; this belief is exemplified by her role as a board member of the travel blogging fundraiser Passports with Purpose. Mara lives in Delaware with her husband and two school-age sons.*

MARCIA DESANCTIS

≈ ≈ ≈

Time or the
Sahara Wind

Both are relentless, and impossible to stop.

In my favorite photograph from my first visit to Morocco, I appear as if on the floor of a canyon. Behind me is a cinematic backdrop: a towering pomegranate-red clay mountainside speckled with clusters of trees. I'm standing on a wide-open restaurant terrace, wearing white Capri pants and a black tank top, sneakers with socks. The wind blows my hair into chaos but one hand pushes the bangs off my face. In the corner, over my shoulder, there is a sliver of Matisse-blue sky. I am twenty-four years old.

I recall arriving at this place, wherever it was, to the staggering sight of the mountains opening up beyond the valley and then, my mother's voice. "I'm just out of words," she says as her narrow foot swings lightly out of the car into the sunshine. "Isn't it something?"

My mother documented that trip to Morocco as she did everything in her life. Perfectly. Painstakingly. With the observant eye of a woman who was born an artist, but in a time and place where it would never have occurred to her actually to declare herself one. Me stroking a carpet or chatting with a merchant at the souk, my sandaled foot in the stirrup of each camel I rode (there were, I'm afraid, more than one), the cluster of mimosa branches that riffled beyond the hotel window—it was all preserved on film. Back at home, my mother's deft hands slipped the photographs into albums, which were left untouched for decades like monuments whose purposes are overlooked or forgotten, and certainly taken for granted.

The photos seem to be brushed with a brownish glaze. Maybe it's the passage of time, but perhaps it was the grit from the *chergui*, the wind from the Sahara that blows west across the Atlas Mountains and through Marrakech, Meknès, Ouarzazat, carrying fine particles of rust-colored sand. It was ferocious that year, the fall of 1985. The dust hung dense but invisible, and may have left a film on the lens of my mother's camera, giving the snapshots a tawny cast that dimmed the brights of morning and churned the milkiness of the clouds.

The fine orange coating on my skin made it erupt with tiny hives upon arriving in Marrakech and some memories of the trip now seem as if they were filtered through a pleasant Benadryl haze. Even the novel I was reading poolside at the Hotel Mamounia—*The Mists of Avalon*—bears remnants of this dry desert wind. The paperback remains on my bookshelf, smudged with fingerprints the color of dried blood. The pages are still stippled from pool water that dripped from my hair and dried in the heat. My mother photographed that, too. Her youngest daughter, asleep in her bikini, stretched out on a chaise under the prickly sun with a book resting on her stomach.

There are no photos of my mother from that trip. This is the fate of many mothers, of course, who are so busy capturing memories for the family archives that their existence is obscured behind the camera. But even if she is invisible, her presence is everywhere in the pages of these two albums, collections of moments she created, assembled and enshrined. In each picture, she is there, reflected in my own eyes that faced both her and her camera. Back then, on the green lenses of her sunglasses, I saw a moving pinprick that was me looking at her. Her arms, legs and face were browned, and her short hair tousled from the stifling wind that rolled across the terrace. She grasped the camera and when the shutter snapped, her engagement ring, and the other one with a row of tiny rubies, flashed white in the sun.

This is the version of my mother that passes through me in dreams. I want not to forget the image of her as she was, vitality intact. Thirty years have passed and today her mind is a vacant chamber, her voice often a profusion of unrelated syllables. Occasionally she can muster up decipherable language, but rarely context for the words that emerge. In Morocco, with her suntan and the skin still tight across her cheekbones, her eyes were almost-sapphire dark. Today, her hair is a tangle of white semi-waves that the staff at her home frequently grooms back into place. That, plus the pale skin on her face render her eyes a vibrant, almost pastel, blue. I have looked at them forever but only really notice them now. Her gaze is direct but tinged with opacity, and I cannot know what it sees. Though she is alive her life is behind her. So I seek her out by studying photographs not of her, but of me. It is in this gathering of images, through the negative space she dominates completely and in every frame, that I understand, miss and grasp most urgently for the woman she once was.

I don't think my mother was searching for much when she first inhaled the sweet, orange-flower air in Marrakech, but Morocco was where she found herself. It was a midlife bloom, the triumphant gift of the empty nest. My father, a Boston cardiologist, was asked to look after King Hassan II's heart and occasionally made a house call to Rabat, Casablanca, Marrakech—wherever the monarch was in residence at the time—with my mother always by his side. They traveled in style on these brief jaunts to North Africa, but that was the least of it. My mother was from humble New England stock, an academic wife and a far cry from a social climber. She was very pretty but plain, barely wore makeup and certainly never colored her gray-streaked hair. In Boston, it was undignified to make pains to turn back the clock. Maybe it was the suntan, or the sudden swoosh of plum lipstick, or the muscular legs (no longer suburban) that descended from her light summer dresses, but in Morocco she blossomed like a teenager into a beauty.

She deserved the extra-big seat on the plane, the little dop kit with Hermès perfume, and once in Morocco, the official car and driver who ferried her to the souks, to other cities and across the streams and valleys of the countryside. In Boston, my father was known and beloved for his dedication to his patients, his medical school students and to medicine—to being a physician and healing—writ large. But his success had a price. He also worked eighteen-hour days, seven days a week, leaving my mother to raise four daughters essentially alone. I can't imagine her exhaustion when she packed me, the youngest, off to college. Sometimes I wish I had asked her how she celebrated that first night in an empty house. If she celebrated. Perhaps she wept, now that the second half of her life sprawled before her and there was no grand plan.

Like most women married in 1955 she had given up her own work to be a wife and mother. It's still not clear to me if it made her happy or if she ever stopped to consider what she was sacrificing, and if resentment simmered beneath her unadorned exterior. I don't know what my mother questioned, if she ever questioned anything. I never asked her that either. I knew she loved us and that was all.

After her first trip to Morocco, it was clear that the country filled the great gaps that had opened in her life. She lunched with new friends. She devoured tagines swimming with

candied lemon peel and tart black olives. She gazed up at the
ramrod-straight palm trees crowned with sprays of leaves
that burst like feather dusters. She reclined by the pool in the
hard sunlight, savored the warm breeze that blew across her
face at nightfall, and loved to divert for a spontaneous meal of
fresh fish and chilled wine on the beach in Essouaria. She trod
her sandals over the rich green tiles and past the bougainvil-
lea that grew in dense thickets along ramparts. She marveled
at the oversized crowns of roses, two feet high and two feet
wide, that His Majesty left in my parents' hotel room on each
visit. She was dazzled by the mottled ochre walls and the lyrical disarray in the souks.

She was delighted that she, that daughter of a quarryman,
could visit the palace (or palaces . . . there was one in every city)
of the king she was invited by, but her real exhilaration came
from how effortlessly she could transpose herself onto this
strange and beautiful place, and freely seek adventure there.
Sometimes she stayed on after my father's medical work was
done, even for a few days—still attended to by minders from
her royal hosts of course, but unscheduled and on her own.
My mother was entirely and happily liberated for the first time
in her life and hungry to explore the country where she felt
embraced and at ease. She was always my father's spouse there,
but more than just a doctor's wife. Morocco dictated the flowing words of her second chapter.

And she wanted to share this new passion with me. As the
youngest of the girls, though not the favorite by any stretch, I
was often the lucky beneficiary of my parent's generosity. I was
the last one at home, suddenly an only child, so during those
two years after my next-oldest sister left, I cleaned up on travel.
My parents took me along when they could: to London, Greece,
the Soviet Union, and elsewhere. Maybe also they felt guilty
about all the hand-me-down clothes I had to wear, the incessant teasing, or the cropped haircut my mother, grown weary of

three older girls in braids, inflicted on me. They certainly made it up to me. That year, in 1985, while I stewed over changes both professional and in love, I was invited to Morocco.

My mother and I explored while my father met with the medical team, but more often the three of us were together, in Marrakech or on the road. We drove to the Atlas Mountains, to Meknès and the great Roman ruins of Volubilis. In the photographs, often there are others alongside me and my father, strangers who were in my life too briefly to remember their names: Moroccan physicians, their wives perhaps, the driver who always joined us for lunch. But in almost every image in the album, I appear.

Here I stand behind my own bouquet of roses—hundreds of red, yellow, pink, and white blooms bursting over a vase—on the terrace of my room. I am wrapped in a robe and my eyes are puffy. I had been crying and though we hadn't discussed it, my mother knew—how could she not? I had received a pleading telegram at the Mamounia from the man I had left for another and my face bore the stain of anguish.

In another, I am standing in front of a massive carved doorway.

"Isn't it beautiful?" she asks as she takes a picture of me. She is impossibly slim, in tan trousers and a light blue blouse. She snaps on the lens cap and stuffs the camera into her canvas tote. She hoists a bottle of water and takes a gulp.

"Are you thirsty, honey?" she asks. "Do you need sunscreen?"

Sometimes she photographed me doing business with the basketmakers in the souk, or buying a round of bread to nibble on, or ordering a glass of tea packed with mint leaves at the hotel restaurant. I am beside a donkey and my hand grazes the saddle. I seem intent while loading film into my own camera, or a tad awkward with a troupe of dancing girls in long brocaded caftans swaying behind me. Shoulders bared, I am in a sarong that is wrapped around me like a dress, seated on a mosaic fountain. In the pool behind me float thousands of roses cut from the stems. I look annoyed. "Mom, please. All you do is take pictures," I likely said to her. "Don't you have enough?"

"You look so pretty, honey," she would have said and then sat beside me on the tiled ledge, listening to the splash of water into the basin.

There are many shots of my father, the driver and me at a restaurant, sitting around a table with her chair empty after she jumped up to chronicle these moments, too. As I look at the album now, I imagine her seated the second before the snapshot, opening our bottle of Sidi Ali water, mothering me to smithereens, asking if I like the stewed pumpkin or the lamb couscous I'd ordered for lunch. I wish it was she who had turned to face the camera once in a while, but I am comforted with the assurance that when I smiled into the lens, I was really smiling at her.

She loved to take pictures when I wasn't looking, as I do now with my own children. She was fascinated by this living entity she gave life to, and the sight of me seemed to never bore or tire her. In one shot, I lean over to inhale the scent of a pile of oranges. She snapped me with my eyes closed on a bench in the Majorelle Gardens. She captured me time after time with my face tilted up to catch the sun. I appear entranced, as if in meditation, but I was only grabbing a moment to turn myself a deeper shade of brown.

My mother was always there.

My mother is always there.

I returned to Morocco many times, several with my parents. I went to weddings and New Year's parties, but they were more rushed affairs, never with the desultory pace of my first trip with them. Occasionally I flew down from Paris, where I was living, with the man I married. My parents returned countless times to Morocco until King Hassan II died in Rabat in 1999. They had seen everything by then and still had never seen enough. My mother shot rolls and rolls of film on her voyages there, but it was only during that first, perfect visit that she documented me with such persistence, as if she suspected I'd reach for these photos as an anchor thirty years later. Those photographs are aging much slower than we are and in them, I feel not just the presence of the woman who loved me. More intensely, I sense a woman I knew, someone exactly the age I am now, who was tackling her hard-earned freedom with wonder, openness, and a sense of abandon. She hurled herself upon the big, open landscape of Morocco and found her place in the world.

Twenty-five years passed since she had first landed in Casablanca, and she was well into her seventies when she realized she wouldn't return. In truth, these cross-ocean voyages were trying, even in first class. Even so, she mourned the end of her travels there with enough grief and nostalgia to make it clear that the sense of loss was for something more than just Morocco and a maybe a decent couscous (something that never quite made its way to Boston).

Then came her decline. It was slow, but inevitable. These days, my mother's sweet little room at her Alzheimer's home is decorated with a few things, now relics, from the souks she roamed so freely. Over the years, she amassed a lot of stuff, most of all carpets that seemed to be delivered to my parents' home with stunning frequency, as if my mother could not resist another tactile remembrance of the place she loved and belonged. There is a small woven basket, a little silver tea pitcher with a long spout. On the wall is a framed menu from one of the king's New Year's parties, engraved with gold and royal blue script, all in French. When I visit her there, I like to chat about her travels to Casablanca, Marrakech, or Fez, as if mention of them might dislodge a secret door to a clear, bright place.

"How many times did you go, about a hundred?" I ask.

"That first trip with you and Dad was one of the best times of my life. Remember how happy you were to show me the Jemaa el Fna?" I ask.

"There must have been a million roses in those bouquets at the Mamounia," I say.

"I hated the bones in pigeon pie," I say. "Didn't you?"

Last time I went to see her, I brought a photograph. It's impossible to know what an Alzheimer's patient is seeing, and least of all remembering. "My favorite picture of me ever is from Morocco," I say. "You took it."

I open my purse and remove an envelope, which contains the shot of me on that great open terrace, under brilliant slice of sky with the clay slopes behind me. Like all the others from that year, the picture is tinged a slight rusty brown.

She looks at it. "Yes," she says.

"You can't see yourself, but you are there," I say.

She nods.

"You took this picture. You were wearing a gray flare skirt, a navy short-sleeved blouse, and little blue flats that day."

She stares.

"In this picture, I am looking at you. You are younger and you are beautiful. You are my age, the age I am now. And you are looking at me," I say.

She stares.

"I am Marcia, your youngest daughter, and you showed me Morocco."

She tilts her head.

"Here," I say. "This is me, and I'm looking right at you."

She turns her face to me. Her hair is unruly, and though she is usually tidy, there are drops of soup on her sweater. She grasps my hand. Her skin is smooth and her touch is feathery, like the drape of a filmy scarf.

"Except I have no idea where this is. Near Marrakech? I just don't remember," I laugh.

She fixates on the photo again.

"Do you know where this is?" I ask. "You know Morocco better than anyone."

She turns her face up to me and a smile unfolds like a handkerchief across her face. The gray creases brighten, her mouth unfreezes, her whole aspect alters in a millisecond from moribund to dewy and bright. Her eyes a shattering blue.

"Yes!" she shouts, startling me. She shakes her head vigorously as if to say, "Of course I do!" My mother takes the photograph from my hand, sets it on the table beside her and closes her eyes. Her lips are still turned upward in a smile, but within seconds her face is glazed with tears. I reach over her and take the photograph, slip it back into the envelope.

She grasps my hand again and squeezes gently. Her fingers graze mine with a light sound, soft as the rustle of mimosa blossoms, yellow as the morning, on a warm night in Marrakech.

❧ ❧ ❧

Marcia DeSanctis is a New York Times *bestselling author of* 100 Places In France Every Woman Should Go. *She is a former television news producer who has worked for Barbara Walters, ABC, CBS, and NBC News. Her work has appeared in numerous publications including* Vogue, Marie Claire, Town & Country, O the Oprah Magazine, National Geographic Traveler, More, Tin House, *and* The New York Times. *Her travel essays have been widely anthologized, including four consecutive years in* Best Woman's Travel Writing *and* Best Travel Writing *volumes. She is the recipient of four Lowell*

Thomas Awards for excellence in travel journalism, including Travel Journalist of the Year in 2012 for her essays from Rwanda, Russia, Haiti and France, and two Solas Awards for Best Travel Writing. She grew up in Winchester, Massachusetts and holds a degree from Princeton University in Slavic Languages and Literature as well as a Masters in International Relations from the Fletcher School of Law and Diplomacy. She lives in Bethlehem year-round with her husband, sculptor Mark Mennin, and her two children Ray, 19 and Ava, 16.

MICHAEL SANO

❧ ❧ ❧

Honey Colored Lies

Secrets surround a romance between a visitor
and local in the mountains of Nicaragua.

The music at the *discoteca* is so loud that I have to shout
to be heard. I'm nodding my head, pretending to listen to one of my co-workers, while searching the green slices
of light on the dance floor for a particular pair of calves. We
are sitting around a group of white plastic tables taking turns
on the concrete *pista de baile*. The tabletops buzz with each
beat of the bass causing a mob of empty bottles to clamor out
its own shaky melodies. One fall could bring the whole clan
down.

A hand lands on my shoulder and I stretch my neck back
to meet his eyes but he's not looking at me. His fingers tighten
on my muscles as he reaches with his other hand for one of my
female co-workers. They sweep onto the dance floor and disappear among the sweaty midriffs undulating to the tempos
of *reggaeton*. I imagine myself out there, watching the rhythm
of his feet, feeling his hand on my hips, his knuckle under
my chin. But he hasn't danced with me all night because he
doesn't dance with me in public. Tonight he spins my co-
worker and sidesteps her thighs. I salsa with his friend's sister;
she's good at pretending I'm leading.

When we leave the club to walk back into town, I lag behind the others and he joins me. We walk side-by-side, shoulders touching, fingers and forearms teasing here and there. He talks to me through his touches. As our groups split, I nod my head, motioning for him to stay, to meet me, something. But he backs away with one last look and that coy, familiar turn of his lips.

We met last summer on my first night in Jinotega, a small town in the mountains of Nicaragua. My co-workers and I were walking its dark streets in search of dinner. The air, so thick during the day, runs away at night, up the mountains at the edges of town, leaving a cool emptiness I had not expected. Jinotega's central blocks are lined with cement homes painted in pastels and stenciled over in graffiti that reveals a bit of Nicaraguan politics. The symbols, similar to those from the 1979 Sandanista revolution, looked stamped, like the pretenses of the president, Daniel Ortega. Once a popular war hero, he has grown into a controversial oligarch. My co-worker, Alyson, who had worked here the previous summer, told us about the province as we walked. Its verdant ranges are dotted with coffee *fincas* and stained with the blood of guerrilla warfare.

We rounded a corner and came chest to chest with three young men. Feet scraped to a stop in the dirt. They looked us over. They were completely silent. One of the men held my stare longer than the others. His eyes were the color of honey and in them I saw a longing, an ache familiar to my youth. It was cloying.

Suddenly the air was full of nervous laughter and moving hands. The men embraced Alyson and began to speak to her in sign language. They fluttered their fingers in front of us telling a story on palms, on arms, in the air. They touched Alyson's shoulder lightly when they wanted her attention, taking turns with it. Though I was surprised and impressed with her fluency, their sign language was more expressive than hers; it evoked space and time and ownership. I watched, trying to translate this language I didn't know.

Laughter erupted and the young men's arms flew up in the air. They were spinning in giggles. Alyson's cheeks spread red like berries.

"I meant to say we have to go because we're hungry," she said, grinding her fists in front of her stomach. "But I said we have to go because we're horny." The boys were still laughing as they backed away and waved goodbye. Before they turned, I met the honeyed eyes again. They yearned for recognition, and in that yearning I saw my own reflected. As he faded into the darkness I felt as though I were watching a ghost slip into hiding.

My co-workers and I spent the next few days readying our house, cramming it with plastic furniture and creating walls with sheets. Steel pickaxes and shovels, caked with mud from years past, piled up in the backyard. We assembled wobbly bunk beds and lined them with mattresses stuffed with recycled clothes. Every surface we bleached. On the walls we hung up colorful signs. We killed the ants again and again and again. Then we taped over the holes they streamed from. The trick, we knew, was to convince ourselves this was home. If we believed it, so would the teenagers who were about to arrive and join us.

"In Nicaragua," I often said, "we dig." In Peru they build classrooms, in Ecuador homes for the elderly. The crews in the Caribbean have constructed houses, medical clinics, and community centers. We do some construction in Nicaragua too, but mostly we dig. For almost a decade our organization had been assisting a local NGO install potable water systems in rural communities around Jinotega. Since the end of civil war in 1990, Nicaragua has become one of the most

peaceful nations in the Americas. The coffee production that
has replaced guerilla warfare in Jinotega, however, is a battle
in its own right. Nicaragua struggles to prosper in a global-
ized economy; it is the second poorest country in the Western
hemisphere. The impact our teens have through our work
here is large, but they contribute shovelful by shovelful in
thick, muddy clay-dirt.

On our last night before the teenagers arrived, the three
deaf men came over for dinner. Though we lacked a shared
language, we conversed through the night. The boy with
the honey colored eyes sat next to me. "Willem" he wrote
on a notepad, pointing to it and to his chest. Then he made a
W with three fingers and bounced it under each of his eyes.
When he handed me the pencil I wrote "Miguel." Willem
placed his finger on my name as he gripped my arm. He ran
a hand along his smooth chin, stroking an imaginary beard
and then pointed at me. After he repeated the sequence, I
understood: I had just been given a sign name. Head bobbing
and lips broad, Willem seemed pleased with his baptism.

As we ate I could feel the heat of his leg approaching mine
under the table and then the skin between his sparse hairs as
he pressed his knee into mine, his calf, his thigh. On the table
I moved my hand closer to his, but he backed it away.

A cake came out, the rum disappeared, and when someone
turned the stereo on we all started dancing. My feet pretended
to find a rhythm in the salsa steps and I shook my hips when
the merengue horns blared. I was a bit dizzy by the time we
were saying our goodbyes. As female cheeks were kissed and
male shoulders patted, Willem caught my eye and wandered
outside. I waited a moment and then followed. In the dark,
he pushed me against the wall. His breath was hot and short
as his mouth approached me. He kissed me hard, his lips like
soft fists rapping on mine. He pushed himself into my groin.

And then he was gone.

I saw Willem from time to time after that. On my days off I would find him and we would share a bench in the park, or a computer in the internet cafe. In the coffee shops around town, we drank the local beans. The baristas didn't talk about the coffee; they were unattached to its farming and the profits it brought to the *finca* owners.

Willem showed me the school he went to, where students swarmed in blue-and-white uniforms on the concrete school-yard. The boys kicked old, slightly deflated soccer balls and the girls bickered over small pieces of colored chalk. When we walked the streets at night, he might dare to hold my fingers in his hand for a moment or hang his arm over my shoulder. Sometimes he kissed me in the dark, in shadowy alcoves off the streets. He never invited me into his home.

I learned how to talk to Willem without using my voice. Through writing, lip reading, and body language I told him about dating men in the United States, about coming out to my family. I tried to show him the possibilities that I never knew when I was in the closet. I knew it was different to come out in Nicaragua, more dangerous. I wasn't out in Jinotega either, though I wanted to be.

Our presence here, we told the teenagers, was an opportunity to exchange knowledge, beliefs, customs, all the things that marked our differing cultures, and to learn from one another. The Jinotegans we met were eager to form friendships with us visiting Americans despite the history of a complex, violent relationship with the U.S. It was from the surrounding mountains that Augusto Sandino emerged to lead the Nicaraguan revolution against U.S. occupation in the early twentieth century. The liberty he fought for was short-lived, however, and not long after his victory the U.S installed a dictatorship that would rule the country for generations. Sandino's legacy inspired a similar revolt a half-century later. The 1979 Sandanista movement culminated in the fall of the

Samoza dictatorship and the civil war of the 1980s between the Sandanistas and U.S.-backed Contras. This war divided Jinotega along fractured lines. Citizens of the same towns and members of the same families placed themselves on opposite sides of a gory counterrevolution. Their memories of this time remain mostly silent.

On other topics, our friends were garrulous. I grew comfortable talking with them about a general acceptance of homosexuality where I lived in California, but I was not comfortable sharing the details of my own sexual identity. I got the sense that homosexuality, though not necessarily demonized, was not demonstrated. Men might sleep with other men, much in the same way they might sleep with women who weren't their wives, but they wouldn't talk about it. This silence was part of a cultural contract I was trying to respect. As staff, our organization had asked us to put our own needs aside for the sake of our group's efforts. But I was struggling to maintain my own self-respect in my silence. I tried to make it clear I was gay without saying so. I said I was not interested in a wife or a girlfriend, though I didn't have one. My silence about my sexuality was similar to my silence at church. I would go to mass in Jinotega, even if I wouldn't say the prayers. It was similar to the silence about the blood staining the surrounding mountains.

Sometimes I wanted to tell my own story of transformation, my personal sexual revolution, but how small it seemed, how insignificant the history of one person compared to that of an entire people. It took me a while to realize a religion is nothing without its saints, a war remembered most for its heroes. But, still, I never came out that first year. Each time I left Jinotega between job assignments, I told myself maybe I would come out when I returned. While I traveled in other parts of Nicaragua and neighboring countries, I didn't face the same challenges to coming out, it felt less intrusive to do so.

The first time I left Jinotega, Willem and I exchanged email addresses to stay in touch while I was gone. The only message I tried to send him bounced back with an automatic reply that I didn't understand.

The following year, a few days after our night out at the *discoteca*, I'm at home alone doing some paperwork when I hear a knock at the door. My breath halts for a moment. The staff and volunteers are off at various worksites. I hope it's a friendly neighbor but fear it's the police or a doctor or some other local official bearing bad news about one of the teens. As I rise, the plastic legs of my chair echo a scrape across the cement floor.

When I open the door it's Willem. As I lean in for a hug, he cuts me short with a handshake. Disappointed but not entirely surprised, I take his hand. I hold it like a fragile souvenir. Willem turns his head and makes a motion to someone out of view and a woman walks up beside him. She smiles and sort of bows at me, her dark bangs bouncing over her eyes. I kiss her on both cheeks, a gesture she accepts but does not reciprocate. Her gaze stays lowered. Her fingers are laced in a net across her navel that catches her stare and my stare and Willem's stare as it holds her protruding belly. She's pregnant.

I look back to Willem to ask him who this woman is, but the proud look on his face says it all. White and wobbly, I force a smile, lift my arms and spread them wide like I'm holding my happiness for him high above my head. "*Felicidades,*" I say, though the syllables come out stunted. Shaking my arms in the air I say it again. Then I hug Willem. I hug this woman.

Stepping back, I look at the couple. Her head remains lowered, his high. He winks at me. Then he begins to talk to me with his hands, but I can't understand. To me he's just dancing, just responding to the beats of the street behind him. I try to keep smiling, but all I can think about is shutting the door and retreating to the quiet of my room.

Finally, Willem says goodbye. I hug him and the woman again before I shut the door behind them. Sliding to my room, I lie down and try to take a nap I don't have time for. But I can't fall asleep anyway and so I just lay in the dark, on a lumpy mattress on the floor. I think about lying in my teenage bedroom when I was the same age as the kids I chaperone here. I remember the boy I had a crush on in high school who I would brush against in benign moments, hoping he would notice, hoping he would look back at me in the same way I looked at him. I wanted him tell me my thoughts. He never did, but there was comfort in his silence. I wonder if my silence about my sexuality here in this foreign place, is an imitation of that comfort from my youth.

When I hear someone knock at the door again, I'm not afraid or hopeful I'm just a bit numb. I open the door and see Darling, our cook, and her wide amber eyes. She's here for her regular shift but she looks at me in a way that I want to believe shows she understands that something is wrong. I always joke with her that I'll marry her, that I'll be her grandkids' granddaddy. I call her *jaguara* because I don't know how to say cougar in Spanish. She knows I don't really want a wife, but I've still never told her why in so many words, or anyone else here in Jinotega. They know I'm not interested in the daughters, nieces, and cousins they introduce me to. They know my secret but they don't want me to talk about it, as they don't talk about their own. Willem's wife doesn't want to know about me. She will allow him his secrets as long he keeps them hidden. Perhaps that's why she kept her head bowed at my door.

Darling tries a smile and stands on her tiptoes to kiss my cheek. Instead, I take her in my arms. She pats my back with an awkward hand. I let her go, then hold her fingers in mine for a moment before I let her slip away. I watch her swagger into the kitchen as I sit down to get back to work.

≈ ≈ ≈

Michael Sano is a wanderer and wonderer from San Francisco. He has spent time living and working in Nicaragua, Panama, the Dominican Republic, and Australia. He has traveled throughout Latin America as well as a few other spots around the world. At home, he supports students in their academic endeavors and writes non-fiction and fiction. His work has appeared in RFD Quarterly *and* Around the World *(Harvard Bookstore Press).*

❦ ❦ ❦

Café Tables

A souvenir becomes a symbol of hope.

At the end of my first trip to Paris, I had come to the Place du Tertre to buy a painting. I could not afford this. I'd just finished an MFA in creative writing and financed my trip with my student loan. But intuition told me that I should not leave Paris without a piece of artwork. I didn't realize then that I would buy something more significant than any souvenir could be. Something I would have paid any price for: hope.

I walked around the *carré aux artistes* twice, dismayed by the caricaturists and the cookie-cutter pictures of Notre Dame and the Eiffel Tower. My flight back to Pennsylvania left in eight hours and a dispiriting panic set in. Not wanting to give up, I made one final lap around the square.

To this day, I believe I conjured that oil painting wedged between two larger canvases. I'm not sure how I missed it before. It was a café scene, and I knew instantly this was the artist I'd hoped to find. I do the majority of my writing in cafés and have always thought of them as sacred spaces, portals to that meditative space where words I never expected flow into my head and shape narratives that help me make sense of the world.

This artist used splashes of color: scarlet and persimmon, cobalt and jade, everything infused with luminous patches that bordered on being abstract. Only under scrutiny did you notice people and tiny tables. In the foreground of one I liked, two ghost-like figures sat together, one in shades of blue, the other in greens and rust. Their small round table glowed yellow, as if with possibility itself. It reminded me of the dreamy blur that cafés can become when I'm in the midst of creating.

I thumbed through the other paintings. *"Vous êtes l'artiste?"* I asked the woman sitting nearby, wanting to know if she had painted them. A petite woman in her forties, she had dark hair and pale skin and a pursed-lip look of persistence.

"Oui," she said.

I thought about how to best phrase that I liked her work. *"Ils sont très beaux,"* I said, then realized that the word for painting is feminine and I should have said *elles sont très belles.* Despite seven years of French and my strong desire to converse easily, my travels had showed me that I was only useful in restaurants and train stations. Every other encounter quickly stymied me. As a Francophile, struggling with the language left me feeling like I was dishonoring France. As a writer, not being able to find the right words was one of the most troubling fates I could imagine.

"Combien?" I asked pointing to a painting. The woman rattled off the price and I tried to quickly translate the number in my head then convert francs into dollars. About $125, I figured. A splurge, but at nearly twenty by fourteen inches, it was far bigger than I ever dreamed I'd be able to buy.

I narrowed it down to two cafe scenes, the one in blue and another, predominantly red.

"Entre les deux . . ." I pointed from one to another, *"laquelle préférez-vous?"* She looked at the paintings and I held my breath, hoping I'd spoken correctly. She pointed to the blue one.

"*Pourquoi?*" I asked.

It didn't matter that I couldn't understand her explanation. For the first time my entire trip, I was having a conversation that didn't involve the words croissant or le train. It felt momentous. Like I belonged in Paris. This feeling lasted until I asked "*Carte de crédit?*" which prompted a series of sentences and gestures toward a nearby establishment.

"*Vous comprenez?*" she asked.

The only part I understood was "*vous comprenez?*" but I smiled and nodded like a dumbstruck fool until she led me toward a storefront then pantomimed the process as she repeated herself. Finally, I understood, though I had misheard the price. It was $250. I flushed, too embarrassed to admit it was beyond my budget. It was art, I consoled myself. It would appreciate, right?

The transaction complete, she led me up a tall, narrow staircase to an apartment overlooking the square where she'd wrap my souvenir for the journey home. Paintings leaned against the walls in thick stacks. Other canvases hung on a clothesline. She gave me a postcard showing a different café scene and her name on the back. Catherine. I stood enthralled by her productivity. I hadn't yet published any stories, and though I had finished a draft of my novel, it was still in need of much revision. This was what I wanted: evidence of my creativity, finished and ready for the world to see.

When I returned home, I had the painting framed and settled into my post-grad life as a writer and lecturer. But within three months, I slipped into a severe depression that left me unable to write creatively for what would turn out to be five years.

My notebooks during that time catalogue my demise. A typical writing session of ten pages quickly dwindles to one, mostly the opening three paragraphs of my novel. The same sentences, about a fourteen-year-old girl driving alone at night, with slight modifications. Often, I complain that the cafés were noisy or the tables wobbly. I'd been working in these spaces for years. It was I who'd become disagreeable.

Days when I found it hard to leave the house, I'd sit on my couch and stare at the painting, the smears and bursts of color transforming into shadowy spirits. The whole thing floats on the canvas like a suggestion or a lovely dream. One figure, possibly hooded, watches from the corner. I imagined that spirit as divine inspiration itself and waited for it to find me.

Weeks of not writing at all became months. I moved to Boston and the painting sat boxed while I mustered the energy to unpack. Unwrapping it was a revelation. I remembered the intuition that had led me to Catherine's work. Now, the glowing table in the foreground seemed a message.

I made room in my studio apartment for a similar café table, and I'd sit with my notebook and pen and envision a tide of words rushing forth, my creativity turning incandescent. At most I'd write a couple of paragraphs of stilted sentences before my attention would drift, but at least I was writing.

On difficult days, I'd look at the painting and remember that the enchanted zone I was currently denied access to did indeed exist. It was there for Hemingway, Colette, Picasso, and the long line of artists who had claimed Paris home. And it was there for Catherine, who'd let me glimpse the life of a practicing artist with her apartment overflowing with canvases. *This is how it's done*, she seemed to be saying to me. *You will find your way here.*

Eventually, words did return to me, and fifteen years later, I revisited Paris. By that time, I had published stories, signed with an agent, and begun another novel when my first didn't sell. I had planned this weeklong visit to be a creative retreat to sit in cafés, write, and wander. I also wanted to search for

Catherine. I'd Googled her name over the years and found only one mention, in an online gallery. If she was still on the Place du Tertre, I imagined telling her how she had gotten me through dark times; that when language all but left me, her painting was hope hanging on my wall.

I didn't know then that I had only a fifty-fifty chance of seeing Catherine, if she was even exhibiting. The nearly three hundred artists annually selected to sell their work in the *carré aux artistes* share their one-square-meter spaces and display on alternate days. Even though there's a ten-year waiting list for a spot and some ten million tourists visit the Place du Tertre each year, a part of me hoped Catherine had moved on to more prestigious venues.

As it turned out, Catherine was sitting right where I had left her, though I recognized her painting's saturated palette first. Seeing it gave my heart a lift, as if something significant was about to happen.

But Catherine herself shocked me. Her hair and skin had the thinness of a woman in her seventies. Had I really misjudged her age before, or had time not been kind to her? She wore a brown plaid blazer and buff-colored Oxfords, the androgynous style popular with Parisians. There was none of the pertness that I remembered. Sitting with her chin on her hands, her eyes cast down, she looked bored. Like she had nowhere else to go.

I considered how to address her, suddenly aware that I had not taken a picture of her painting hanging on my wall. It would have been so easy to show her and say, look, I bought that. Fifteen years ago. I look at it every day.

Finally, I approached Catherine, exchanged a simple *bonjour*, and leafed through her paintings. These were slightly more abstract, depicting the arches of doorways and hints of buildings, instead of cafés. I glanced at her twice, wanting her to recognize a kindred artistic soul. But Catherine didn't look up. I leafed through her work a second time, trying to form the words that would tell her what a profound effect she'd had on my life.

But I couldn't remember how to say fifteen years ago— *il y a quinze ans? Ça fait quinze ans? Depuis* something? Why hadn't I planned out what I would say?

I wanted to ask about the changes in her art and whether she still painted cafés, what work lined her apartment walls. But I couldn't force words out of my mouth. I was too aware that my bumbling French would never convey all I wanted to say. And I wouldn't understand her response anyway.

I also couldn't shake the fact of Catherine, old and tired, sitting in that same spot on the Place du Tertre. In retrospect, I think I feared hearing weariness in her voice, when I needed to know that all the time I clung to her hope, all the time I spent waiting to be surprised again by words, hasn't been in vain. That the result of a creative life is a feeling of satisfaction and fulfillment, not despair.

We owe it to artists to tell them when they've touched us, but I can only imagine what it would have meant to Catherine. I wish I'd had the courage to tell her in my imperfect French. All I have now is the next best thing: honoring Catherine by using the very language her painting ensured me I'd find my way back to.

❧ ❧ ❧

Amy Marcott writes fiction and nonfiction, and her work has appeared in Salt Hill, DIAGRAM, Necessary Fiction, Memorious, Juked, *and elsewhere. Her prose has been nominated for a Pushcart Prize and been awarded in* Glimmer Train's *Very Short Fiction Contest, among others. She currently resides in the Bay Area, where she's at work on a novel and is a member of the Lit Camp Board of Directors. Read her work at amymarcott.com.*

～～ ～～ ～～

Sister

The ties that bind strongest are often unseen.

Lahssan streams hot tea from an ornate silver pot into a colored glass stuffed with fresh mint leaves and sugar cubes, and sets it on the table.

"This is your last night in Maroc, Sister. What you think?" he asks in accented English, using the French word for Morocco and the name he's called me since we'd met four days earlier.

"I've fallen under the spell," I say. "I love your city of Fez and can't wait to return."

Lahssan's eyebrows press together, so I repeat myself slowly.

His eyes spark with comprehension and a smile spreads across his cheeks as he places a blue and white plate of cookies in front of me, then puts his hand over his heart.

"You are most welcome, Sister," he says.

Dressed in a burgundy-hued *djellaba* and white leather slippers, he shuffles through a doorway and out of sight, leaving me alone in the *riad's* courtyard.

Back home, being called "Sister" by anyone other than my actual brother would have felt as threadbare as someone saying, "Yo, girlfriend!" or "What's up, Bro?" Yet somehow when Lahssan says it, I know it comes from a treasure chest deep inside him where his English words are stored and selectively gifted. Only a week earlier, I'd heard my brother utter the same word. I was lounging on a metal chair in the Tuileries Gardens in Paris when my phone rang. I recognized the number right away, and since I hadn't spoken to my brother in a while, I answered.

"Hey, Rickley!"

"Hey, Sister, how's it going? I hope I'm not bothering you, but I have a few questions about Paris."

"That's *so* weird," I responded. "I'm actually *in* Paris right now."

He feigned surprise, but we both knew it wasn't really so weird. As twins, we were used to such uncanny coincidences.

A favorite movie of ours when we were growing up in the '70s was *Escape to Witch Mountain,* in which a twin brother and sister, Tony and Tia, move things without touching them, and communicate with one another using only the power of their minds. Though we never produced the showstopper twin magic of that movie, we can still look at one another and laugh without saying a word, as if our twinness has an inside joke, and we always seem to reach out to one another at just the right time. He once called me to ask about migraine headaches, not knowing I'd been in bed, thousands of miles away, suffering from one. More recently, I'd locked myself out of my car while out to dinner. Instead of calling a taxi or a roadside service, which I'd normally do, I had the urge to call my brother's cell phone instead. He was working late and driving home, and was only a few blocks from where I was stranded.

In school, friends often asked silly questions like, "Can you read your brother's mind?" or "If I punch you in the arm, will he feel it?" I said no, because it was the truth. At the time, I didn't understand that the motive behind these inquiries was curiosity about the unseen link twins are perceived to have. I never thought much of them either since many siblings boast strong bonds, but as I grew older, it made more sense that twins would have more enigmatic ties. After all, we'd been given a nine-month head start on forming a relationship while sharing a space the size of a watermelon, then set out on parallel paths through childhood and adolescence to endure the same stages and phases at the same time. My brother and I not only share 50 percent of the same DNA and a birthday, but until we were about two we also shared a bedroom, our cribs pressed one against each wall, where my mother says we'd peer at each other through the slats as we fell asleep, talking in our own unintelligible language.

Now here was my brother, a sound effects editor from California, calling to ask me about the noises found in the subway stations of the French capital, where I just happened to be. Fifteen minutes later, I stood in the Metro, holding my phone out as arriving and departing trains pushed and pulled air through the underground tubes, their doors swishing open and thudding closed, then sent my brother the recording.

Lahssan had started calling me Sister the morning I arrived in Fez. I was chatting with Sue, the *riad's* manager, before setting out to explore when Lahssan shouted from an interior balcony overlooking the courtyard.

"Sister, wait. I have something for you."

I nodded O.K., then asked Sue if "Sister" was perhaps a common term young men used to address solo female guests, or foreign women.

"Neither," Sue said. "In fact, I've never heard him call anyone that."

My heart warmed and flickered a little, much like the candles inside the lanterns shimmering in the entryway. I'd been drawn to Lahssan immediately, too. Not in a romantic sense, but with that peculiar pull kindred spirits feel when locking eyes for the first time.

"Sister, take this map," said Lahssan when he finally reached me.

I unfolded it and began to laugh. It was a map of the medina, the walled-in old city of Fez, whose depicted streets took on the form and usefulness of cooked spaghetti noodles dropped onto a piece of paper.

"It's no problem," he said, interpreting my hesitation as confusion.

Lahssan opened the front door and we stepped into the sheltered lane that smelled of damp cement and forgotten daylight.

"You keep walking up," he said, pointing into the medina's maze.

For even the best navigator, the medina is Fez's greatest riddle. When I first saw it, from outside the ancient walls, it looked dehydrated; sun-toasted to a golden hue the color of parchment paper; lifeless and inert. But once I walked through the keyhole gate, Fez awakened.

A melodious mix of colors, sounds, and smells, the medina reinvented itself every day like an enchanted jewelry box that, when wound, produced a dazzling new gem and tune. Men sloshed clothing in plastic buckets overflowing with saffron and indigo dyes, turning the cracks between cobbles into tinted streams. Arabic and French, the two main languages of the medina, picked at either ear as I explored the city's arches and alleyways.

"Balek! Balek!" "Attention!" I pressed myself against a wall as a worn and matted donkey loaded with goods clattered past on gawky legs.

Another day, an incessant clang and ting lured me to a crowded square where metal craftsmen thumped mallets against brass, plying it into lamps, mirrors, cauldrons,

and jewelry from sunrise to stardust. The arrhythmic beat
vibrated the fillings in my teeth and jiggled my eyeballs in
their sockets.

Even in its most static state Fez thrummed, and the only
way to grasp it was to let go and get lost between the stone
walls that have witnessed a couple millennia of history, always
trusting that the path would lead to somewhere. At times I
found myself so deep in the medina that only the slivers of
blue between buildings and the hazy fingers of filtered sunlight through a latticed cover reminded me I was on the surface of the Earth, not below it. Every now and then I pushed
deeper inside, once opening a cracked doorway and following
a dark crevasse until it gave way to a garden where a bench
sat in the shade of a lemon tree drooping with yellow orbs.
I sat there for a few minutes, savoring the silence, a rare flower
in the medina's cacophonic bouquet.

The song "Eye of the Tiger" rolled toward me at another
turn. For an instant, the music carried me back to the summer
of 1982 and Niagara Street in suburban Los Angeles where
my brother and I rode our bikes. We'd just seen the movie
Rocky III and as we pedaled up and down our driveway,
we sang the lyrics and boxed at the air in tune with the song's
opening instrumental salvos. The modern tune was incongruous in the medina, and I searched for its source. It was literally
a hole in a wall, as if a supersized Rocky Balboa himself had
punched his giant fist through the stones. Inside the cave-like
space, a boombox blared next to a thirty-something-year-old
man who, beneath the light of a single bulb, maneuvered a
clacking wooden loom over colorful threads that would eventually become a scarf, a tablecloth, maybe a rug.

There were thousands of shops like this that were nearly
indistinguishable when closed, easily absorbed into the human
routine of disregard. Once opened, they bulged dirt to rafters
with handmade sticky nougat candy, gold jewelry, crockery

and spices, oils, and pointy *babouche* slippers in gumball colors sold by leathery-skinned troubadours telling and selling their histories and heritage. Bargaining was expected, but I was not good at it and paid way too many Moroccan dirhams, I was later told, for the *djellaba* I'd purchased.

"Sister, why didn't you tell me you were shopping? I would have gone with you," Lahssan said when I arrived back at the *riad*, a plastic bag in hand.

"You don't need to do that," I said.

"No," said Lahssan, putting his hand on his heart. "It's my job to help you, Sister."

"*Shukran,*" I said, putting my hand over my heart, too.

Lahssan really didn't need one more job. He lived in a small room on the top floor of the *riad*, which explained why he seemed to be at work day and night, pouring tea, hauling luggage up and down the steep stairs, serving warm bread and jam each morning and dinner to guests who decided to dine in each night. Even so, he still found time to leave extra candles in my cubbyhole room one evening, which I'd never asked for, though admittedly I had been thinking about the extra light.

I sit alone in the *riad's* courtyard, the sugar from the freshly poured mint tea sticking to my teeth and coating my tongue. I hear the muezzin's tinny call to prayer pour in through the open ceiling. It's bellowed five times a day from the mosques and minarets that pierce the sky over the medina and it trickles down the blue and green Moorish tiles that encrust the *riad's* walls and floors. I let it finish, making a mental note to tell Rickley about the evocative sound, then dash up to my room to grab a few things before heading out for the night. On the way back down, I see Lahssan talking to Sue at the bottom of the stairs. Gone are his white leather slippers and the burgundy-colored *djellaba* he was wearing earlier, and in their place are a red and blue soccer jersey, flowing shorts, socks, and sneakers. I sit down on the stairs so we are looking eye to eye and smile, happy to see this boyish side of Lahssan. I ask him what he's up to.

"Playing soccer with my brother," he says, a smile carving its way across his mocha-colored cheeks.

He looks like any American boy back home. In my head I see the picture of my brother in sports clothes that hung in our hallway. Sue interrupts my thoughts.

"Did you know Lahssan has a twin brother?"

Goosebumps prick my skin. I rest my chin in my hands, my elbows on my knees.

"No, I didn't," I say.

Our eyes meet.

"This might surprise you," I say. "But I, too, am a twin. I also have a twin brother."

Lahssan smiles and puts a hand over his heart, a gesture I've come to associate with him.

"Sister, now we are four in our family."

When I return later that night, the candles in the lanterns have been blown out and it's dark beneath the door of Lahssan's room as I pass it on the way to the rooftop where I stare silently out at thousands of staggered, flat-topped houses unfurling in all directions. Fez has existed for more than a thousand years and will likely exist for a thousand more, I think. Suddenly I feel like a solitary speck of a stone in the history of this place, one that will eventually crumble to dust and blow away through a keyhole gate. It makes me think of another question someone once asked me about twins.

"They come into the world together, so I wonder if it is common for them to leave the world at the same time, too?"

I'd dismissed it as another silly question until a few months ago when I was having dinner with my brother and he told me he's always felt as if he'd never live beyond fifty years old—just three years away. Hairs tingled my neck.

"That's *so* weird," I'd replied. "I've never told anyone this, but I've always felt exactly the same way."

We both knew it wasn't so weird.

From the roof, the methodic hymn of the mosques sounds anew, and I imagine all the unseen people below moving about, kneeling, praying; a reminder that in places, as within people, what is essential, much like faith, is also often invisible.

The immensity of all that remains unseen overwhelms me, so I do what I've climbed up here to do. I take out my phone and record the muezzin's haunting call so I can send it to my brother, thousands of miles away, but also, somehow here in Fez with his sister.

૨ઃ ૨ઃ ૨ઃ

Kimberley Lovato is a freelance writer and author based in San Francisco. Her work has appeared in magazines and websites including National Geographic Traveler, American Way, Celebrated Living, BBC Travel, travelandleisure.com, *and many more. Her culinary travel book,* Walnut Wine & Truffle Groves, *was the 2012 recipient of the Lowell Thomas Award book of the year, and her essays have been recognized with Solas Awards and have appeared in* The Best Women's Travel Writing *volumes 8, 9 and 10.* www.kimberleylovato.com

KEVIN MCCAUGHEY

≈ ≈ ≈

An Occurrence
of Nonsense at
N'djili Airport

Sometimes you just have to go for it.

I have heard savvy travel stories in the common rooms of youth hostels and guesthouses. The raconteur tells of his quick thinking in the face of bureaucracy or venality or danger, narrates how he sidestepped a wicked border guard, sliced through red tape, or just had the wherewithal and impeccable timing to pay somebody off: "So I slipped him twenty ducats."

That's not me. In travel, as in daily life, I am much more likely to refuse an extra fee than to arrange one. The only occasions when I have paid dubious fines—and half the time I couldn't tell you if they were bribes, tips, or legitimate transactions—I've done so only after officials have pulled me with embarrassing patience, like a donkey up a stairwell, to that outcome.

I do not know how to outwit officials. I always prefer to *outwait*. That suits my sometimes nervous, sometimes passive, and usually lazy nature (behavior which, sadly, breaks all the rules of good story plotting).

This is to say that I am *not* a savvy traveler.

However, there are moments on the road when I become goofy. It's not a strategy. It's more of a character defect, I think. I can't predict when it will happen, and I can't always explain why. But it happened not long ago in the middle of Africa.

N'djili Airport in the Democratic Republic of Congo was, according to some online forum I had browsed, a cauldron of bureaucratic molestation. Passengers crossed the sun-warmed tarmac from South African Airlines Flight 50 on foot to a terminal painted the color of couscous. But inside, the arrival hall felt darkish. We formed lines and edged past concrete columns, blue to the halfway point and white to the ceiling. Officials with stubble-shaved heads that were beaded with sweat whirred here and there, their underarm musk trailing like a scarf behind. Ahead were wooden kiosks where uniformed women checked passports.

In front of me was a Spanish businessman who'd been coming to Kinshasa for three years. We'd exchanged a few words during the flight. He had his coat folded over his arm, and in his hand was a passport. I noticed the yellow edge of a document protruding from that passport. That yellow thing was an international vaccination card, as any savvy traveler knows. They will also know that a vaccination against yellow fever is required for entry into the DRC.

I often experience, when traveling, a sudden panic that I've lost or am missing something. *Where the hell is my ticket? Where's my passport?* A wash of heat spreads over me. This reptilian-brain stress-out lasts anywhere from a few seconds to a few minutes—until I discover my passport or tickets in the outside pocket of my shoulder bag or in the pages of a book I'm reading. It's a weird self-induced panic, when the body physically creates a worse-case scenario based not on evidence, but on doubt, uncertainty, and fear.

On this day in Kinshasa there was no doubt. There was no uncertainty. I had an International Vaccination Card with evidence of inoculation against yellow fever, and I knew exactly where it was.

It was in the top drawer of my desk. My desk was in the school where I taught English in Kuils Rivier, a town not far from Cape Town, South Africa.

The oozy warmth spread from my face and neck down my back, moving the same way liquidy oatmeal would, if someone had tipped over a bowl on my head. Sweat followed and gripped at the fabric of my shirt.

In the second most corrupt bureaucracy in Africa, I had just set myself up for a royal screwfest.

"Excuse me," I said, to the Spaniard, who had some experience in Congo. "Do you have an International Vaccination Card?"

"Yes," he said, and showed me. "You must."

"I forgot mine," I said. I wanted a reassuring reply.

"That is not good," he said. And then there was a space of a few seconds, and he repeated, "That's not good."

Someone ahead finished at the arrival kiosk, and we shuffled forward a few steps. Now the Spaniard was standing on a red line painted across the floor. He was next to passport control. Then me.

The Spaniard turned to me and said, "Just be strong." The tone of this was somewhere between warning and advice. "If not, perhaps they will give you the injection here. You do not want an injection here. Be strong," he said again.

I did not have much time to formulate a plan. How should I go about being strong?

Now, the Spaniard moved ahead to the kiosk. A girl of twenty-five took his passport from a half circle cut into the bottom of a pane of glass. For a moment I saw her face— menacing and put out—it takes special training to get this effect from healthy young women—then she lowered her head.

What scared me most was the nurses. They milled about on both sides of the arrivals kiosks, in their white blouses with red epaulettes and neck scarves. They were checking vaccination cards.

I was now at the red line on the floor where the word STOP was painted. The nurse spoke to me in French. I did not reply.

Ignoring isn't a good strategy, but once in a blue moon it works and a problem will just—poof—disappear. I didn't have a better plan.

When the Spaniard moved off, I stepped ahead and pushed my passport through the semi-circle into the window.

The young customs lady spoke in French. The hall was a swirl of sound, heat, smells, and voices. I stopped and pushed my forehead up to the glass.

"Repeat, please," I said in French.

She wanted to know if I was a South African citizen.

"*Non*," I said. "*Americain*." And I pointed through the glass at my passport, which she was holding and on which were printed the words "United States of America."

"Where did you receive this visa?"

"Embassy of the Democratic Republic of Congo, in South Africa. Johannesburg."

She flipped through my pages. There were a lot of them. It was a jumbo passport. She took some time and punched at her keyboard. I straightened to find that I had left the print of my forehead on the window. I refused to look to my right, where the nurse was still hovering.

The passport girl lifted her face, spoke to me through glass and the smudge of my brow.

"You can not receive a visa in South Africa. *C'est impossible*."

This seemed strange. I had a visa. It was there in my passport. Ergo, I *can*. But it would not do to have an attitude. So I kept to the facts.

"I have a visa. It is there."

The nurse was now at my side. "*Votre carte*," she said.

The Spaniard's advice jumped into my head: *Be strong.* I did not know what that meant.

The kiosk girl was talking again. I had to push my ear closer. "Your nationality is *not* South African?" she said, fingering my American passport.

"No, it is American."

"Applicants must apply for visas in their own country. You must apply in America."

No doubt this was terrific advice for some. Less so for Americans at N'djili Airport.

"I applied in South Africa. And I obtained a visa. Here is the visa. In my passport. I am an American."

This information seemed to irritate her, and she stood up and exited the back of the kiosk.

The nurse saw her chance and moved in again: "Your international *carte* of inoculations. Do you have it?"

"Yes."

"Show me."

"One moment. It's on my computer."

"No, you must have a *carte*."

"Yes. I have a *carte*. I have a *scan* of the *carte* on my computer."

"No," she said. "You must have a *carte*."

The customs woman re-entered the kiosk. "Go with him," she said.

Now on my right appeared a blue-uniformed customs officer, my passport in his hand. He fanned it, in a gesture to fellow him. For a moment, my hopes rose as he led me *forward*— inexplicably past the line of kiosks in the direction of baggage claim—and deliverance. But then, just as inexplicably, we looped left to the far wall and around the crowd, crossing back again to end up at a row of small offices, only thirty feet from the kiosk where we'd started. At least we'd lost the nurse.

The office contained several desks and officials, a few passengers and not much else. Everyone was talking to someone. My escort said, "Wait here," and he pointed at a chair facing a desk, then he went away. I sat down in the chair directly across another official, blue-suited and stubble-headed like the rest. But he was older, physically wider, more brooding in expression than the younger ones. He stopped the conversation he was having and looked me over. "What are you doing here?"

Forgive me for interrupting myself, but here is where the story might take a savvy twist:

Here I am in Kinshasa, Congo, facing off with a bureaucrat with beads of sweat on his pate. He wants to know just what I'm doing in a chair at *his* desk.

"Let me explain," I say in excellent French.

I open my wallet. His eyes follow. I remove my Santa Clara County Public Library card, which really, is mostly blue, and doesn't look like anything. But I get my finger on the word *Library*, which he will recognize from the French *librarie*, a book store, and I inform him that I have been sent to Kinshasa to ease the procurement of a shipload of children's books from SCCL, which is a small but esteemed international organization that works indirectly with Livres Sans Frontiers—which I'm sure *monsieur* has heard of—and how I would love to get these books, *tout de suite*, to the noble but needy children of his country.

"Hmmm," he says to me, rising. "This sounds so legitimate, well-arranged, and philanthropic that it would be a shame if we delayed your entrance into our country a moment longer."

He extends his hand.

To be on the safe side, I slip him twenty ducats.

But I had no library card. So back to reality:

"What are you doing here?" the official wanted to know.

"I'm waiting," I said. The closed-ended nature of the questions I'd been getting, coupled with the limitations in my French, necessitated absurdly literal answers.

But the wide man seemed to find this answer acceptable, and he resumed his conversation.

Soon my young official returned and asked me to sign a long form written in very small French print. After looking it over, I determined it to be an admission that despite all regulations and good sense I had premeditatively, with full knowledge that I was an American citizen, obtained a Congolese visa from Congolese diplomatic mission in South Africa. Was I certain about that? No. There could have been hidden confessions of treason and criminality. (It's easy to understand how people can sign things under duress. It had taken me all of five minutes before giving in.) The young official went off with my document and passport.

Not long afterward, a new young official came for me. He was the most chipper I'd encountered. He took me outside the little office, back through the noisy hall and outside into the hot and seeping daytime. He said in English: "What is wrong?"

"I don't know."

And it was true. It was often the case in my travels, despite having visited a hundred countries and lived overseas for ten years, that I often didn't know, that I was often just bewildered.

"Yes," he said. "I see."

We walked away from the terminal directly toward South African Flight 50, on which I'd arrived.

Was it conceivable that some junior official would suddenly escort me back to the plane, without even a whiff of a chance for bribery? In fact, I realized, even though I'd had exchanges with five or six Congolese officials at this point—as brief and tautological as they'd been—not one of them had made the slightest overture that a payment might resolve matters. Nor had they left any obvious pause in negotiations in which I was to explore that avenue. Or if they had, I had completely missed them. No, everyone had for the most part been wandering to and fro in a way that, like worker ants seen from outside the society, appeared to be chaos but must have had some kind of purpose.

"Everything is good," my young man said, practicing his English. I liked that. And I liked the South African plane sitting there. It was comforting. If everything went to pot here at the airport, if they refused my visa, or they demanded to jab me with a needle, I could just refuse, jump ship as it were. O.K., some money would be lost by the agencies sponsoring my week of teacher training in Kinshasa, but governments are accustomed to that. I could be on that plane. In two hours I'd be in Jo'burg. In another two hours I'd be back at my apartment in Cape Town where my Belarusian girlfriend was waiting. Maybe there was even some sherry left in the cupboard.

Everything is good.

Without any conscious understanding of my actions, I put my hand on the young man's shoulder. And since my hand was on his shoulder, I called him "*mon ami*," which I hope did not sound as corny or captious as "my friend" would in English. "Everything is good."

This was not calculated to achieve anything. It was not a play. I didn't know what I was doing. But the stress and uncertainty was gone, replaced by a wonderful apathy. I suddenly didn't care.

My *ami* looked around the tarmac, and then not seeing what we wanted, turned and walked us back to the terminal.

He got my passport from somewhere, guided us to the same kiosk as before, and handed it to the unhappy woman behind the glass. She looked things over, took a stamp, and pounded my passport. And that was that.

Except the nurses hadn't forgotten. Most of the other passengers were gone by now. They were waiting.

"*Votre carte*," the main one said.

I was not nervous in the least. I was happy to fly back home to South Africa if need be.

"*Bonjour mademoiselles! Ne vous inquiétez pas—ma santé c'est extraordinaire.* I have a scan on my computer. I will show you."

"No," she said, shaking her head. Stern.

"Are you sure?" I asked. "It's a nice photo. *Tres beau.*"

"No. *Carte.*"

"I have many photos. You will like them as well."

"No, you pay a fine."

"Ah hah. *Les jeux sont faites.*"

"I will give you a receipt," Mademoiselle Nurse said.

"You really know how to sweeten a deal," I said in English.

The Mademoiselle Nurse took me into a little one desk-office cubicle, three other nurses following us. They offered me a seat at the little desk.

"How much must I pay?" I was already fingering a five-euro note, and putting on an air of magnanimity.

"Fifty dollars."

"And in euros?"

"Forty euros."

"Unacceptable!" I said. "Exchange rate—terrible. *Pas juste. Pas juste.*" Outraged, I slapped my five-euro bill on the desk. "*D'accord. Vous avez gagné. Cinq euros.*" You win. Five euros.

"No," she said, "Fif-ty."

"*Oui, oui,*" I said, "Fifty," and pointed at my fiver.

The nurses were looking at each other and wondering what was wrong with me. Mademoiselle Nurse got out a piece of paper. In large letters she wrote "50."

I leaned forward to examine the figure. "*Exactement!*" I said. And with one finger I tapped at the digit five.

"No, fifty!" She used two fingers to touch *both* of the digits. We went back and forth on this for some seconds until everyone thought I was a complete moron. But they had started to smile about it.

Finally, I produced forty U.S. dollars, which aside from my five euros, was all that I had—visibly at least.

"Fifty!" I said, pointing at it.

"O.K.," she agreed. "Fifty."

She took the forty dollars and wrote up a receipt. She even returned my five-euro note. Everyone seemed happy.

Mademoiselle Nurse gave me her email address. I took her photo, we said our goodbyes, and I entered the Democratic Republic of Congo.

≈ ≈ ≈

Kevin McCaughey is a traveling teacher-trainer. He began wandering a week after his eighteenth birthday, alone and shy in Europe. Since then he's been to more than one hundred countries.

AMBER PAULEN

❧ ❧ ❧

The Spinster of Atrani

Life stories from the old can change
the direction of life for the young.

S omeone called my name and a figure came toward
me—a shadow against the yellow lamplight of the road,
and beyond that, of Atrani. It surprised me that someone knew
me. I had been in the small town for only three hours and spent
most of that time sitting in a damp cove where hearts and ini-
tials were etched into stone, watching the gray sky become
night and the sea turn black and shimmery.

It was a midwinter evening obscured by loneliness, as the
clouds earlier had obscured the blue of afternoon. But what
could be done about loneliness? I had left my family, friends,
and country with the finality of a one-way ticket. I was
twenty-two and thought I could take on anything. After five
months of lugging a backpack through Europe, I should have
been buoyed up by my independence.

Yet here I was feeling sorry for myself, upset that my
efforts to see my ex-boyfriend in Rome had proven fruitless.
I told myself I wanted to see him because I needed a break
from the anonymity of traveling alone, a conversation with
a familiar person. But he hadn't replied to my email during
the five days I was in Rome, so I traveled south. The only

plan I had made before traveling was that there was no plan; where I went, what I did, was guided by my whims and desires, precarious things.

As I crossed the road, I saw that the figure was Bernard, the talkative painter who lived alone up the mountain in Ravello: the guy I had met on the bus.

"This is great!" Bernard exclaimed when I stood before him, his curly russet hair filled with light. "I just left Grosdana's to find you. She wants to meet you. She agreed. You can stay at her place." Bernard took off walking and I followed. "I had a feeling you would be on the beach and I think you'll really like Grosdana. She's a superb woman. Su-*perb*!"

I kept pace with Bernard, under the brick arches, through the empty piazza, as I had done earlier that day when we got off the bus together and he led me to the hostel. He had told me not to stay at the hostel but with a friend of his who needed money. I hadn't expected anything to come of the imperative, but now we were standing at Grosdana's door. Above the apartment, its neighbors ascended the steep hill like a picture on a postcard of the Amalfi Coast. Bernard rapped, and light from the open doorway poured around the shape of a woman. "Bernard? You're back. And Amber? Come in."

A heavy green shawl hugged Grosdana's shoulders. Her hennaed hair sprang on end. She walked deliberately to a long couch that consumed most of her studio apartment and lowered herself onto the cushions, which seemed to absorb her on contact. I sat next to her. Under the lamp, gold veins glinted in Grosdana's ash-green eyes, tired and alive. She pulled a cigarette from a light blue pack labeled *Ms* and offered me one. Bernard sat on my other side, his hands gripping his knees, bouncing.

"Bernard says you're staying at the hostel," she said and lit her cigarette. She passed me the lighter, then leaned against the couch's bolster. As I would learn, Grosdana's every action was mirrored by inaction.

"Yes." The hostel had white walls and a long row of empty beds. It was part of what had driven me out to the beach in such a gloomy, lonely mood.

"Who owns that? Ah, yes, the Guarellis? Right, Bernard? I don't trust them completely. They're charging you more than it's worth, I think. Stay here with me for a week for one hundred euros. A good price for Atrani in the winter."

I agreed. But it wasn't up to me, I knew; the decision had already been made.

"Come here at eight to pick up the keys. And now, are you hungry? Bernard, stay and talk to Amber while I make pasta."

"That's O.K.," I said. "I was planning on getting a sandwich."

But Grosdana insisted I stay for dinner. I think I gave her the impression that I needed to be cared for: months of eating on a budget had intensified my thinness, and my clothes were frayed and worn. After dinner we three retired to the couch, where she and Bernard filled the apartment with conversation of the war in Croatia, Grosdana's homeland. Their presence and words were blankets I wrapped around myself, a warmth and temporary respite from the effort of moving alone through the world.

The next morning, I left the hostel early and met Grosdana at her door. She handed me a ring of keys and went off to work. When I returned in the evening from exploring Atrani and Amalfi, she was already home. I handed her a 100-euro bill, and with the note balled into her palm she headed across the piazza to the tiny *alimentari*. Grosdana would insist on making me dinner every night of my stay.

Like the night before, once the table had been cleared, we went on Grosdana's lead to the couch. Her studio apartment had no windows and the open room was sparsely decorated with ethnic knickknacks, such as a long-necked wooden woman with breasts that hung from her chest like long goat teats. But her stories filled the space.

Now, I have trouble pulling apart what she said and what I have since imagined.

"I'm a spinster," Grosdana told me. Pleasure animated her aquiline face, sparked a flare of wrinkles around her eyes. "Which means I can do whatever I want, whenever I please." A cigarette vacillated between her mouth and the ashtray. Occasionally, Grosdana's soliloquy would suffer a fit of interminable coughing, followed by a minute of silence as her breath came back. I waited in silence.

"The old men of Atrani think I'm crazy to live alone and they tell me. A few have asked, 'How can you possibly live without a man?' And as they talk, I watch their fake teeth bumping in their gums. I laugh at them and ask back, 'What can you offer a woman at your age?' They think a woman's happiness depends on a man. Ha! I tell them, 'I'm happier alone than stuck with a wrinkled prune like you.' I don't mind them thinking I'm a little crazy. Their wives aren't any happier than me.

"The longer a woman is alone the longer she'll be alone. You see, I can never live with a man again. Imagine, if along came an old prune! Maybe, if we lived in separate houses and he provided for himself, cooked his own dinners and if he had money. Money would be good. The problem with old people is they get stuck thinking people need to be one way. They're so rigid. And me too! I don't have patience for men anymore. Men are like children, wanting to be taken care of, and that's part of why I never married.

"I was with a man for many years though. I was in love with him. We had a son. When you are in love, then you'll do anything for a man, even pretend to be someone you're not and that's fine, but be careful. How you are in the beginning creates a habit in the relationship. Then, years later, the man still expects you to be like you were—and that, of course, goes for your expectations of him, too.

"When this man and I were living together, I liked to read in bed. One night, when the man came to bed, he asked me to put down my book, turn and pay attention to him. He wanted to make love but I wanted to keep reading. Then he closed my book.

"We fought and I knew then that the relationship wouldn't last, that I would leave. I didn't think he would be that kind of a man. And eventually I left.

"I've never put down my book for a man. I have friends who set down their books when they are asked, and these women have nothing for themselves. Their husbands are uninterested, their children grown and gone. You can only give so much until there's nothing left. When these women are alone they don't know how to be alone, they know nothing about themselves. It's as if they throw out their person when they set down their book.

"Remember what I tell you, so if you find yourself in a similar situation you can think, 'This is what the old spinster in Atrani told me!' Remember, a woman experiences herself as a person first and then as a woman. Whereas men think a woman is first a woman and second a person. It feels good to be a woman, but no woman wants to be a woman all the time. Many women are married to a life that only supports one half. I hope this will change."

The soft mattress of Grosdana's bed was unlike any I had slept on in the hostels; the downy pillows and comforter surrounded me as I stayed up to read and write in my journal. Her heavy breathing from the couch downstairs deepened into snoring that sounded like a chainsaw cutting through the apartment. I supposed, because I was paying, this bed was mine, but I didn't feel I deserved it. Grosdana's experiences towered over me. Against the wishes of her family, she had left Croatia when she was young, had adventures, and regretted nothing. And here she lived alone in the twilight of life, not indulging in loneliness or debilitating self-pity.

Grosdana's experiences had created a towpath through long grasses. Not even in books had I come across a character, a female character, I could hold up as an example, who had journeyed away from home as I had, tossing away family expectations like the maps of cities already traveled. Before I told my family I was leaving the country, I had dropped out of university so I could save money for my journey—first one shock and then the other. I drew strength from Grosdana, and I think she sensed it.

Grosdana's life was replete with domesticities and rituals that bound it together. Today, as she had done every morning, she made Turkish coffee and served it in porcelain cups so thin that the light shone through like lace. She said: "Don't think during your first cigarette and coffee. The best way to start the day is with an empty mind."

When only a sludge of coffee grounds remained at the bottom of her cup, Grosdana bemoaned the climb up the steep hill to the hotel—owned by a friend—where she worked. I lingered at the kitchen table after she left, but without her the apartment was lifeless.

I went out, taking the path to the right. It ascended back and forth past the stacked white houses of Atrani, arched over a ridge and finished down the hill in Amalfi. At the top of the ridge the wind blew in from the sea and I leaned my elbows on the low wall overlooking it. Wind played with my hair and I held it down. At the bottom of the hill, I passed through Amalfi and its shop displays of bottles of bright yellow limoncello, to the trails that led me up through the Lattari Mountains.

Grosdana never asked what I did with my days on the coast in the off-season, but if she had, I wouldn't have known what to tell her. I sat in the sun when it shone or walked in the forest that climbed the cliffs of the coast. I sought unobstructed vistas where the cloudy sky and gray Mediterranean were a blurry, two-toned painting, the horizon barely a line.

I thought about where to go next. I was supposed to leave Grosdana's in three days. My ex had finally emailed me, inviting me back to Rome, and I turned over the idea. If I went back to Rome, it would be the first time I saw him since our relationship had ended in the States.

Part of me wanted to know if he still liked me. Part of me wanted some familiar conversation. And another part of me wondered if I could keep on going without it.

In the evening, I returned to find the aroma of bread baking filled the windowless studio. Grosdana was sitting at the table smoking when I opened the door, nothing before her but an ashtray, a distant look in her eyes. At first I thought I had interrupted her, absorbed in the practice of one of her maxims, but she smiled warmly and stood, pushing back her chair. "Just in time," she said. "Let's check if the bread is ready."

For dinner we ate pieces from the tan wreath of bread. Its soft texture was broken up by toasted hazelnuts, and the butter I spread on melted immediately. The outside was a perfect layer of crust. As I ate, I asked for the recipe.

Grosdana's eyes betrayed pleasure while she continued to chew. "I thought you would like it. I'll show you how to make it," she said. "The best part about this bread is it's cheap. And if you add nuts or olives or whatever you like, it tastes different every time."

On my last day in Atrani, in the narrow hall that was Grosdana's kitchen, she taught me how to make her spinster's bread. I had decided I would go back to Naples for the night, call my ex and then probably catch the train to Rome. After she had deftly kneaded the lump of dough, Grosdana peeled off the scales it left between her fingers and brusquely rubbed them together under warm water. She dampened a tea towel and draped it over the pallid ball. "Now, leave it to rise in some warm place," she said.

We waited on the couch for the bread to rise and, later, to bake. Grosdana lit a cigarette and, leaning back into the couch, picked up her monologue from the previous nights. "I've been thinking again about the man I was telling you about. I almost married him. When I first met him I never thought he would get so upset over my reading in bed.

"When we were first in love, he invited me to go with him on a business trip to Tunisia. He went a few days earlier than me. During our days apart, I had the most intense daydreams, him and me in a foreign country, palm trees, exotic foods, a luxurious hotel room, the clothes I would wear, the sleepiness his eyes got after making love, how we would walk hand-in-hand through the dusty streets."

Grosdana's laugh shook her body and lit the gold in her eyes. "Sometimes it's like these things happened to me in another life, like I was another person. As I tell you about them, the time doesn't seem so far past. I can picture everything so clearly. When you're my age, you'll see.

"Life is a mystery," she added. Her voice had dropped in sudden seriousness.

"When I stepped off the plane in Tunis I entered my dream. As I rode in the taxi to the hotel it was as if I were drunk on the strange city. From the windows, I saw men dressed in traditional robes, the deep blue of the doorways and shutters. I smelled street food and spices mixed with dust.

"The taxi stopped at our hotel. While it waited before the big glass doors, I was to get ready for dinner and even though

I knew it was waiting, I took my time. In front of the full-length mirror, I changed into one of the most beautiful dresses I've ever owned. Long and black, it caught the littlest light and shimmered. I prepared myself slowly. It's good to leave a man waiting, to build his anticipation.

"The taxi driver opened the car door for me and as I stepped into it I became nervous for the first time. But as we drove through Tunis's streets, through the blur of city lights, my nervousness left me. I opened the window and let in the warm, fresh air. I was being driven through a foreign city, wearing a beautiful dress, going to see the man I loved. I don't know what happened to me during that moment, but it was as if everything was perfect and right, beautiful in a way I cannot explain. I fell in love with the country.

"At the restaurant, nothing was what I expected. The man put his arms around me and kissed me, but not with the passion I had imagined. I had completely forgotten about his business partners. After introductions, my lover pulled out my chair where I sat and we ate dinner as the men had a boring conversation. The best parts of the trip were the taxi rides through Tunis, when I had been alone.

"Of course, the man couldn't be who I wanted him to be. I was smart to fall in love with Tunisia. Since that trip I have gone back many times. Have you ever been to Tunisia?"

I shook my head and told her I had never thought about going to Tunisia. But as she talked about the country and showed me the things she had bought there, the pastel tunics and the pail of blue paint, my curiosity was piqued.

"You must go if only for the color blue. It's the most beautiful blue I have ever seen. In a city not far from Tunis, Sidi Bou Saïd, there are whitewashed houses with doors and windows painted this blue. You must go there. I don't have many years left, but I want to live some of them in Sidi Bou Saïd. I am drawn there. Some days I think of nothing else."

Grosdana stubbed out her last cigarette of the night and pushed herself off the couch to get ready for bed. I remained there until she was done, picturing a Tunisia where villages looked almost Greek, scattered between the desert and sea.

Early the following morning, I stood on the main road waiting for the bus back to Naples. From Naples I would take the overnight train to Palermo in Sicily, stay a few days, then go to Trapani, where I would catch the ferry to Tunis, as Grosdana had explained over breakfast. In Palermo I could sort out the details online at an internet cafe. Rain fell while I waited for the bus. The only other faces passed alone in their cars. Tires pulled up rips of water, windshield wipers oscillated frantically, and headlights smeared white on the wet pavement.

When the bus came, I tossed my dripping backpack on the floor and rested my head against a steamed window. I felt crazy pushing on like this, going to a continent I knew nothing about. North Africa made Europe seem easy, similar to the States, familiar. I thought of Grosdana and the pride in her voice when she said that word, *crazy*. I felt it, too.

܀ ܀ ܀

Amber Paulen is currently finishing her bachelor's degree in Creative Writing at Columbia University in New York after a fourteen-year break in her education. During that time she lived, traveled, and worked in and out of Europe, and spent nearly a decade in Rome, Italy. "The Spinster of Atrani" was previously published in Front Porch Journal *and nominated for the Push-cart Prize.*

≫ ≫ ≫

Ma Ganga

There are many ways to say good-bye.

Acorpse wrapped in gold foil—lightly balanced on the shoulders of a group of men—jostled past me. Its bare soles bobbed as they disappeared into the dark crowded alley leading down to the river. I stared briefly while skirting the cremation ghats—burning fires and dense smoke—and barely avoided falling on the twisting cobblestones of Varanasi as I caught up to Raju.

"You don't allow women at cremation rituals here in India because you are afraid they might still throw themselves on the fire?" I asked, knowing the old custom of *sati*—widows practicing self-immolation—had been illegal for years.

"Oh, perhaps it started for that reason," Raju replied, politely oblivious to my cynicism, "but now it is part of our culture. Our brothers, fathers, and husbands perform this sacred ritual." Without interrupting his effortless weaving through the crowd, he continued, "And who performed your own good husband's cremation?"

Saved from an immediate response by another jostling corpse, I stopped to watch a skinny, nearly naked black man weighing large pieces of wood for the pyres that were lit hundreds of times daily in this most holy of places.

I was spending several weeks on Ma Ganga—Mother
Ganges—the heart and soul of India's Hindu culture. For
days we floated on small boats covered by old cloth canopies,
each rowed by two young, gently muscled dark-skinned men
wrapped in *lungis*—the six-foot-long cloths that cover, from
the waist down, most Indian men in all but the centers of
large cities. Often the banks of the river were quiet, just oxen
mingling with night herons, an unexpected perspective on
this vibrant land. But during the Sonepur Mela celebration in
Bihar, near the confluence of the Ganges with the Gandak, we
joined over 1 million people bathing in the river at this auspi-
cious moment—the November full moon.

Moments—like snapshots—imprinted themselves:

A small boat floats along a placid channel, the water pale blue,
the sun gentled by constant haze. We—three startlingly white
women—relax against colorful pillows, facing oarsmen who lie
asleep in the prow while the minimal current does their work.
Beneath our idle gaze a group of large black birds—crows or
ravens—alights on a body-shaped floating object.

Smoke on a garbage-strewn rocky bank clears to show three sinewy men cremating a young family member. A brother reaches
quickly into the fire to pull out remaining shards of bone and
throw them in the river. Water is splashed onto the flames in the
final step of the ritual.

Our boats approach the night's campsite—a broad expanse of
sand that forms an island in the low post-monsoon river. I jump
ashore, avoiding a round white object. Our oarsman says it is a
skull, but a fellow traveler laughs and assures me it is an old piece
of styrofoam. Tents are extracted from beneath boards that were
softened by our bed pillows during the trip on the water; dried cow
patties are quickly set on fire for our afternoon tea.

Beneath a quiet alcove a holy man setting up his morning gratitude ritual invites me to sit. In an intensely personal ceremony
he steers my soul to my deceased husband and welcomes him to
the circle of the blessed. I chant along and toss bunches of seeds,
gripped with my thumb and middle two fingers, onto the fire in
time with his rhythm. A sense of peace and a decorated forehead
testifies to my participation in this *puja*.

I walk during the Mela with increasingly dense crowds towards the broad river, lined by cement ghats—the ever-present stepped platforms full of life along Indian waterways. A barber snaps his scissors overhead advertising his availability for a child's first ritual head shaving. This day many parents cannot reach the river for the density of the mob, so bald babies are trustingly passed above the crowd, assuring their dunking before the rising sun flashes on the water. Even in this intense swarm people save a smile for my visibly foreign face.

The Ganges flows for a thousand miles through India, its life-giving force evident all along the way. In death, people aspire to bring their loved ones to sacred spots like Varanasi and Haridwar to assure peace for their souls. Tourists also flock to Varanasi—at sunset the river is full of twenty-passenger boats rowing up and down between the two large cremation ghats, visitors staring in rapt amazement at the fires. The evening religious ceremony there is now performed under glowing neon lights. Seven priests in gold, in a carefully staged performance, swing flames to loudly broadcast chants. Prosperous Indians fill the front sections, and, in spite of the strong tourist presence, it is believers who crowd the banks.

Standing above this melee, I watched a hawker entice a baby with a poodle-shaped balloon—the father too polite to chase him away, the hawker intent on getting the child to demand the toy. The whole scene could fit somewhere between St. Mark's Square and a country carnival.

I headed for the cremation ghats where work continued into the night. Each body is allocated a large amount of hardwood straight from some diminishing forest. The flame is brought from a perpetual fire—lit by Shiva thousands of years ago, they say—and the fee for its use is based on the wealth of the recipient.

The men in the family stay the three to ten hours it takes to complete the cremation, having brought the body on their shoulders through the town. The government, concerned about conservation, has built a sophisticated modern crematorium that sits ignored. People wish their loved ones' ashes to enter Ma Ganga in a traditional manner, and the ceremony is a joyous time in which the soul is freed.

The intensity of India keeps pulling me back, and I feel protective of experiences that touch me in unexpected ways, often dissipating disbelief. When I later share stories of the trip, questions about dead bodies in the river dominate conversation, seconded by awe over the intensity of the cremations and revulsion over the crowding, filth, and chaos. It is in this revulsion that I recognize how far my own perceptions have moved.

My mind returns to that one question, innocently asked by a young Indian in the alleys of Varanasi: "And who performed your own good husband's cremation?" At that moment I was horrified to realize I had no idea. Complete strangers—men—took my husband's body away from my home.

I later received his ashes in a polished wooden urn that I had selected in the sterility of a crematory along the freeway not far from my house. The beautiful small mortuary in the heart of my small town of Healdsburg, California had been torn down and replaced by a lively restaurant. In our society the real estate was simply too valuable to waste on the dead.

The moment I seriously considered the question about Harold's cremation, I saw my world through the eyes of my Indian hosts. Their rituals of death, the normality of corpses and skulls, the belief that a river can ease the passage to the afterlife—these are all ways in which people accept the unacceptable—the loss of a loved one. Our ways might seem as impersonal and foreign to them as dead bodies floating in rivers are unimaginable to us; our horror might be perceived as callously judgmental.

The floating object with black birds on it did in fact turn out to be a dead body—a lost corpse. The styrofoam ball really was a water-smoothed human skull. The boatman who drank river water from his fingers moments after we passed a corpse was vibrantly alive at the end of our trip. My friends ate river fish at our campsite and suffered no ill consequences. I didn't choose to dunk myself in the river but I did fall in and survived unscathed. No one drowned on the packed ghats of the Mela in spite of intense crowding and shoving. And the water and air around Varanasi—subjected to the burning of hundreds of bodies daily—mysteriously has no unpleasant odors.

I could not leave Ma Ganga, unchanged. An old fear of crowds dissipated. Faith and fantasy cohabit with greater ease in my scientific Western mind. Death harmonizes more naturally with life today than it did before those weeks I spent on her, and Harold's spirit roams more freely.

Early one morning at my riverside campsite I watched a holy man appear out of the mist. He roamed alone in a land of a billion people, on his river, oblivious. I carry that scene with me, and the memory helps me walk in serenity. From my low angle I saw him effortlessly walk out onto and over the water. *Of course*, I thought.

᠉᠊ᡱ   ᠉᠊ᡱ   ᠉᠊ᡱ

Tania Amochaev is a writer, traveler, and photographer who loves luxury and ease as much as the next senior citizen but can't resist the next bend in the road, wherever it may lead. On a recent trip in China it led to muddy roads, drivers near tears, conversations without language, and the questionable joy of one more night on a hard floor. You can follow her travels at TaniaAmochaev.com.

❧ ❧ ❧

Speaking in Hats

The language of fashion may be difficult to decipher,
but in Panama, a fashion accessory may be more
difficult to keep on one's head.

After decades of nonreligious life, my churchless streak had been broken. But not for any spontaneous rediscovery of God. Apart from attendance at the occasional wedding or funeral, a humble straw hat was the unlikely force that had finally prodded me to sit in a holy pew.

Years of travel had snapped the brittle fibers at the base of my hat's brim, fiber by fiber, mile by mile. I had just crossed the tiny, leafy plaza in San Francisco, a small town in central-west Panama, when the wind rushing down the nearby continental divide had almost finished off the sombrero I'd purchased in the country on a previous visit. The hat was receiving a rough homecoming. The tears had coalesced into one large frowning gash. With needle and thread in hand, I discovered that the town's house-sized church, with its stone walls blocking the gusts of wind, would serve as a tranquil place to mend my hat.

The only light snuck in from the open doors. The church's architectural details had been carved more than three hundred years ago by converted Amerindians who added details that

reflected their own interpretations of Christianity, including
a varnished, doll-like Virgin Mary dressed up in a fabric robe
and chiffon cloak, her humorless eyes demanding an apology
for my choice of stitching venue.

I was not the only irreverent one. The town's priest had
just left the back of the church with his lively puppy on a
leash, even though a sign had been posted to remind patrons
to refrain from bringing their pets inside. I continued sewing.
Fashion can be a nonverbal method of communication, and
I didn't want to transmit the wrong message about myself.
As I would learn the following week, a Panamanian hat can
speak for its wearer in matters much more diverse than I'd
ever imagined.

I was in the region Panamanians refer to as El Interior, a
stretch of agricultural lands west of the capital, but I was
beginning to think of the area as Hat Country. Two years ago,
I had acquired my flat-brimmed sombrero in the neighboring
province of Coclé, where markets and roadside stands selling hats are almost as widespread as crosses marking tragic
highway deaths.

The most common locally woven hats, known as *sombreros pintados*, have angled brims and appear on waiters, on men
hunched over daily tabloids in the town square, on bar-goers
wearing pressed *guayabera* shirts and spit-shined black shoes.
They outfit residents riding in roofless water taxis, the gusts
of wind somehow unable to yank off the hats, as if the hats
had been woven into the wearers' hair. Hats are painted into
the imagery of murals on the concrete walls of open-air restaurants, worn by grinning models in billboard advertisements for
ready-made sauce packets, even atop fruit vendors at indoor
markets, even though the men were not in want of shade.

I was reminded of the delicious voice of Silvia de Grasse,
one of Panama's renowned singers from the mid-twentieth

century, who immortalized the hat in the song "Sombrero Jipijapa," referring to the type of palm-like plant used to make the straw. The country's proud attraction to an article of apparel, made from locally available palm trees, resembles the likeness of religious devotion. My own devotion to patch up my hat, and the pilgrimage to replace it with another, could be interpreted similarly. Perhaps it was appropriate that I had chosen a house of worship in which to make the repairs.

Panama is not alone in claiming a hat that has transcended fashion to become a piece of wearable culture. The American cowboy hat roams freely between pasture and party as a symbol of style and Western identity. In her book *Fashion and Its Social Agendas: Class, Gender, and Identity in Clothing*, sociologist Dr. Diana Crane reveals that hats hinted at one's social rank in nineteenth-century America and Europe. While hats, such as bowlers, were worn to indicate one's bourgeois standing, they were soon commandeered by other social strata to blur class lines. In El Interior, any past blurring of class lines is complete: the *sombrero pintado* has become a wearable symbol of the region.

But the style of hat I refer to may not be the hat you're imagining. The fabric-banded, fedora-style hat known as the Panama hat, preferred by Hannibal Lecter, Jessica Alba, and rookie gangsters, is made in Ecuador. The Panama hat acquired its misleading name when the hats were seen passing through Panama en route to Europe and the United States. A few know-it-all onlookers (as early as 1834) associated the hat with its transit point, not its country of origin, and the name stuck.

The California Gold Rush cemented the accessory's name in history when Ecuadorian entrepreneurs shipped thousands of their hats to Panama to outfit the gold miners on their journey across the tropical isthmus. At the start of the twentieth century, President Theodore Roosevelt donned a Panama hat during his visit to the Panama Canal's construction site, elevating the accessory from utility to fashion statement. Later in the century, Hollywood icons from Paul Newman to Johnny Depp insured the hat's timelessness.

My sewing job had failed by the time I reached the town of La Pintada, a couple hours further east on the Pan-American Highway, where 5,000 artisans in and around the town weave most of Panama's sombreros. My hat's frowning gash had grown. The hat had lost its style, and perhaps its social acceptability. My wife, also in search of a hat, had joined me in the public minibus on the ride up the pasture-blanketed foothills of Panama's Coclé province. The mountain range's rough peaks poked up as if the horizon had been torn, and the air had grown cool and restless.

The Panamanian *sombrero pintado* took its name from this town, which used to boast the only painted (*pintado*) house in the area a century ago. Since the hats were woven here—and since Panamanians tend to be partial to landmark navigation as opposed to being reliant on street names—the town was named after the house, and the hats after the town. Like any self-respecting Panamanian town, La Pintada is easily navigable owing to its central plaza, complete with requisite gazebo, benches, and manicured grassy area. Fellow passengers on the bus had told me to look for the store run by Reinaldo Quiróz, La Pintada's most famous hat maker.

The living-room-sized store faced the central plaza and was covered with a corrugated aluminum roof. Rows of sombreros—some with dyed black rings, others with dashed weaves, others simply the natural sandy color of dried palm leaves—were attached to cords strung across the walls with clothespins. Quiróz found us inspecting the circular wooden molds onto which the crowns are woven. He had a compact frame but stood up as straight as a pillar, betraying none of the fatigue that might be expected from the monotony of fabricating the same article over the span of a lifetime.

"Hats are part of our culture," Quiróz began when I asked him about the uses of the various hats he offered. Farmers usually buy two hats: a basic sombrero with a coarse weave and a large brim for work in the field; and another, the finer and more costly *sombrero pintado* for daily use.

"Sombreros were made in Panama over two hundred years ago, before the arrival of Ecuadorian Panama hats," Quiróz explained. He unclipped a hat and held it up, spinning it slowly, as if it were a jewel. "A Panamanian sombrero does not have indentations on the crown like an Ecuadorian Panama hat. It is made of woven rings sewn together in a spiral," he said as his finger followed the outline of the brim. He explained that the materials are purely Panamanian: the black rings within the weave get their color from natural dyes used by the Emberá and Wounaan Amerindians of Panama's easternmost jungle provinces.

Near the end of the nineteenth century, the popularity of the Ecuadorian Panama hat threatened to topple the actual Panamanian sombrero industry. "Because of the great demand for Ecuadorian Panama hats," Quiróz explained, "the Panamanian government, around the year 1890, brought in artisans from Ecuador to teach Panamanians how to make the Ecuadorian Panama hat." It was a one-two punch: a foreign product had hijacked Panama's cultural identity, and local artisans were being told to manufacture foreign Ecuadorian hats as a replacement to their own sombreros.

At that time, Panama was still a far-flung and rebellious province of Colombia. But when Panama gained sovereignty in 1903, the artisans, vitalized by their independence, began to teach their pupils how to make *sombreros pintados* instead of Ecuadorian Panama hats. "Thirty years later," Quiróz added, a glowing smirk growing across his face, "classes on the fabrication of *sombreros pintados* were obligatory in the primary schools of the Coclé province."

Panamanians have also discovered that their sombreros offer a versatility that most molded Ecuadorian Panama hats do not, thanks to basic geometry. The *sombrero pintado's* round crown and slightly slanted brim have given Panamanians the ability to change the hat's shape. Since human heads are oval, not round, the act of wearing the round hat distorts the crown, which in turn distorts the brim into a front and back flap. Each flap can be toggled up independently. And not just for vanity. According to Quiróz, the bus drivers and fruit salesmen may be attempting to communicate their current temperament through their sombrero's brim. He began decoding the head-bound language of El Interior by sliding on a *sombrero pintado* in a well-practiced motion and flipping up the front brim. He shook his fists and, while holding back a chuckle at his overemphasis, he said, "This style means that he is looking for a fight." The angled-up accessory did not immediately register with me as an extension of angry posture, but I made a mental note to give such wearers a wide berth.

Both brims up? An economically successful man. The front up and the entire hat tilted back? You would be facing a strong worker, since the extra tilt allows the wearer to wipe the sweat off his forehead. And like any language, this too has its regionalisms. "There are several interpretations from different parts of the country," Quiróz said, flipping up only the front flap. In Coclé, unlike other areas, this wearer may not be ready to throw punches, but instead may be keeping secrets and cannot be trusted. A ladies' man, for example. I surmised that both etymologies could share a common ancestor, one of manly overconfidence.

Any aspiring hat flap interpreter must also consider that wearing only the back flap up holds its own ambiguous pitfall.

"In the Azuero Peninsula, this style means that the wearer is looking for a girlfriend." In Coclé, however, the same style indicates that the wearer is an intellectual. I wondered what confusion might occur if a proudly educated lad from Coclé travels south to the neighboring Azuero Peninsula. How would the women know whether he was displaying the sartorial equivalent of a Facebook relationship status update or harmlessly preparing to bombard them with boring literary references?

Hat-flap etymology has also been known to evolve over time. Many years ago, Quiróz explained, when a man wanted to kiss his girlfriend, he would use his hat to conceal the tender moment. When both flaps were down, more of the action was hidden. Today, wearing both flaps down currently holds a meaning that has morphed from the joy of a sneaky smoocher into a general mood of calmness and agreeability.

I glanced back at my mortally wounded sombrero. With its flat, damaged brim, I knew it was not a real *sombrero pintado*, and thus was unable to articulate mood. Silent as it was, it still had something the *sombrero pintado* lacked: a ring of black and white yarn woven into a repetitive geometric pattern. I asked Quiróz if he knew what it was. He lifted it up and studied it. "This is a weave made in a different part of Coclé. The cotton design is an indigenous motif. It's a newer design." I enjoyed finally discovering that my hat was a newer—yet obscure—cousin of the *sombrero pintado*. But after learning of the latter's influential history, I began trying on several from Quiróz's wall.

My wife, eyeing my torn hat, asked Quiróz what would be the average life expectancy of one of his creations. "Four or five years," he answered, "but if it is worn every day, then less. In Panama, there are people who change their hats every year." I felt marginally better knowing that I was not as obsessed as Panama's fashion slaves.

While the hats with finer weaves—up to $500 for one with
twenty *vueltas* (rings), requiring a month to make—are more
desirable, I opted for a coarser, seven-*vuelta* selection, one
which could accept a makeshift neck strap without causing
weave damage. My wife selected one with an accented pattern of birds. It was one of Quiróz's modern designs, one that
has expanded his clientele base to both sexes. Since his father
started the business decades ago, Quiróz has introduced new
patterns—fifty-nine in all—further shaping the evolution of
the Panamanian sombrero.

In 2011, the Panamanian National Assembly formally
recognized the cultural and economic importance of the hat
by declaring October 19th the Day of the *Sombrero Pintado*.
An annual festival takes place in the town of La Pintada and
includes the participation of weavers from the surrounding
area of Coclé.

While Panamanian hat makers have confidently reinstated
their sartorial heritage in their own country, the misleading
name of the Ecuadorian-made Panama hat is still causing
trouble in Ecuador. In a 2012 article in the *Miami Herald International Edition*, Alba Cabrera of the Ecuadorian Institute of
Intellectual Property remarked, "In Ecuador it is prohibited
to say 'Panama Hat.' Here, it is the Montecristi," referring to
the coastal town that produces many of the finest hats in the
country. When I visited Ecuador in 2006, however, the hat
vendors I'd spoken with still casually referred to their products as Panama hats without any signs of unease.

Several tourism websites and online clothing retailers have
also thrust themselves into the arena of thorny nomenclature by
diplomatically referring to the accessory as the Ecuador Panama hat—but no matter what the hat is named, its popularity
is on the rise. Ecuador's hat makers reported that sales were up
25 percent in 2014 as compared to the previous year. The trend
would have been even steeper if it weren't for the competition

from cheaper, Chinese-made imitations, which some Ecuadorians refer to as "false Panamas"—a term the Panamanian sombrero weavers just might relish as fitting justice. I had taken three steps out of Quiróz's store when the wind made off with my new *sombrero pintado*. It didn't matter how I adjusted the brim—as the intellectual, the agreeable chap, or the belligerent hothead—the gusts tore it off just the same and sent it rolling across La Pintada's manicured square again and again.

Arroz con piña, or rice with pineapple, was the drink of the day at the bakery near the square. I was now in Penonomé, the capital of the Coclé province, about ten miles from La Pintada. I had just returned to the counter for another forty-cent Styrofoam cup of *arroz con piña* when a man in a light yellow *guayabera* and a *sombrero pintado* sat down at an outdoor table with his daughter. The weave on his hat was fine and smooth. Twelve, maybe fifteen *vueltas*. Both front and back flaps were up. He could have been alerting the bakery of his acute business sense. But I was more interested in how the hat stayed on his head, as my scientific side assured me that the upward flaps should provide lift.

I complimented him on his sombrero and asked him if he has had problems with Penonomé's wind, a non-stop gusher of a breeze that gleefully joyrides down the slopes of the nearby mountains and into town. He nodded dismissively. How did he manage to keep it on his head? He probed me for a moment, freezing his pensive eyes on me, and then answered, "It's the correct size."

By that logic, I have never owned a hat of the correct size. I did not let that prevent me from wandering past the town's quiet rows of colonial-era houses, admiring their stained and varnished doors that appeared as if they had just been constructed. The houses were lined up neatly, creating a wind tunnel. I kept one hand on my new hat, and I was mildly disappointed that there was no way to communicate frustration by means of brim manipulation.

My wandering led me to a dead end—the town's cemetery. Many of the above-ground tombs had been adorned with pastel-colored tiles, the same all-purpose tiles one can find covering sidewalks, walls of churches and the floors of Panamanian bakeries, giving the cemetery an unusually welcoming and lively small-town atmosphere. Such a feeling was enhanced when I read the inscriptions and realized that almost everyone in and around Penonomé, both dead and alive, seemed to have one of two surnames, either Quiróz or Arosemena.

I was still carrying my old sombrero in a plastic bag. I couldn't bring myself to throw it in the trash, but I knew I had to rid myself of its needless bulk. Reflecting on the hat's journey and how I had ushered it back to its home country and province, I placed it on an empty plot, somewhere between the tiled tombs of the Quirózes and the Arosemenas. Back to its old stomping grounds.

As I walked back past the row of colonial houses, one of the varnished doors had just opened and a thin young man in his late twenties emerged with a swagger. Nightfall was arriving, and the back flap of his hat was up. Cruising for ladies or signifying readiness for philosophical debate? Or both? Perhaps neither. One thing was certain: his hat was the correct size.

≈ ≈ ≈

Darrin DuFord is arguably the only connoisseur of both wine and slow-cooked jungle rodent. He is the author of Is There a Hole in the Boat? Tales of Travel in Panama without a Car, *silver medalist in the 2007 Lowell Thomas Travel Journalism Awards. He has written food and travel pieces for the* San Francisco Chronicle, BBC Travel, Roads & Kingdoms, Gastronomica, *and* Perceptive Travel, *among others.*

ERIN BYRNE

❧ ❧ ❧

In Vincent's Footsteps

What else except pain and suffering
can we expect if we are not well, you and I?
—Vincent van Gogh, in a letter to
Theo van Gogh, February 1889

What if all you can do is all you can do? Curl up.
Breathe. Exist. Breathe, exist. In. Out.
This was not what was meant to happen here.

During the two years Vincent van Gogh lived in Arles,
1888-1889, the *mistral*—the keening, tree-leaning, untamed
wind of the south of France—pummeled him and gave his
mind what he called *a queer turn.* He fixed his easel in the
ground with iron pegs, tied everything down with ropes,
and let the mistral gust the colors through his body, out of
his hand to the brush, and onto the wobbling canvas. Sometimes, *a very spiteful and whining wind* forced him to lay the
canvas flat on the ground, crouch over it, and work on his
knees.

The wind rattled the shutters in my tiny hotel room in
Hôtel d'Arlatan, each *tat-tat-tat* a nail into my head. I curled
tighter into the fetal position.

The train brought Vincent to this Provençal town. He was full of high hopes of creating an artist's colony. He had fresh plans. A house! Creative inspiration! Friends! He found a house near the train station and called it the Yellow House. Vincent painted a picture of it with supplies his brother Theo had sent from Paris. He would decorate the house with bright paintings and invite specially chosen artist friends to join him. They would all create together in this Artist's Colony of the South.

The air, Vincent wrote to Theo, did him good. One of its effects on me is quite amusing, a single small glass of cognac here goes to my head. His blood was circulating.

The train had spat me out in the underground station with my two suitcases and a bulky carry-on bag. Each seemed to bulge with additional books and boots, every second growing heavier and heavier. I shivered in the cold at the bottom of three flights of stairs, looked up toward the sunlight, hoisted my bags in aching arms, and clomped up, feeling as if a magnet were pulling me from behind.

At the top of the stairs, Bienvenue à Arles. As the seconds ticked by, what I knew about Vincent's life here simultaneously unfolded.

Each day, Vincent emerged from the Yellow House loaded up like a porcupine with sticks, an easel, canvases. He puttered around from site to site, happily painting the different aspects of Arles. I even work right in the middle of the day, in full sun, with no shade at all, out in the wheat fields, and lo and behold, I am as happy as a cicada, he wrote.

He made friends with the postman, Joseph Roulin and his family, and other artists and townspeople. He painted Roulin in his blue uniform with gold trim, thinking the postman looked a bit like Socrates.

Vincent did a self-portrait of himself jauntily setting out, his portable studio on his back, a whimsical likeness in which even his shadow seemed perky.

He painted the Langlois drawbridge; the women gathered on the banks of the river washing clothes appeared to move in rhythm, cheerily chatting away.

He painted people on leisurely promenades and clean still life works of bright pitchers and lemons.

I saw no taxis at the summit of the stairs. It was Sunday. I'd have to drag my burden through the town to my hotel. My map was buried, and I scanned for signs, hauled the carry-on upon my back and rolled/dragged/stopped every few feet. The joints in my fingers hurt, my energy twisted strangely.

There were signs everywhere for The van Gogh Walk: Over there was the park he'd painted so prettily, up ahead was the Arena, a small Roman coliseum, and around that cor-ner was Place du Forum where Vincent had painted the café at night in festive yellow and blue. All the sites were labeled with poster-sized prints of the paintings and little vignettes of Vincent's activities in each spot.

Clusters of van Gogh lovers huddled together reading the placards, ran their hands along the backs of benches, railings, and chairs where Vincent had once existed, and scurried here and there, maps in hand.

I reached the top of a hill near the Arena and the colors of the coliseum, the sky, the trees, and people's clothes ran together in dizzying swaths.

Much later, the youth of the town threw cabbages at Vincent. The people of Arles turned against him and called him "Fou-roux" (redheaded madman). In the end, Vincent was smacked from all sides.

I checked into my hotel and, still oddly achy, went to a hammam where I was slabbed face down on a table. Hands

pummeled my shoulders, squeezed my neck. This was supposed to feel good, but my muscles shrieked, my joints
gnashed together. The grip felt as if the huge hands of Vincent's washerwomen were kneading me to a pulp. I returned
to the hotel and crawled into bed.

If you are coming down with something, it turns out that a
massage can call the illness forth in a rush.

Inside the Yellow House, Vincent covered the whitewashed
walls with paintings of sunflowers, six in all. He carefully
decorated the bedroom for his friend Paul Gauguin, who had
agreed to come, even putting up a painting he'd finished of the
bedroom itself, an asymmetrical picture done from a skewed
perspective. He wrote to Gauguin that he hoped the delight-
ful garden near the house would stimulate his imagination.

> My bony carcass is so full of energy. . . . However clumsy this
> attempt may be, it may show you perhaps that I have been thinking
> of you with great emotion as I have prepared your studio.

Vincent prepared and prepared. He put flowers in vases,
purchased bread and cheese, made the bed carefully.

I'd filled the map of Arles with my own notes ahead of time:
Find the Yellow House. Have a glass of wine and live inside
the painting, Café Terrace on the Place du Forum at Night.
Stand on the banks overlooking the river, near where he
painted Starry Night Over the Rhone. Visit Espace van Gogh.

I had prepared and prepared. Hopes were high.

On Day #1, I'd planned to place my feet, clad in black ballet slippers, directly on the path Vincent had taken through the
park, to sit on a bench and contemplate the life of the artist. I
would visit Espace van Gogh, the hospital where he'd stayed
later, when things went bad, a tall building that I knew had
a courtyard in the middle (which Vincent had painted) with
another bench on which to ponder. Later that evening I would

linger outside on the terrace of the café Vincent had made appear so inviting and cozy, and gaze at the stars in rapt admiration.

That morning, I swung my feet over the side of the bed, and the walls of my hotel room tilted into a trapezoid.

Vertigo. Nausea rose and fell in swells.

Chills, heat rising, teeth chattering, hot, cold, thrashing, still.

My hip joint seeped poison into my side, into my legs, into my back.

All I'd wanted to do this day was to meander through the park and sit quietly in the courtyard at Espace van Gogh, which was right around the corner from my hotel.

I went nowhere. Instead, I was visited with lurid visions in hideous reds and greens, scenes inside the other café Vincent painted, the place he'd lived before moving into the Yellow House, Café de Nuit. A pool table with one harsh light over it, sad, slumped, depressing figures, the painting Vincent had said was the ugliest he'd ever done.

People on The Walk that day were enjoying the café on Place du Forum, but I was in the grip of the other painting, about which Vincent had written, *the café is a place where one can ruin oneself, go mad, or commit a crime.* This place where *"Night Owls" can take refuge if they haven't enough money to pay for lodgings or are too drunk to be taken in anywhere* was not featured on The Walk.

Café de Nuit filled my fever-dreams.

My system had failed me in the most unpredictable, devastating way. Even if I could move, my intestines insisted on my staying. On top of it all, lugging my suitcase had carved a strip of agony from my arm up my shoulder up the side of my neck to my ear.

I was trapped.

Vincent came to Arles convinced that two things were his destiny: to paint and to bring artists together. He had not yet sold a painting, but here he felt as if he sailed on the cusp of his creative powers. He painted an Arlesienne, a woman with delicate, angled features, her chin resting on a slender hand, and a Zoave, an Algerian soldier, who he rendered in vibrant oranges and blues, *a young man with a small face, a bull neck, and the eyes of a tiger.*

Gauguin was the first of the artists to arrive. It was happening, Vincent's destiny was opening. He poured happiness and hope into his work, and kept up a brisk pace, spending hours out in the blazing sun and wind.

Vincent and Paul painted together and often enjoyed vigorous discussions that lasted late into the night. *Sometimes when we finish,* Vincent wrote to Theo, *our minds are as drained as an electric battery after discharge . . . We have been right in the midst of magic . . .*

I had gradually begun to suspect that two things were my own destiny. I had won this trip by writing the winning essay at a conference I attended annually. I'd been first to Rome, of which Arles was a miniature replica. Next I'd gone to Geneva, then to the writing seminar in the Jura, where rich friendship and creative collaboration had increased my certainty that I was destined to travel and to write. This pilgrimage to walk in Vincent's footsteps fulfilled both, and was a dream I'd had since I was a little girl and had first seen an image of van Gogh's *Bedroom.*

All I wished to do on Day #2 was stroll over to Place Lamartine to finally see the Yellow House, but crunched up in bed squinting at my guidebook through a searing headache, I read, to my own stupidity-laced surprise, that it had been destroyed in the World War II bombings of 1944. How had I missed that? That night I'd hoped to gaze at the starry sky from the quai and feel what Vincent had felt as he painted *Starry Night Over the Rhone*, wishing *to express hope by some star.*

Inside this tiny space, seconds crawled to hours, day to starless night. I was alone with no hope of salvaging my time in Arles.

It turns out, Vincent learned, that sawing your ear off with a razor brings madness forth in a rush.

He began having bouts of melancholy and soon he teetered on the edge of psychosis. One evening, Gauguin was strolling through the gardens near the house and Vincent pounced on him, threatening him with a razor. Paul met Vincent's eye and calmed him down, but left to spend the night in a hotel. Vincent hacked off part of his ear and carried it to a nearby brothel, where he plopped it, gloppy and bloody, into the hand of an unsuspecting woman named Rachel.

"Take good care of this," he said, and returned home and crawled into bed. It must have been an excruciating night, for he had severed an artery. His ear burning as if on fire and gushing red onto the pillow, his mind spinning and screeching, his heart broken, Vincent must have willed himself to take each breath, his thin chest puffing out, then caving in. The police found him unconscious there, but there is no picture of blood-stained sheets, of Vincent's pale, tortured expression, or of his hands unable to hold a paintbrush, his immobile feet. He was taken to the hospital, wracked with fear and heartache.

I awoke on Day #3 still feverish, dizzy, and now beginning to feel stabs of anxiety. I gaped at the tropical scene on the curtains. How would I get to my next destination, Aix? (Considering Paul Cézanne's miserable temperament, what the hell was in store for me there?) I had planned to take the train, but could barely shuffle to the window. I picked up my three-inch cloth makeup bag and my finger joints weakly released it to clump to the floor. Equilibrium was almost within reach, I could feel it, but there was no way I could take the train. I phoned a driver.

Vincent, trapped in the hospital, was miserable, wretched. He later wrote to Gauguin, In my mental or nervous fever or

madness—I am not too sure how to put it or what to call it—
my thoughts sailed over many seas.

When he returned home from the hospital, his equilibrium
fluctuated. He experienced moments when he was *twisted
with enthusiasm or madness or prophecy,* but he knew he had
lost Gauguin, and his dreams of the artist's collective and his
life's work were at risk of crashing down upon him. Everything Vincent loved was in turmoil.

Vincent tried to start afresh, but his presence caused uneas-
iness all over Arles. The people filed a joint petition, and the
mayor ordered him locked in an isolation cell in the hospital
for a month while police searched the Yellow House.

By the time he was released, Vincent had come to think
of his madness as a disease and had made plans to stay in an
asylum in nearby Saint-Rémy, but he would not be allowed to
paint outside at first. He'd be imprisoned there, too.

Vincent packed up his things inside the Yellow House, his
studio, *now come to grief.* He had painted and sketched 300
works here in Arles. He wondered whether it was all a losing
battle, this weakness of character. Had it been the drink that
had gone to his head, the sun, the *mistral?* The artistic and
intellectual stimulation of having Gauguin near? How had he
missed the signs?

He wrote to Theo that everything was vague and strange. He
pondered the condition of an artist in nearby Marseilles who had
committed suicide: Vincent didn't think it had been too much
absinthe that caused the man to kill himself, but who knew?

As he left Arles, Vincent was filled with a limb-numbing
remorse. He had failed himself.

A large, solidly built man in shades with a short, trimmed
beard easily tossed my baggage into the trunk of his car.

"*Vous êtes malade? Je suis désolé,*" he crooned, then gestured
to the big car and pointed around the corner up ahead. "*Les*

rues est très petites." The streets were too narrow for the car. We'd have to take the long way out of town.

I slumped in the back seat as the car rolled up the street. On my left was Espace van Gogh, the place Vincent had suffered so.

We passed the hammam where my condition had been unknowingly aggravated.

A thought tugged at me.

We turned the corner and there was a group of people, noses to a placard.

We drove over Pont van Gogh, across the Rhone where I'd missed the starry night because I'd been incapacitated.

A couple stood holding up their map, then the man pointed ahead and they walked in Vincent's footsteps.

It was all I'd wanted to do.

Then I knew.

What if all you can do

is

all

you can do?

Curl up.

Breathe.

Exist.

Breathe, exist.

In.

Out.

This was exactly what was meant to happen here.

❦ ❦ ❦

Erin Byrne writes travel essays, poetry, fiction, and screenplays. Her work has won numerous awards including Grand Prize Solas Awards for Travel Story of the Year, the Reader's Favorite Award, Foreword Reviews Book of the Year Finalist, and an Accolade Award for film. Her writing appears in publications including

Vestoj, Burning the Midnight Oil, Adventures of a Life-time, *and The Best Travel Writing anthologies. She is editor of* Vignettes & Postcards from Paris *and* Vignettes & Postcards from Morocco, *author of* Wings: Gifts of Art, Life, and Travel in France, which won the award for best travel book at the Paris Book Festival, *and writer of* The Storykeeper, *an award-winning film about occupied Paris, made with Dutch filmmaker Rogier Van Beeck Calkoen. Erin is occasional visiting instructor at Shakespeare and Company Bookstore, and teaches on Deep Travel trips. For details, please visit her website: www.e-byrne.com.*

JILL K. ROBINSON

❧ ❧ ❧

War Memories

The past recedes but is always with us.

Motorbikes stacked with baskets of produce and crates of chickens cross in front of the car, causing me to hold my breath as we navigate the route.

My driver doesn't seem concerned.

"Now in Vietnam," he says, "everything under construction." His arm sweeps the horizon as we drive through Da Nang, more than forty years since the end of the American War, as it's called here. It seems every other building is a casino resort in the country's desire to turn the beachside town into a Las Vegas rival. We weave through slow "sticky rice traffic," and are soon zipping along the road to Hoi An, where he assures me things will be different.

Soon, the presence of vehicles on the road is the only clue that we haven't transported back to another time. On either side, emerald rice paddies stretch into the distance, tended by chunky water buffalos with crescent-shaped horns and people wearing *non la* conical hats.

This day trip is a solo journey for me. All my other excursions in Vietnam have been organized by the small luxury cruise ship on which I'm traveling—along with 115 other passengers. Each morning in another port, we meet in the ship's

248

lounge, form groups based on pre-determined tour interests, and board buses that take us deeper into the country.

Among the passengers are a handful of men who have visited Vietnam previously, during the war—although "visit" isn't exactly the description they use. From Marine to Army pilot, all are here to see the country anew, some more enthusiastically than others.

"I think the only reason I'm here," says Chuck Molenda, a former army captain and pilot stationed in Hue Phu Bai who flew an OV-1 Mohawk over Laos and North Vietnam, "is to see if I can find Tia."

He shows me a black-and-white photo he'd taken of a fourteen-year-old Vietnamese girl, and explains that she was the "hooch" girl, who cleaned the tent and Marine jungle hut that he and three other pilots called home for a year.

"Tin roofs, screened sides, and plywood floors," says Chuck. "Pure luxury."

In the photo Tia has a shy smile, and isn't looking directly at the camera. It's as if she was intrigued and yet cautious all at once.

It seems a far distance to travel for someone who might not be the closest of friends. But the war, for many, changed the personal borders they had with others—making them thinner, or even far thicker, than one might have at home. Was Chuck motivated to make the trip because he was always worried for Tia, or did his experiences with the war and their aftermath push his thoughts of Tia's whereabouts to a more comfortable place—until it couldn't stay quiet any longer?

While I'm spending the day in Hoi An, Chuck has hired a driver to take him to a village about a half mile off the end of the runway they used during the war, where he plans to ask residents if they recognize the girl and perhaps know what has become of her.

"I'm prepared to be disappointed," he says. "I know the odds aren't good, and I'm almost sure I won't find her, but if I don't try, I'll be thinking about it for the rest of my life."

Leaning on the railing of the bridge that spans Hoi An's Thu Bon River, I watch fishermen setting their nets while wooden tour boats sit empty along the banks. The boats' painted eyes silently gaze at the Japanese merchant houses, Chinese temples, and souvenir shops with Viet Cong pith helmets and t-shirts exclaiming "Buddha is my Omboy." During the American War, Hoi An, with the cooperation of both sides, remained almost completely undamaged.

The Ancient Town is small—one street running along the Thu Bon with three more streets parallel to the river. They're intersected by smaller streets and alleys, and in a few hours, visitors can cover it all. Detours into the alleys reward me with glimpses of Buddhist altars, scrolled lampposts, families eating breakfast, and women loading baskets of goods for market.

Near one end of the Ancient Town, a Japanese covered bridge emerges from rose-colored walls, linking previous Japanese and Chinese communities. I walk past monkey guardians at one end, before entering a tiny temple built into the bridge. The deep red wood glows under silk lanterns, and smoke curling up from a forest of incense sticks never quite reaches the ceiling before an oscillating fan blows it gently away.

Looking out from the covered bridge, I spy Vietnamese teens in suits and *ao dai* tunics posing for photos near the river. Tourists emerge from shops with new treasures, and backpackers perch on tiny plastic chairs to sample street food prepared in front of their ankles. The fisherman hauls in his net, arranging fish in his boat with painted eyes, and casts the net again.

It's still morning as I walk along the river toward Hoi An's Central Market. My eyes are focused on the ground, to avoid

stepping on the buckets of fish on one side and the baskets
of peppers on the other. I don't see her coming. The light
punch on my shoulder, delivered with an expertly closed fist,
is her only communication. I turn quickly to see a tiny older
woman, with salt-and-pepper hair pulled into a bun underneath a conical hat, scurry away through the market crowd.
Resisting the urge to run after her and ask her motive, I
scan the faces of the market vendors around me. They'd been
quietly observing, and now with my gaze on them, turn back
to their tasks—whether selling cucumbers, lychees, shrimp,
dragonfruit, or the hundreds of other types of merchandise at
the Central Market.

Their disinterest makes it seem as if a tiny elderly woman
is regularly scheduled to punch someone every day at around
this time, like the clock parade at It's a Small World in Dis-
neyland, the changing of the guard at Buckingham Palace, or
even the Bellagio fountains in Las Vegas. I must have missed
important advice if the Hoi An Central Market's punching
lady is merely part of the entertainment.

My growling stomach lures me to a stall with a sign that
advertises "Pho, Cao Lau, Hu Tieu, Kinh Moi," and I take a
seat as I wait for the rich pork broth with light yellow noodles,
slabs of tender pork, bean sprouts and fresh herbs to be ladled
into a bowl.

"She's still mad about the war," the vendor says, handing
me the bowl of *cao lau*, a specialty of Hoi An. "She lost many
people in her family."

"She knows I wasn't here in the war, right?" I ask, wondering just how old I look.

The woman smiles and nods, and as I pull money out of my
pocket to pay, she waves her hand to communicate that this
bowl of *cao lau* is her treat. A minor blow for a bowl of porky
goodness is a fair trade.

I wonder how Chuck is doing with his search, and recall a conversation I had the day before with Geoff, the ship's travel anthropologist, about the likelihood of finding Tia.

"If she made it through the war and is still in the area, which for a number of reasons is unlikely," said Geoff, "the North Vietnamese would have identified her as a sympathizer or even considered her a combatant, and life for her would have been very difficult, to say the least."

He added that for many men who supported the South Vietnamese campaigns (or worked with the United States directly), "reeducation camps" were the norm. Higher-ranking people may have faced forced labor, aggressive treatment, or execution.

"For women, while they may not have been killed directly, it's highly possible they may have been abused at the discretion of the men who found them, in ways unthinkable," said Geoff.

I find myself slowing down as I walk through Hoi An, watching women tend to their daily lives. How many of them had been lucky enough to escape torture and death? How many others had been from the other side? How large would today's population of Hoi An be if there had been no war?

Hoi An extends far beyond the old architecture and shops of Ancient Town. Eager to get a longer look at life outside old Hoi An, I walk past the boundaries to see what most of the tourists are missing.

I find a vendor who sells me a glass of *bia hoi* (fresh beer brewed only in Hoi An) and sip it while watching residents and visitors pass by. The rain falls lightly at first, and then begins to pour. I stand under the vendor's umbrella, and the woman lifts a stack of t-shirts from a chair, motions for me to sit, and then plunks a *non la* hat on my head.

"Wait for rain," she insists, sitting in a chair under the umbrella and miming drinking a beer, so I'll understand.

Traffic stops, and for a moment, it seems that we're in our own timeless cocoon. We take turns offering simply worded observations about passersby as we wait out the rain.

She shows me a stack of old photos—dog-eared sepia-toned remnants of the American War. I flip through the stack to see images of soldiers, villages, beach activities during down time, even simple portraits of Vietnamese people. Every once in a while, I linger on a photo, and she leans over and touches it. Both our hands hold it together as we gaze into the past.

The vendor appears to be in her mid-fifties, around the same age Tia would be today. I wonder how long she's had the photos, and if now they were such a part of her memories that despite the prices she'd penciled on the back, she might have a hard time letting go of them.

We finish looking through the images, and I hand them back to her. She tucks them inside a silk scarf, and then behind the last pile of t-shirts, decidedly not on display, or for sale. Like many things that challenge us, causing both pleasure and pain, placed just out of reach.

When the rain stops, I finish my glass of beer and hand it to her, along with the loaner hat. In return, she tucks a small pink flower behind my ear. Our goodbyes are nearly drowned out by the sound of motorbike traffic, but our smiles are enough to convey the sentiment. I skirt puddles as I head back into modern Vietnam, and eventually to the car that will take me past casinos and resorts. Back to where everything is under construction.

On the ship, I find Chuck sitting in our regular spot—on the deck near the bar. I ask the question that's been on my mind all day.

"No, I didn't find her," he answers. "I didn't think I would, but I'm glad I came."

He looks disappointed, but claims not to be. Once they return to the ship, the other vets check in with Chuck—all with the same question. Some of them ask silently, with raised brows. Others have more questions: "Was she there? How was it? Is it what you remember?"

They linger over memories with their drinks, and I give them some time alone. I wasn't part of their experiences, and feel as it I'm trespassing on their memories. The ship's engines growl, and we slowly pull away from the dock in Da Nang.

I pick the pink flower from behind my ear and turn it over in my fingers for a few minutes before letting it flutter down into the East Vietnam Sea. For Tia, wherever she may be.

๛ ๛ ๛

Jill K. Robinson is a freelance writer and photographer. Her work has appeared in the San Francisco Chronicle, AFAR, National Geographic Traveler, Outside, American Way, Every Day with Rachael Ray, Robb Report, Coastal Living, *Travelers' Tales books (*The Best Travel Writing *and* The Best Women's Travel Writing*) and more. This story will also appear in an upcoming issue of* The Saturday Evening Post. *She still craves* cao lau, *but perhaps without the added punch. Follow her on Twitter @dangerjr.*

❦ ❦ ❦

Breathe In

A last-minute dash into a dodgy looking market leads
to some lasting insights about Italy and its people.

"We won't find anything for dinner here," I whispered
to my wife, Chris. "Look at that pitiful tomato."
I pointed to a solitary, withered blob in a wooden crate
outside the shop. There was little else to suggest the entrance
led to a grocery, other than the word *Alimentari* painted care-
lessly on a weathered board. Shops in Tuscan hill towns usually have colorful outdoor displays to lure customers inside,
but this market tucked into a corner of a sunny piazza had
no alluring bin of flowers or vegetables, no baskets swollen
with panettone or shimmering bottles of limoncello. Only the
slumping tomato and the afterthought of a sign.

"I don't think we have a choice," Chris whispered back.
"It's siesta time and the other place is already closed. We'd
better hurry while this one's still open."

Peering inside, I could barely make out the shop's dark
interior. The sunlight streaming in illuminated a small shelf
of produce along one wall. Opposite the shelf, a bare, incandescent bulb dangled over a narrow counter. A small, battered
ice cream freezer sat in front, emitting a dim, fluorescent glow.

Perched on a stool behind the counter, with arms crossed, sat an elderly, white-haired woman in a threadbare sweater.

We were in Montisi, a village in the Crete Senesi region of Tuscany. It had a single main street that was so narrow in places, even the tiny Piaggio trucks had to maneuver carefully to avoid scraping the walls of adjacent buildings. We were renting an old farmhouse on the outskirts of town. After four days, we had yet to adjust to village siesta time. On several occasions, we had rushed around to shops or cafés only to find them closed. Our tardiness today had put us in a bind. We were leaving the village until evening and needed groceries for dinner. This pathetic little market was our only hope.

Fighting every instinct I had that it was a fool's errand, I stepped across the thick stone threshold into the cave-like room.

"*Buon giorno,*" said the old woman halfheartedly as she shifted on her stool.

I returned her greeting, then glanced furtively around the room, letting my eyes adjust to the dim light. There wasn't much to see; the store's provisions appeared limited to the paltry offering I'd seen from outside.

As I studied the shelf of vegetables, I could feel two pairs of eyes boring into my back like tiny heat lamps: the old woman wondering what could be taking so long, and Chris, willing me to invoke some spell to magically make more produce appear. I disregarded a yellowing cabbage and instead plucked two small potatoes from a box. If nothing else, we could bake them, though I held little hope for scoring a stick of butter.

"You're supposed to let her choose the produce. Remember?"

Chris was referring to the part of *Under the Tuscan Sun* where Frances Mayes learns the etiquette of buying produce at an outdoor market. I should have told the old woman I wanted two potatoes and let her pick them out. I glanced back at her self-consciously. She seemed content to let me help myself.

I grabbed an onion, a bulb of garlic, and a limp bunch of spinach and placed them on the counter. I glanced down through the glass top of the ice cream freezer. It was actually a small dairy case containing milk, cheese and a few other items. I added a carton of milk to my meager supplies. The old woman looked at me with patient eyes, a faint smile hovering lazily in the corners of her mouth. She looked cold and tired. She was probably anxious for siesta: a pot of hot tea then a nap on a sunny terrace, far from this gloomy dungeon.

I peered into the shadowy corners of the shop, searching for some sign of more merchandise. There was another doorway farther back, but it was dark and unpromising. Out of options but still determined, I asked, "*Dove è il pollo* (Where is the chicken)?" I managed to butcher the language and sound plaintive at the same time.

"*Ah, sì,*" she replied, showing a sudden burst of energy.

She hopped off the stool and came around the counter, burbling in a warm, Italian lilt. I couldn't understand what she was saying, but followed dutifully behind her as she walked back through the darkened doorway. She waved an arm in the shadows for a moment, then the tinny sound of a pull chain unleashed a hundred watts of light on a largish room lined with shelves. There were cans of vegetables, loaves of bread, coffee, boxes of crackers and cookies, toilet paper, cleaning supplies, cooking oil. A large freezer occupied the center of the room. The old woman had been sitting in near darkness to conserve electricity. Any local would have known this. Only her clueless American visitor suffered such confusion.

She rummaged around in the freezer, then pulled out a small frying chicken. She held it up high, arching her eyebrows victoriously, and said something indecipherable, perhaps the Italian equivalent of *voilà*.

As she closed the freezer and reached for the light cord, I held up my hand, signaling her to wait.

"*E el vino?*" I asked, hoping to complete this modest feast with a bottle of wine. I stressed the word *vino*, stretched it out, let it dangle expectantly in midair. There was no wine in sight, but I was feeling suddenly lucky. After all, I had just seen a chicken materialize out of thin air.

The woman said nothing, but motioned for me to follow her. We passed through a doorway into another darkened room. Once again, she fished in the air for a pull cord. Once again, the tinny sound yielded bright light, illuminating a room that served as a small *enoteca*. Bottles of local reds lined the shelves: Vino Nobile, Brunello, Dolcetto, and Negro Amaro, as well as wines from nearby regions. Feeling pressed for time, I resisted the urge to study the labels closely. My hand hovered briefly over a Chianti then came to rest on a bottle of Rosso di Montalcino, or Baby Brunello, as it was often called.

"*Oh no, signore, è speciale!*" the old woman said in a deep, somber voice. She was warning me that it wasn't table wine, but rather a more expensive variety reserved for special occasions. We were in Brunello country, but the locals drank simple wines with their meals, usually something lighter made either by themselves or their neighbors. Table wine ran five or six euros. The Baby Brunello was twenty.

"*Va bene* . . . umm . . . *celebrazione,*" I reassured her in my best broken Italian. It was indeed a special occasion. If nothing else, we could celebrate finding enough food for a decent dinner. But we were also in an idyllic place, enjoying a rustic farmhouse that overlooked the vineyards and olive groves of Tuscany. That was reason enough to splurge for a special bottle of wine.

As we walked back toward the front of the store, she patted the frozen chicken, burbling again in her motherly Italian. Though I couldn't really understand what she was saying, I was certain she was advising me about how to cook the chicken. I imagined her saying: *You'll want to rub this with olive oil and salt, then lots of garlic. Then stuff it with bay leaves and lemon wedges. Use lots of rosemary. Don't overcook it now.* When we reached the counter, I glanced back at the two previously dark rooms and shook my head in disbelief. The dingy little grotto we had entered so tenuously was really a sprawling emporium and the listless old woman, a warm and lively surrogate mother.

That evening, after we'd returned from our sightseeing, I rubbed the chicken with coarse salt that I found in our kitchen, then with olive oil that had been pressed from the trees outside. I added a generous dose of crushed rosemary that I'd picked from the bush by the kitchen door.

In a short time, we were sitting down to dinner in the spacious dining room of the old stone house. Other parts of the house could be dark and cold, but the dining room was always bright and cheerful. The double doors to the garden were open and a soft, warm breeze blew in over the rolling hills outside. The smell of roast chicken mingled with that of spring grass and olive trees and pungent sage. The sun was low on the horizon and a rosy-golden hue was spreading across the sky. As we ate our simple meal and sipped our *vino speciale*, I felt a deep sense of gratitude. The food, the wine, and the magnificent landscape had merged into a single, pervasive sensation that provoked all of my senses. It was something to relish, something to savor.

Savor, from the Old French *savorer*, means to taste, but it also means to breathe in. That's what was happening at that moment: I was breathing in everything around me and making indelible recordings of the experience.

We never returned to the little market in the piazza, but I found myself recalling that day at other times during our trip, times when I felt reticent about sampling something or eating in a restaurant that was a bit frayed at the edges. I would picture the kind old woman and the two dark rooms in my mind and remind myself that there is really only one way to experience Italy. Don't doubt. Don't hesitate. Just breathe in. Deeply.

◆ ◆ ◆

Keith Skinner writes fiction, memoir, creative nonfiction, and travel stories. His story "Inside the Tower" about Robinson Jeffers was a 2014 Grand Prize Bronze Solas Award winner. He published the hyper-local blog Berkeley Afoot, and his work has appeared in the San Francisco Chronicle, Berkeleyside, *and* The Woven Tale. *He is currently at work on a historical novel set in nineteenth-century Mendocino County. He lives in Berkeley, California.*

❧ ❧ ❧

Paddling with Marigolds

Death sat on her shoulder reminding her
that everyone is going to die. Even herself.

"We burn the bodies and then float the ashes with
marigolds, the flower of the dead," the owner of
the kayak shop told us as we drove over a river on the shuttle
to the Mahakali River where he'd drop us off for our two-
day expedition. "Nepalese believe in reincarnation—the river
takes us to better place in next life."

"Do the Nepalese consider water holy?" I asked, pressing my head against the window of his Jeep, not wanting to
miss my first glimpse of the Himalayas. As a former kayak
instructor, I'd reluctantly settled down to a desk job, con-
soling myself with the promise of whitewater vacations, a
promise that had brought me to Nepal to whitewater kayak
with two skilled paddlers, Josh and Kimberly. Paddling,
if not exactly holy, had become the closest practice I had
to religion. Rivers were the sacred place that connected me to
paddlers who had become my dearest friends and took me
to amazing places I'd never have visited if not for the chance to
paddle new rivers.

"Holy, yes. Safe, no. Most villagers think kayakers crazy.
Water dangerous and Nepalese can't swim," he said as we

drove by roadside temples. The most elaborate ones were five-roof gilded buildings topped with towers soaring so high that I craned my neck to see them. Rainbows of prayer flags waved in the air, long strings spanning the distance between the temples to nearby trees, some strands bright and others faded by the sun and rain. The steps leading up to the temples were laden with marigolds, candles, and trinkets.

He turned onto a gravel road surrounded by lush valleys. Dozens of porters carried containers on top of their heads and one man drove a pack of mules transporting supplies to nearby villages. In the distance, terraced gardens decorated the hillside, striped yellow and maroon by blooming marigolds. The hills grew steeper, giving way to jagged white peaks that pierced the cobalt sky and punctuated the horizon. I sat in awe of those mountains, their lines so sharp and size so commanding even from that distance, half listening as he explained how a simple fall near the river often meant death. As he told us how the villagers needed the river to bathe, wash their clothes, and gather the driftwood that floated down from forests, their sole means of heating their villages during the cold winter, I imagined a simpler and purer lifestyle than my own.

He parked at the put-in, and we unloaded our kayaks from the roof and gathered our gear. We planned to paddle fourteen miles down Class IV rapids to a teahouse, where we'd eat dinner and spend the night. We didn't have to pack much food or sleeping bags, a luxury to paddle lighter boats on a multi-day trip. Kimberly and I stuffed our small boats with the little gear we did carry—a spare paddle, a first aid kit, a box of energy bars, water, and sleeping clothes, while Josh studied the map, jotting down notes about rapids and the location of the teahouse and take-out on the deck of his kayak with a waterproof marker. The map was out of print and belonged to the kayak shop owner, so we couldn't buy one or take his on the river.

Josh spread the map on the hood, pointing to a bend in the river. "Is this where the teahouse is?"

The kayak shop owner nodded. "Written on rock in river—arrow pointing to path that will lead you to teahouse. Kayakers before you have gone there. No worries." Josh pointed to a spot of the map. "And this is the take-out?" He shook his head and circled his finger around an area much farther down river. "No, here, at village. Bus there goes to Kathmandu. Seven hours, maybe more, depending."

Josh took another long stare at the map before handing it over to the kayak shop owner who in turn wished us a safe paddle before driving away. I stood there watching the dust swirl behind the Jeep until it was a tiny speck in the distance and the road a cloud of brown. We were alone, not having passed another car, house, or person for the last hour of the drive.

Josh and Kimberly had already hoisted their kayaks on their shoulders and headed down a steep path toward the river. I double checked to make sure nothing had been left behind before following them. We put on in an eddy, the calm spot formed because a huge boulder blocked the flow of the water, giving us time to attach our spray skirts to our kayaks and get situated in our boats.

We peeled out of the eddy into a fast-moving current of holes and waves. The water churned until it seemed to tumble off the horizon and disappear. My stomach gurgled with fear as I contemplated what line to take, studying the water far below to see where most of the river flowed. Josh paddled into the lead and aimed his toward a slot between two large boulders. I took a long draw of air, summoning my courage to paddle with precision into an unknown rapid. I trusted Josh and had followed him down many rivers in my home state of California, but still, it required something akin to faith to follow his line without scouting. I concentrated on my every stroke, knowing that staying upright and in control was the only way to make sure I didn't end up in a dangerous undercut rock or sieve.

The slot was a ramp of turquoise water through other boulders and drops until finally we paddled into a clear pool at the bottom between walls of rock. Sheer granite with patterns of intricately marbled caramels and browns rose from the river, making me feel as if we had somehow gotten inside the mountain itself and were paddling through it. A single waterfall cascaded down the mountain, its icy water joining the river a few feet from where we sat in our kayaks.

Something about how the swirls and designs etched into the rocky mountainside, the melody of falling water and the rushing river, and the prospect of kayaking halfway around the world from home struck a perfect chord inside me. I swelled with the possibility of adventure, of what lay beyond the next horizon line, tingling from being alive in that perfect moment. I wished to somehow become part of the mountains and river and to stay there paddling that river forever.

Josh turned to us. "We've got to pick up the pace or we won't get there before dark." He scanned the horizon. "I sure as hell don't want to camp out here with no gear."

The river bent to the right. Josh paddled into the fast current, dropping out of sight. Kimberly followed. Huge water stacked up against boulders into piles of frothing white. One wrong move and I would be upside down, pinned against a rock, the rushing water overhead creating an impassable wall between me and the air. I froze at the prospect and hesitated too long. The others were gone. If anything happened to me, they'd be too far downstream to see me, much less help. I studied the water for a good line through the churning river, trying to anticipate how I'd react to each lateral wave and rock. The air was cold, but still sweat dropped from my brow.

Between surges of breaking waves, something scarlet on the other side of the river caught my eye. I was still in an eddy, but the water bobbed my boat up and down as it refracted off the rocks. I steadied myself on a rock to get a better look across the river. Sprays of whitewater and the peaked waves made it difficult to be sure.

Scarlet underwear.

I blinked in disbelief. I squinted and could barely make out a pair of dark legs and arms.

A man.

The water was so clear—I couldn't tell whether he was above or beneath the water. *Was he alive or dead?* I'd never prayed before, but I did then, even though I wasn't sure who I was praying to, God, the universe, or the river itself. *Let his head be above water. Let him breathe.*

The need to reach that man consumed me. Strong current separated me from him, leading into the steep drop. I pulled on my paddle to ferry across and help him, thinking of one thing. *Let his head be above water. Let him breathe.* But even my hardest effort was no match for the river's strength. The powerful water grabbed the bow of my kayak and turned me downstream as soon as I paddled out of the eddy. Dropping into a huge hole, I leaned my body forward, reaching my paddle blade into a wall of water and pulling with all my body force. I needed to reach Josh and Kimberly fast. I powered through hole after hole until I saw the tallest horizon line of the day.

Without hesitating, I took decisive strokes. *Let his head be above water. Let him breathe.* Leaning over the drop, I timed my stroke at precisely the right moment to propel my boat into the air. I was flying over the burly water. Josh whistled in appreciation as I paddled toward them.

"A man." I panted. "Up there, we've got to help him." I'd already pulled my boat onshore.

"Are you sure?" Josh asked. "We haven't seen anyone all day."

"C'mon." I scrambled up boulders and they followed me a hundred feet up the bank.

I pointed. "See that bit of red? That's his underwear."

Josh dashed ahead and Kimberly and I trotted after him, joining him on a massive boulder that skirted out into the river directly above the body. We crept to the edge and peered over. The man was at least a foot under the water's surface, one foot stuck under a rock and the rest of his body floating downstream as if even then he was struggling to free himself. The force of the river made his head and arms move with the surge of the water. Looking at his body aglow in the late-afternoon light, I felt an upwelling of sadness and my eyes blurred with tears. Kimberly clasped my hand as we stood there in silence, staring at the body.

"Entrapment," Josh said, identifying why the man had drowned. As paddlers, we learn one of the first lessons of the river is to never try to touch the bottom. If a foot gets stuck under a rock, it becomes almost impossible to free it once the powerful current wedges it into a crevice. Often rivers are so powerful that the flow knocks people underwater.

I saw with unforgiving clarity how it might have happened. The man was planning to bathe when something slipped from his hand. He walked farther into the river to retrieve it, unwittingly stepping into current stronger and water deeper than he expected. He would have tried to free his foot from the rock's grasp, but the rushing water pushed the rest of his body downstream so that he couldn't use his hands to wiggle the rock and free his foot. He fought the water's power until it was too much and he lost his balance, getting swept off his other foot. He would have gasped for air, even as the water flowed over his head, his lungs taking in water.

"He's gone," Kimberly said over and over.

It seemed so unfair. The man hadn't taken risks the way we had. He wasn't flirting with wild water, seeking the thrill of paddling new rivers, and pushing his skill level. He was simply living, using the river to survive, the way his village had done for centuries before him.

Josh turned to us. "We need to keep paddling. We're not going to be of any use here."

Kimberly pointed to a stream of men walking down the green slope, men wearing long-sleeved robes falling slightly below the knee and tied at the waist with a cloth sash carrying a bamboo gurney. Women wore floor-length dresses, balancing woven baskets brimming with yellow and crimson marigolds. "Not yet. They may be from his village, but they don't know whitewater like we do. We need to stay and help."

Kimberly ran up the slope to meet the villagers.

Josh crossed his arms. "We've got to keep moving. The longer we stay here, the less likely we are to find the teahouse before it gets dark, and paddling this water in the dark is a death wish."

Minutes later, a slender Nepalese man followed two paces behind Kimberly. His face was tear-stained and he repeated one word. "Brother."

Perhaps Josh had a brother, because that one word caused him to grab all of our throw ropes and sprint upstream toward the dead man. Kimberly and I trotted behind him, and by the time we caught up, he was thigh deep moving through the water toward the particular rock under which the dead man's foot was stuck. He turned and threw us the other end of his throw rope so we could rescue him if anything happened. Tentatively he negotiated slippery rocks, making sure his footing was secure before committing his foot to the riverbed. When he reached the rock, he stood directly in front of it in an effort to lessen the powerful current. Holding onto the rock with one hand, he reached down with the other in search of the man's foot.

After minutes of searching, he shook his head, indicating he hadn't found the man's foot and beckoned to me to join him in the water. I scooted out into the rushing current, using the rope tied to Josh and secured by Kimberly for balance. When I reached him, I grabbed onto Josh.

He steadied me. "I think his foot is over there. Stand right in front of it and hold onto my lifejacket. I'm going underwater."

He disappeared and I struggled to maintain a grasp on his lifejacket as he worked to free the dead man's foot. I saw the dead man's body jerk and then Josh reappeared holding the foot. The dead man's body was so limp by then that whenever Josh moved, the body followed, having no movement of its own.

I held onto Josh's lifejacket as he tied another rope around the dead body and threw the other end to the Nepalese man who had repeatedly said "brother." The Nepalese man reeled him in, just as any other day he might have done with a fish.

Josh and I held onto each other as we made our way back to the shore, Kimberly keeping the rope taut to help us. After we climbed out of the water, the Nepalese man walked up to us, first bowed deeply, pressing his hands into prayer position and then looked into our eyes, saying *"Namaste"* to each of us.

I wanted to express my condolence, to recognize his loss. But I knew only one word, so I bowed and returned his greeting, watching Kimberly and Josh do the same. We stood for a few minutes, looking at one another with the wide eyes of grief before Josh nudged me.

"C'mon, we've got to make up for lost time."

We bowed one last time and scrambled over the boulders to our kayaks. Josh and I sat in our boats and started paddling around in the eddy to warm up.

"Get a move on it," Josh called up to Kimberly.

"I need a minute." She kicked a rock.

Josh scowled. "We've got to make up for lost time if we have any chance of finding the teahouse before dark."

The river posed at challenge for my skills in the light. Once it got dark, there was no way we could keep paddling. And the steep gorged-in river meant suitable campsites were few and far between. Besides, I'd already started looking forward to a warm dinner before snuggling into a sleeping bag on a real bed. We didn't have proper gear to spend the night in this weather. I stared at the water, silently willing Kimberly to paddle.

Kimberly looked up, a tear streaming down her face. "My father drowned last summer."

Josh sighed. "Fuck. I'm such an ass." He swallowed hard. "We'll take it slow, but we've got to keep going. Besides, they're going to burn the body soon. We don't want to intrude more than we already have."

The wind blew the smoke downstream. I was grateful it smelled only of burning wood and not burning flesh. Even though I couldn't see that far upriver, I could hear the men chanting and I imagined them lifting the dead man onto the gurney. The women would be lacing his body with marigolds and straw before the men carried it to the top of a slab of flat granite. In my mind I saw the Nepalese man who had repeated "brother" lighting the straw, and minutes later flame would engulf the marigolds and the body.

I steadied Kimberly's boat for her and looked into her eyes. "I'm so sorry."

Our pace slowed by half. Death seemed so capricious in who and when it claims what's rightfully his. As I paddled, I felt death sitting on my shoulder, reminding me that everyone is going to die. Even me. Everywhere I looked, I saw death beckoning. Rocks looked undercut. I envisioned myself stuck upside down underneath a granite overhang, unable to roll up or move forward, and eventually drowning. The fear played out in my strokes, which became short and tentative. I no longer anticipated the water underneath my boat so instead of moving with it, I reacted to the waves as they threw me backward, bracing at the last minute to stay upright. In turn, the more my paddling deteriorated, the more likely I was to let the river have its way with me, pushing me into dark, dangerous pockets.

The rush of paddling, at the edge of my paddling abilities, had been replaced by the realization of the danger all around me. I no longer cared about adrenaline or testing my paddling on faraway rivers. All I wanted was to be off the water, safe at home. I wanted the security of the familiar, my own bed and a hot shower. I didn't want to die, not yet, not ever. Fear consumed me, dulling my senses until it was as if I was watching my body from far away, seeing the evening unfold, but not actually part of it.

The sun lowered in the sky, the glare from the rays making it difficult to read the water. We peered into the distance, hoping the teahouse would be right around the next bend. When the gray of twilight made it impossible to distinguish waves from rocks, we decided that it was too dangerous to continue and stopped on an island in the middle of the river, a beach of pebbles and driftwood.

We ate energy bars around a fire in the comfortable quiet shared by good friends. By then, Kimberly and Josh seemed like family members after witnessing death with one another. I stared into the fire and saw images from the day—the kayak shop owner driving away, the jagged mountain peaks, waterfalls cascading into the river, the dead man wearing scarlet underwear, his arms waving helplessly under the water's surface, the baskets brimming with marigolds, and the rapids stretching one after another. I saw the river's gradations of blue leaping in the fire's flames. That day had been so long, and yet, after seeing death up close, a lifetime seemed too short.

I tried to sleep, but couldn't keep my eyes closed. Painted on the back of my eyelids were bright orange and yellow petals with crimson hearts—marigolds, the flower of the dead. Their vivid colors burnt alive in my head. They seemed impossibly bright, perhaps, because eventually they would fade before disappearing altogether.

The embers turned to ash as I thought about how the dead man's body would have been ashes by then and his family would have scattered them into the river along with marigolds. I wondered if any of the marigolds had floated down to our campsite during the night. And I thought how the lessons of the dead man I'd never met would stay with me. I would still be afraid at the top of a rapid and feel the sadness that surrounds death. But instead of retreating into a comfortable numbness, distancing myself from my own life, I vowed to experience every minute of paddling with marigolds. A sense of joy and profound relief filled me. I was alive in Nepal.

Ky Delaney regularly contributes feature articles to the print edition of Blue Ridge Outdoors Magazine *and a weekly online advice column titled "Mountain Mama" for their website. She's a certified whitewater kayak, sea kayak, and ski instructor. Currently, she practices law at a non-profit legal aid office in Asheville, North Carolina, where she solo parents her young son, Tobin Creek.*

DON GEORGE

🙢 🙢 🙢

Piecing Together Puzzles

He needed a few days to understand
why he had come so far.

As Mr. Kim navigated his car onto the puddled, pot-
holed road that led to Banteay Chhmar, he turned to
me. "Where are you staying?" he asked.

"I don't know.".

He looked at me out of the corner of his eye. "There are no
hotels in Banteay Chhmar."

"I know. I arranged a homestay. On my computer."

"O.K. Where is the home?"

"I don't know."

He swiveled to face me. "Where should I take you?"

This moment seemed to symbolize my entire Cambodia
trip: Where was I going? Why was I here?

I had arrived in Cambodia after a week-long tour con-
sisting of lectures, book readings, and writing workshops in
Melbourne and Singapore. When I was planning that tour
half a year earlier, I realized that Siem Reap was just a short
flight from Singapore. I had been wanting to visit Siem Reap
since childhood, when I had seen a photo of Angkor Wat in
National Geographic. Some kind of seed had been planted, and

over four decades, its stony tendrils had blossomed into an irresistible longing. I had to see that place, touch its ground, smell its air. Now it would be just two hours away by plane. I booked a one-week visit.

Over the ensuing months, as I was researching Siem Reap, I discovered a village about one hundred miles to the northwest called Banteay Chhmar, where an organization named Community-Based Tourism (CBT) arranged home-stays. There was scant information online, but what I found promised amazing ruins and kind people. At first I thought I would base myself in Siem Reap and spend one night in Banteay Chhmar. Then I decided to make it two nights. As time passed, the image of going off the map to little-visited Banteay Chhmar took hold of me, and I ended up reserving a three-night stay through the CBT website.

Mr. Kim met me at the airport to take me to my Siem Reap hotel. During the twenty-minute drive, he spoke easily and impressed me with his knowledge, English fluency, and calm, kind air. I asked him about getting to Banteay Chhmar. A few years earlier, he said, the drive would have taken most of a day, but recently a paved highway had been built almost all the way to the village, and now the journey would be about three hours by highway and just thirty minutes along bumpy, unpaved paths. "Of course," he added with a wry smile as a sudden downpour turned the windshield into a washing machine, "it's the rainy season, so it might take longer." I asked if he could take me, and he said sure, that he liked that part of Cambodia and had served in the army there.

Over the next two and half days, I immersed myself in a giddy, deluge-dodging round of ruin-hopping and restaurant-gorging in Siem Reap. I saw Angkor Wat at dawn and dusk, mysterious strangler-figged Ta Prohm, the benevolent, beguiling faces of Bayon, and exquisite Banteay Srey.

I slung back Indochine Martinis at the seductive Miss Wong bar and savored a six-course seasonal feast at acclaimed Cuisine Wat Damnak. I was exultant to have reached the place I had dreamed of for decades, but somehow among the thousands of balloon-panted, sarong-wrapped, selfie-snapping foreigners, I sensed Cambodia eluding me. Even immersed in the cultural heart of the country, I felt somehow distant from the place.

So it was that on my third morning, filled with a mixture of apprehension and anticipation, I set off with Mr. Kim for Banteay Chhmar. The drive was spectacular—palm trees, rice paddies, cassava fields, stilt houses, bright-eyed children waving and calling "Hello!"—and it was only when we arrived at the outskirts of the village that I realized I literally had no idea where I was going. The emailed reservation confirmation had said to check in with the CBT office when I arrived in Banteay Chhmar, but I had been too distracted in Siem Reap to think about re-reading emails, and the only thing I could remember was that I had arranged a meeting the following morning with a man at the Global Heritage Fund (GHF), an international organization that was working to restore the main ruin in Banteay Chhmar.

"So you are staying at the Global Heritage Fund house?" Mr. Kim asked.

"No, I don't think so."

"Anyway, we go there," he declared and turned back to the road. A few minutes later we saw a sign for the GHF and Mr. Kim pulled into a fenced, two-building compound. A dignified man strolled toward us and asked if he could help. This, it turned out, was Sarun Kousum, the assistant director of the GHF project and the man I was supposed to meet the following day.

"Is Mr. Don staying with you?" Mr. Kim asked Sarun.

Sarun looked uncomfortable. "No, no, he is not staying here."

"He says he made the reservation on the computer."

"Oh, that must be through the Community-Based Tourism office," he said. "You need to go there."

After bouncing, sloshing, and skidding along the main street for another ten minutes, we reached the two-room, thatch-and-metal-roofed CBT office, where a smiling young man named Sokoun Kit greeted us.

"Ah, I have been waiting for you!" he said. "Welcome! Please fill out some paperwork and I will take you to your home. It's just a short walk from here."

As I wrote, Sokoun explained that since my host family was not equipped to serve meals to guests, I would take all my meals at the CBT office. The village had electricity from 6 P.M. to 11 P.M. each night. He would be happy to lend me a flashlight.

"How about Internet access?" I asked.

"I'm sorry," Sokoun said. "There is no Internet access."

A few minutes later, Mr. Kim parked at the edge of an unpaved road outside a muddy compound of stilt houses, and sloshed my suitcase on his shoulder through the muck and around the puddles, scattering chickens as he walked, to the two-story home where I would be spending the next three days.

Sokoun joined us in the spare, open-air, concrete-floor living area under the second story of the wooden house, where a middle-aged couple stood to greet us.

"Don, these are your hosts," he said, gesturing to the man, who was wearing a polo shirt and shorts, and the woman in a bright patterned sarong. They both smiled and bowed slightly, and the man said something to Sokoun. "They don't speak much English, but they are very happy to have you here," Sokoun said. I smiled and bowed in return, and said the one word I had learned in Khmer, "*Agung!*"—thank you.

Their eyes brightened momentarily, then the man gestured toward a wooden staircase that led to my bedroom. Mr. Kim kicked off his sandals and carried my bag up the stairs. I sat on a child's red plastic chair that had been placed at the bottom of the stairs and laboriously liberated my feet from my muddy shoes. With a quick nod, I ascended with my backpack.

Sokoun and I had arranged to meet later that afternoon, and after calling out, "Make yourself at home," he left to take his lunch. Mr. Kim had said he would stay with a friend who lived nearby, and we confirmed that he would meet me at the CBT office four days later for the drive back to Siem Reap. He left too. Then I was alone.

I sat on the edge of the mosquito net that covered the queen-size four-poster bed that occupied most of my room. The noontime sun blasted through the room's barred windows. The humidity hammered on my head. Outside I could see a half dozen wooden stilt homes surrounded by muddy patches and palm trees, a clothesline hung with shirts and sarongs, tree branch kindling stacked under a storage shed, a scrabbly vegetable garden where smoke plumed from a dying fire. Roosters strutted and crowed, dogs barked, babies wailed, adults called from home to home.

Suddenly I felt overwhelmed: What had I gotten myself into? My hosts didn't speak English. I was cut off entirely from the outside world. The roads were a muddy mess. I had no means of transportation and no idea what I was going to do for the next three days. Sweat poured down my face. Was there a shower, or even running water? And what about the toilet—where, and what, was that? What had I been thinking when I booked three nights here?

It took all my energy simply to lift my mosquito net and crawl into its cocoon.

The next morning, over coffee in the GHF courtyard, Sarun Kousum told me he had first visited the main Banteay Chhmar ruin in 1997. "It was a huge surprise," he said. "Only a little bit of the dirt and trees had been cleared at that time, but already you could tell from the size of the ruin and the quality of the work that it was an important site." GHF began its efforts there, under the directorship of John Sanday, in January 2008. "I have been a part of this project from the beginning," Sarun said, and his face glowed with a quiet pride.

After coffee Sarun grabbed a couple of umbrellas and took me on a tour of the site. As we walked toward the ruin, Sarun explained that the Banteay Chhmar complex had been commissioned in the late 12th century by King Jayavarman VII, the architecturally ambitious ruler who had also commissioned the magnificent Ta Prohm, Angkor Thom/Bayon, and Preah Khan complexes. When it was completed in the early 13th century, Banteay Chhmar was one of the largest and most important religious sites in the kingdom, rivaling Angkor Wat in size and grandeur.

We reached the spectacular 180-foot-long wall that greets visitors who approach from the eastern entrance, now the principal entry to the site, and Sarun said, "One of our first projects was to secure, stabilize, and restore this wall."

The restoration showcases a stunningly detailed bas-relief depicting battles between the Khmer and their long-time enemies, the Cham. In one section, long ear-lobed Khmer soldiers bearing spears and shields march over a battlefield under the command of their larger-than-life-sized king. The Cham soldiers, identified by their curious headwear, which looks like lotus flowers plopped upside down on their pates, flee from the advance. As the narrative unfolds, the Khmer offer the heads of their now vanquished enemies to the king. Later, musicians and dancers perform in a palace celebration.

"The builders in the 12th century were very skilled," Sarun said. "Even though their tools were unsophisticated, the quality of the carvings they did is astonishing."

A gentle rain began to patter on the leafy boughs that covered much of the site, and Sarun led me along a muddy path to an area where a concrete-floored, metal-roofed storage and work space had been built; beyond that a portion of wall about thirty feet long had collapsed into a jumble of stones.

"I was here in January when this wall fell down," Sarun said. "There was a big wind during the night, and the next morning when we came to the site, we were surprised to see this toppled portion. In all, 214 stones fell over, and we are using computer imaging to put the wall back together. We paint a number on each stone, then we carve the number on the stone. Then we take pictures of each stone, do hand-drawings, and put the pictures and drawings on the computer. Then we begin to put the pieces back together on the computer. It really is like a puzzle, based on the shape of the rock and any carving on the stone. The experts know what they're looking at and are very skilled in reconstructing."

We toured the ruins for an hour without encountering any other visitors, and this poignant place—sculpted stones scattered as though a giant had smashed the temple with his club—cast a spell on me. As we exited by the western temple wall, Sarun showed me perhaps the greatest of Banteay Chhmar's masterpieces: two breathtakingly detailed depictions of the Buddhist god of compassion, Avalokitesvara, one with thirty-two arms and the other with twenty-two arms. A gaping hole in the wall next to one of these marked the spot where looters made off with two other Avalokitesvara reliefs. Happily, Sarun said, these were intercepted near the Thai border and are now on display at the National Museum in Phnom Penh. Unhappily, another stolen section with two more reliefs has never been found. Sighing, he said, "We must preserve these for our culture, our heritage."

Sarun's pride in these ruins was so evident that before we parted, I couldn't resist asking him one last question. "You've been working here non-stop since January 2008. These ruins must be so deeply a part of your life by now, do you ever dream about them?"

He looked at me with smiling eyes. "Oh yes, sometimes. . . ." he said, and then he looked away with a shy laugh.

That afternoon I met Sopheng Khlout, the slight, smiling, twenty-something CBT president. Sopheng had kindly arranged to be my guide for the rest of my stay, and over the next two and a half days, through an ever-changing flow of sunshine, light showers, and deluging downpours, he went far out of his way to give me an exceptional tour of Banteay Chhmar. We began by visiting two of the region's nine satellite temples. The first was Prasat Ta Prohm, just a few minutes' ride by motorbike south of the main temple. Ta Prohm is a four-sided tower, elaborately reinforced by modern carpentry, that soars about forty feet out of the surrounding vegetation, with Bayon-style faces—a prominent, wide nose; thick lips upturned into a slight smile; and protruding almond eyes—on each side. It looked entirely overgrown, but Sopheng knew a trail that wound through the vines, bushes, and branches to a hollow under the tower itself, where I was surprised to find not only ancient inscriptions but also fresh incense and candles. There was a red cloth wound around the tower, and Sopheng said that the cloth showed that this was a living temple where locals came to leave their offerings and to ask the gods to answer their prayers.

Next we motored eight miles south past tranquil rice paddies and simple stilt houses to Banteay Torp, a temple built to honor Jayavarman VII's troops for their defeat of the Cham. The most impressive feature of this sprawling, densely overgrown, crumbling complex was three towers that rose teeteringly over the ruins. For me, the place poignantly represented the destiny of all ancient temples, and it gave me an even deeper appreciation for the dedicated efforts of John Sanday,

Sarun, and the GHF—and other individuals and organizations like them—to rescue and restore these sites.

"It's hard to imagine what this must have looked like 800 years ago," I said to Sopheng.

"Yes," he replied, gazing over the ruins. "Mostly people come here to picnic now. I think this temple has become a place to worship nature."

Finally we visited a reservoir formally known as Boeung Cheung Kru, but more popularly called the Pol Pot Baray (*baray* means reservoir), because it was built during the reign of the Khmer Rouge under Pol Pot. The scene was blissfully beautiful: a placid expanse of water with patches of lotuses floating here and there, birds swooping and settling, children splashing, adults wading with fishing nets. On the horizon, green hills marked the border with Thailand. The peacefulness of the scene belied its past.

"Yes," Sopheng said with a pained smile. "It is hard to believe how much suffering took place right here, to build this *baray*. We hear the stories. People worked at least twelve hours a day, every day, and they were fed only a little rice or soup. People were killed without reason."

For a moment his face darkened, and he turned away. After a long silence, he said, his voice tight, "We don't understand these things."

Immediately I recalled a moment in Mr. Kim's car, on the ride from Siem Reap. We had talked about Siem Reap's main tourist sites, ancient Cambodian history and Khmer culture, Buddhism and Hinduism, and the Cambodian economy. Now he was telling me about current politics and how the government was seeking to unify the country and focus on the future after being brutally ripped apart during the Pol Pot years from 1975 to 1979.

I had been reluctant to bring up the subject of Pol Pot, but this mention seemed to open a channel in Mr. Kim's mind. Suddenly the words streamed from his mouth.

"You can't comprehend what it was like during those years," he said, shaking his head. "No one who didn't live it can understand. Before the civil war, nine million people lived in Cambodia. After the war, there were six million left. Pol Pot killed one-third of the people. One-third!

"I was lucky. I was a commander in the Cambodian Army against Pol Pot. But I know so many people who were not so lucky.

"They took all the people from the cities—educated people, teachers, office workers—and put them to work in the fields. Then in the fields, if someone got sick, they would be killed. If someone wasn't working hard enough, they would be killed. Sometimes even if you just looked at a soldier the wrong way, you would be killed. These were Cambodian people, killing Cambodian people."

He stared straight ahead and his tone barely changed, but his words spewed with an almost terrifying urgency.

"Pol Pot wanted to break up all the families. The Khmer Rouge would separate children from their parents. And to break them, to make them loyal only to the Khmer Rouge, they would make them do terrible things. Do you know what they did? They made them kill their own parents. They would bring the parents before the children, and then tell the children, 'You must kill your mother. You must kill your father. From now on, your only loyalty is to the Khmer Rouge.' If the children hesitated, they would threaten to kill the children.

"You are a father. Can you imagine? These were children!" he said and his voice suddenly broke.

And then I broke too. Huge convulsive waves of sobbing shook my body, coming from some deep well I didn't even know I had, the tears streaming down my face, sobbing and sobbing so hard that I shook the car and the air writhed in agony around us.

Mr. Kim kept driving steadily, in silence. He never looked at me but simply exuded what felt like a kindly calm.

I covered my eyes but the tears kept pouring and the deep sobs kept racking my body. After what seemed an eternity, I finally stopped, embarrassed.

"I'm so sorry," I said. "I'm so sorry. . . . I just don't understand how any human being could do that to another fellow human being. I just don't understand how people could do that. I don't, I don't . . . understand," I said, and I started sobbing again.

"I know," Mr. Kim said quietly. "We don't understand either. We think, 'How could our fellow Cambodians do this?'

"This is why I don't tell my children about this," Mr. Kim continued. "I don't want them to think about this and to feel such sadness. I want them to feel happy. I want them to think about the future, about what they can do with their lives. Cambodian people don't want to think about this. Life is better now. We have human rights and freedoms. We don't want to dwell on the past. We want to focus on the future now. . . ."

At the Pol Pot reservoir, Sopheng was silent, staring at the water and the horizon beyond. When he finally turned back to me, his smile seemed somehow refreshed, lightened, as if he had buried some burden in the landscape.

"Now we use the *baray* to water the fields and for fishing. The *baray* is giving back to the people," he said. "We can't change what's past. We can only make sure that the future is better."

On the first night of my homestay, I ate dinner at the CBT office and then slipped and sloshed back down the road toward my house. It was supposed to be about a two-minute walk, but in the unfamiliar dark I missed my house and continued on past more stilt houses. I could see families gathered by fluorescent light or lantern light in the paved, open-walled, under-stilt portions of their homes. In some, multiple generations were gazing at the television. In others, adults were eating, drinking, and talking around picnic tables. Here a mother carefully combed a child's hair. There an older sister bathed a sibling, both erupting into peals of laughter. When thickets of trees appeared on my left and rice paddies stretched away on my right, I knew I had walked too far. I walked back and finally discerned the small "Homestay" sign that marked my house.

At about 4 A.M. one of the most torrential rains I have ever experienced drummed on the metal roof above me. As it went on and on, I felt like I was living under a waterfall. It was unsettling being in an unfamiliar place, with unfamiliar weather, at the mercy of strangers. After about twenty minutes, men's voices shouted from house to house and footsteps scrambled on stairs. Then I heard splashing and urgent cries outside. I didn't know what they were doing or what I should be doing. So I simply fretted. After another twenty minutes, the voices stopped and peace returned, but still I couldn't sleep under the percussive pounding. Then I thought: This is not an unusual occurrence. This has been happening for decades, centuries, millennia even. You're just part of some cycle so much older and bigger than you that there's no point in worrying about it. This village has survived for centuries. These people have survived for decades. You've just become part of some huge natural whole that you were never aware of. Lucky you. Now just surrender to it and go with the flow.

The next thing I knew, cocks were crowing and sunlight was streaming through the window.

On the second night of my homestay, as I walked back to my house, children waved and called, "Hello! Hello!" Mothers holding babies smiled and laughed. Teenagers nodded as they passed on their bikes, and the men talking around the picnic tables saluted me with their beers. Even the renegade dogs yapped in a more friendly way.

On the final evening of my homestay, I lay in the hammock in my home's ground-floor living area. Behind me Mom and Grandma were sitting on their haunches, chopping dandelions and radishes by a boiling pot, and Dad was rocking three-month-old Baby to sleep. I took out my journal and wrote:

> I can't believe this is already my last night here. I don't want to leave. I feel so comfortable here now, so completely at home. There's so much to love. The super kind and innocent people. The beautiful landscapes. The simple stilt house life. The kids running around playing with their makeshift stick-and-cloth toys; one kid has a red truck and that's as sophisticated as it gets. There's such a community feeling, everybody talking with everybody, sharing with everybody. When a huge rain poured my first afternoon, everyone worked together to carry plastic buckets of rainwater to the ceramic storage vessels and to construct a temporary dam so the soil wouldn't erode so quickly.
>
> And my god, the smiles! There are smiles everywhere, especially the kids with their big smiles and their incredibly bright, innocent, hopeful eyes.

The village cocks started their incongruous round of evening calls. Dogs barked. Frogs croaked. In the distance a tractor rumbled, and scratchy music wafted from speakers at a nearby Buddhist festival. The seven-year-old from the house across the way raced by on her bicycle and gave me a big wave. The boy with the red truck suddenly appeared carrying a coconut and held it out to me. Baby issued a blissful burp, and we all laughed.

"Thinking about leaving tomorrow," I wrote, "I feel like I could cry. . . ."

For our last tour, Sopheng told me he was taking me somewhere very special, a place he didn't usually take visitors. I hopped behind him on his trusty Honda motorbike, and he maneuvered onto the rain-mucked road once again. The road to this temple was the worst yet. There were deep pools of water separated by thin islands of exposed road that looked too slick and mucky to even attempt. But like a moto magician, Sopheng turned the handlebars this way and that, minutely steering a course between puddles, somehow avoiding the slickest spots that would have sent us flying, gunning the engine moments before we got stuck, fording puddles when that was the only way, and all with a serene smile. Against impossible odds, we didn't topple over even once.

When we reached an especially submerged section of road, for the first time Sopheng stopped and said, "We'd better walk here." So we dismounted. I must have been quite a sight: I had rolled up my trousers to my calves, showing a patch of alarmingly white skin between my blue socks and khaki convertible trousers. My walking shoes were thickly caked in mud. I had a red bandanna on my head and another around my throat, and I was wearing an electric blue t-shirt under a long-sleeved blue work shirt. We sloshed along on foot for about one hundred feet until we had passed the worst section.

We re-mounted the motorbike and slow-motored down a series of ever narrower, branch-littered paths, between groves of lush green trees and rice paddies. Prickly bushes grasped at us. We passed a couple of stilt houses, and a bent woman with a leathery lined face suddenly crinkled into a smile and called out a greeting. The trail ended at a dense patch of jungle, where Sopheng stopped the engine and parked. One narrow, crushed-grass walking path led to the left through high grasses and bushes. Another led to the right through similarly forbidding growth.

Sopheng took neither. "Follow me," he said, and plunged straight into the impenetrable jungle. As I followed him, silently cursing, the barest brushstroke of a path materialized, a muddy, leaf-strewn depression. After a few steps, that depression disappeared and all I could do was try to exactly match Sopheng's footsteps as he burrowed into a world of densely overhung, intertwining vines, bushes, and branches, sharp rocks and slick tree trunks, all crawling with slimy insects, I was sure.

Soon the trail led onto a jumble of moss-covered stones with sharp sides. As sweat poured down my face, neck, arms, and legs, everywhere sweat could pour, I gingerly picked my way over the rocks, noting the fat brown millipedes on all the smooth surfaces. We crossed into deep green shadows, heavy with the weight of damp branches, dripping ferns, wet leaves and grasses. The air smelled of earthy wetness, a musky, primordial scent.

We stepped over another jumble of rocks—me slipping on one and missing a millipede by a millimeter as I grabbed a rock to steady myself. Then we turned a corner and the foliage gave way to a clearing and Sopheng smiled. "Look!" he said.

Just behind him rose a stone tower with a huge carved face—smiling lips, bulbous nose, protruding eyes. Its appearance was so unexpected, so hallucinatory, that for a moment I couldn't process what I was seeing.

Then it all came into focus: a single tower, thirty feet high, topped with a massive magnificent carved face, surrounded by the jungle, with no one else around for miles. We scrambled a few feet forward, then Sopheng said, "We can't go closer than this. It's too dangerous."

I stopped and tried to grasp the moment: I was gritty, grimy, and exhausted from a day of clambering and bumping and sloshing through the jungle, surrounded by bulbous leaves and drooping, dripping branches and vines, balanced precariously on mossy, vine-woven rocks, gazing at a tower of stone blocks, placed painstakingly block by block, hand by human hand, some eight centuries before.

I laughed and Sopheng laughed, and I took out my phone and took sweaty photos. "This is incredible!" I said. "This is like a dream!"

"I found out about this temple only in 2009," Sopheng said. "The people who live nearby told me about it. Just a few foreigners know it. If tourists don't have a local guide, they cannot find this temple. It's too complicated to find on your own. Even if you are standing right in front of it, you won't see it." He paused. "I don't usually take people here," he said, with a wide smile.

My last grand adventure of the trip occurred as Mr. Kim drove me from Banteay Chhmar to Siem Reap. Mr. Kim knew this was my final full day in Cambodia, and after I had waved a long and lingering farewell to Sopheng and Sokoun at the CBT building, he looked at me and asked, "When do you have to be back at Siem Reap?" Not until dinnertime, I said, and his eyes shone. "Do you want to go to the Thai border? There are two temples there I want to show you. Twelfth century. We go?"

"Of course, of course!" I said, and off we went.

We drove north through heart-stoppingly idyllic landscapes—glistening, rainwater-filled rice paddies and lush cassava fields, towering palm trees and groves of green deciduous trees, interrupted occasionally by settlements of a few dozen wooden stilt houses. For a change, the sun was shining and the sky was a deep blue backdrop for a spectacular succession of pure white clouds—streaks and puffs and mounds upon mounds.

Mr. Kim was pleased. "I was here during the war," he said. "I was a commander here. There were many Khmer Rouge soldiers in this area." Looking out at a landscape that moments before had seemed the very picture of purity and innocence, I struggled to absorb the idea that Cambodians had been torturing and killing Cambodians here just a few decades before, that corpses almost certainly underlay parts of this pristine ground. My mind was spinning.

"We go to the temples on the border," Mr. Kim said. "Even just a few years ago, there was fighting there with the Thai soldiers. Many people died."

In the spring of 2011, he explained, Thai troops had seized the temples' grounds, claiming the areas belonged to Thailand. Cambodian troops had rushed to repel them, and for a month, artillery shells and gunfire from both sides had claimed at least fifteen lives.

"Now it is peaceful," Mr. Kim said, "but still, there are many Cambodian soldiers there, just to make sure the Thais don't try to move the border again."

We reached the first temple, Ta Moan, in less than an hour. The last section of road corkscrewed into almost unimaginably dense jungle mountains that marked the border. This was the territory where Pol Pot's troops had been based, Mr. Kim said, close enough to scurry into Thailand when necessary, and in vegetation so thick that it would be almost impossible to spot an encampment until you had literally walked into it.

Ta Moan turned out to be a sleepy site, about the size of a football field, with brown rock remains of walls that outlined one central building with some still visible decorated doorways and corridors, and half a dozen subsidiary structures. A couple of Thai soldiers sat on stones at the far end of the site, and a Cambodian border policeman and soldier stood at the near end, talking quietly. It was surprising to see these soldiers from both countries simply strolling around the grounds, and even more surprising when they sat down together and talked like old friends; a breath of hope seemed to rise in this peaceful air where blood had been shed just three years before.

The second temple, Ta Krabey, was even more moving. Mr. Kim knew the commander here, and we were

accompanied by a military escort of a half dozen soldiers up
a winding jungle trail to the mountainside temple grounds.
Ta Krabey was essentially a single tower in a clearing about
100 feet square, surrounded by massive trees and jumbled,
moss-covered stones. There was a much larger military presence here. Eight Thai soldiers were lounging on the site when
we arrived. The soldiers nodded and smiled at each other, and
one of the Thais greeted the Cambodians in Khmer. As they
shared cigarettes and talked easily with each other, the Cambodian commander showed us bullet holes and scars from
artillery fire in the temple stones.

"Now, we are friends," he said, gesturing toward the mingling soldiers. "But a few years ago, we were shooting at each
other."

He then walked down and clapped his Thai counterpart
on the back, and before I knew what was happening, I was
being herded along with a contingent of Thai and Cambodian
troops to a prime photo spot in front of the tower's entrance.
One Thai and one Cambodian soldier were dispensed to take
photos, and the rest of us put our arms around each other's
shoulders and smiled.

"We'll call this 'Tourist at the Peace Temple,'" the commander said, and as his words were shared and translated, the
soldiers nodded and laughed.

After a half hour of cigarette-sharing and photo-snapping,
the commander led us back down the trail to a roofed, open-
walled meeting area with a table where he bade us sit and
brought us tea. He then disappeared for a few minutes and
reappeared with a dozen of his soldiers, including the six who
had accompanied us to the temple. When all had been seated,
he stood and gave a speech, which Mr. Kim translated, welcoming us and telling us what an honor it was to have a foreign guest among them. He also spoke about the history of the
conflict over the border temples and how happy everyone was

to have peace in the area now, and how they hoped the only visitors in the future would be tourists—he smiled at me—and not soldiers.

He sat down to applause and I rose and gave a brief speech, through Mr. Kim, saying how very honored I was to be welcomed at this ancient and important site, and how tremendously moved I had been to see the Cambodian soldiers talking so harmoniously with the Thai soldiers. I told them how very inspiring that was to me, and how that kind of peace and understanding between people was the prime reason I traveled and why I believed so fervently in the power of travel to transform the world. I said I would always treasure my photo of the Peace Temple and my visit with them.

I sat down and all the soldiers burst into smiles and applause, and then, quite unexpectedly, a very young-looking soldier at the end of the table got up and began to speak. His voice quavered at first, but as he continued to speak, the words flowed out of him with a pure passion.

"I am just a simple soldier," Mr. Kim translated. "I have not traveled far or seen much in my life. But today is a very special day for me." He looked directly at me. "Our honored guest is the first foreigner I have ever seen in my life, the first foreigner I have ever met. I am so excited and happy to have met you and talked with you. I cannot quite express what this means to my life. This makes me think how big the world is, and gives me a kind of hope. Please when you go back to your village, tell the people about the soldiers you met at Ta Krabey. And tell them about the peace you found here. I will never forget this day for the rest of my life."

He stopped, looking embarrassed, but his comrades burst into applause, and I leaped to my feet, pressed my hands to my heart and said, "*Agung! Agung! Agung!*" Then I asked Mr. Kim to say that I would definitely tell all my fellow villagers about the kind soldiers I had met at Ta Krabey and the inspiring peace I had found there. And that I too would never forget this day.

Mr. Kim dropped me at my hotel in Siem Reap at 5 P.M., and we parted with assurances that we would see each other again. I had thought I would visit Angkor Wat one last time, but instead, I decided to have dinner at the hotel and spend the night in my room. I had a day's worth of flying ahead, but even more important, I wanted to end my stay in the place where Cambodia had come alive for me, in Banteay Chhmar. So I sat in my room scrolling through memories of the days just past, until one scene stopped me.

On the second morning of my stay in Banteay Chhmar, I awoke before dawn to explore the main ruin where Sarun had taken me the day before. I made my way by flashlight along puddle-pocked paths to the eastern entrance and admired the bas-reliefs of warriors and dancers again. Then, just as day was breaking, I followed a footpath to the right that led past the collapsed wall and into the heart of the temple.

Alone in the ruins, I lost all sense of time. I picked my way over mossy rocks, extricated myself from clinging vines, slowly stepped up and over stairs and crumbling walls, butt-slid down precarious inclines, then turned to find a beautiful carved maiden encased in a tiny niche, an intricate carving of a Buddha under a bodhi tree, an ornamented head here, a shield-bearing torso there, a half dozen bodhisattvas buried among grasses and leaves.

I moved deeper and deeper into the ruin, sloshing through puddles, slashing through vines, clambering over toppled stones, avoiding millipedes, swatting at mosquitoes, parting branches, and plucking persistent stickers. At one point I stopped for a swig of water, and when I slapped at the whining mosquitoes that danced on my neck and hands, I slipped and slid over some tumbled pieces of rock, grabbed at branches to

stop my fall, and landed just in front of a bas-relief of warriors, maidens, and fish alive in stone.

Sweat poured into my eyes, and as I mopped the stream
with a sopping bandanna, I saw a stony face—lips, nose,
eyes—at the top of a tower of tilting stone. I fumbled with
my camera, and rain started to fall, first a pitter-patter on the
forest canopy and then an insistent downpour that penetrated
the branches and leaves.

I stood in the downpour and felt electrified, closer to the
wild heart of life than I had been in a long time. I was sweaty,
dirty, dripping, exhausted, utterly alone in the wild and connecting with things so far beyond me I could barely comprehend them.

Part of me was transported back to this same stony spot
eight centuries before, gazing in wonder at that tower face
in pristine splendor, wrapped in the awe this kingly complex
compelled. And part of me was exploring the woods behind
my childhood home in Connecticut, wondering at the stone
walls I found there and the thrilling sense of communion with
older histories and hands that they bestowed.

I thought of puzzles: the puzzle of the GHF archaeologists
attempting to restore the ruins piece by piece; the puzzle of
this enchanting, elusive country—its glorious ancient past and
agonized recent past, the promise and peril of its present; and
the puzzle of my own ruins, from the woods of Connecticut
to the wilds of Cambodia.

Why was I here? Why had I chosen this path?

Now, in the jungle gloom of my Siem Reap hotel room, a
glimmer of understanding grew. This is what I do, this was as
close to the wild core of me as I could ever hope to get: I follow the compass of my heart, venturing off the map, making
connections, asking questions, going deeper, trying to penetrate the essence of a place, so that I can understand it better
and bring back precious pieces to share. Piecing together the

puzzle of Cambodia was a way to piece together the puzzle of me.

I thought of the soldier at the Peace Temple, of the speech he had made and how he had waved and waved as we had driven away. I thought of Mr. Kim, Sarun, Sopheng, the towers of Banteay Torp and Ta Prohm, the Pol Pot Baray, the unforgettable face in the jungle, my stilt house home. Here I was, a temporary traveler on a spinning globe, alone yet connected to every single one of these: a piece in a puzzle of a journey whose design I would probably never know, but whose path had restored my sense of the whole, in the ruins of Banteay Chhmar.

❧ ❧ ❧

National Geographic *has called Don George "a legendary travel writer and editor," and he has been lauded as one of the most influential travel writers and editors of his generation. Don has been exploring new frontiers as an author, editor, and adventurer for almost four decades, much of which is in his most recent book,* The Way of Wanderlust: The Best Travel Writing of Don George. *He has visited more than ninety countries on six continents, has published hundreds of articles in dozens of magazines and newspapers around the world, and regularly speaks and teaches at conferences, campuses, and companies from San Francisco to Singapore to London.*

Acknowledgments

"The Train to Harare" by Lance Mason published with permission from the author. Copyright © 2016 by Lance Mason.

"We'll Always Have Paris" by Mara Gorman originally appeared in November 2015 on BBC.com/Travel. Reprinted with permission from the author. Copyright © 2015 by Mara Gorman.

"Time or the Sahara Wind" by Marcia DeSanctis published with permission from the author. Copyright © 2016 by Marcia DeSanctis.

"Honey Colored Lies" by Michael Sano published with permission from the author. Copyright © 2016 by Michael Sano.

"Café Tables" by Amy Marcott published with permission from the author. Copyright © 2016 by Amy Marcott.

"Sister" by Kimberley Lovato published with permission from the author. Copyright © 2016 by Kimberley Lovato.

"An Occurrence of Nonsense at N'djili Airport" by Kevin McCaughey published with permission from the author. Copyright © 2016 by Kevin McCaughey.

"The Spinster of Atrani" by Amber Paulen originally appeared in *Front Porch Journal*. Reprinted with permission from the author. Copyright © 2016 by Amber Paulen.

"Ma Ganga" by Tania Amochaev published with permission from the author. Copyright © 2016 by Tania Amochaev.

"Speaking in Hats" by Darrin DuFord published with permission from the author. Copyright © 2016 by Darrin DuFord.

"In Vincent's Footsteps" by Erin Byrne excerpted from *Wings: Gifts of Art, Life, and Travel in France* by Erin Byne. Reprinted with permission from Solas House, Inc. and the author. Copyright © 2016 by Erin Byrne.

"War Memories" by Jill K. Robinson published with permission from the author. Copyright © 2016 by Jill K. Robinson.

"Breathe In" by Keith Skinner published with permission from the author. Copyright © 2016 by Keith Skinner.

"Paddling with Marigolds" by Ky Delaney published with permission from the author. Copyright © 2016 by Ky Delaney.

"Piecing Together Puzzles" by Don George excerpted from *The Way of Wanderlust* by Don George. Reprinted with permission from Solas House, Inc. and the author. Copyright © 2015 by Don George.

About the Editors

James O'Reilly, publisher of Travelers' Tales, was born in Oxford, England, and raised in San Francisco. He's visited fifty countries and lived in four, along the way meditating with monks in Tibet, participating in West African voodoo rituals, rafting the Zambezi, and hanging out with nuns in Florence and penguins in Antarctica. He travels whenever he can with his wife and their three daughters. They live in Leavenworth, Washington and Palo Alto, California, where they also publish art games and books for children at Birdcage Press (birdcagepress.com).

Larry Habegger, executive editor of Travelers' Tales, has visited more than fifty countries and six of the seven continents, traveling from the Arctic to equatorial rainforests, the Himalayas to the Dead Sea. In the 1980s he co-authored mystery serials for the *San Francisco Examiner* with James O'Reilly, and for thirty-one years wrote a syndicated newspaper column, "World Travel Watch." Habegger regularly teaches travel writing at workshops and writers' conferences, is a principal of the Prose Doctors (prosedoctors .com), and editor-in-chief of Triporati.com, a destination discovery site. He lives with his family on Telegraph Hill in San Francisco.

Sean O'Reilly is editor-at-large for Travelers' Tales. He is a former seminarian, stockbroker, and prison instructor who lives in Virginia with his wife and three of their six children. He's had a lifelong interest in philosophy and theology, and is the author of *How to Manage Your Destructive Impulses with Cyber Kinetics and Authority*. He is also CEO and Founder of the Auriga Distribution Group, Johnny Upright, Fifth Access, and Redbrazil.com, a bookselling site.

Ms. Joni Is a Phony!

Pictures by

Dan Gutman

Jim Paillot

HARPER

An Imprint of HarperCollinsPublishers

To Toby Katz

My Weirdest School #7: Ms. Joni Is a Phony!

Text copyright © 2017 by Dan Gutman

Illustrations copyright © 2017 by Jim Paillot

Library of Congress Control Number: 2016935897

ISBN 978-0-06-242929-2 (pbk. bdg.)–ISBN 978-0-06-242931-5 (library bdg.)

Typography by Kathleen Duncan

17 18 19 20 OPM 10 9 8 7 6 5 4 3 2

❖

First Edition